DELHI

THE HEART AND SOUL OF INDIA

SUKHENDU CHATTERJEE

INDIA • SINGAPORE • MALAYSIA

ISBN
Paperback 979-8-89610-680-7
Hardcase 979-8-89610-778-1

Dedication

This book is dedicated to my illustrious father, Late Shri Bholanath Chatterjee, scientist by profession and a scholar of Sanskrit and English literature and to my loving mother Late Shrimati Shobhana Devi, for her unflinching care and devotion and her strength of character inspiring me to embark upon this onerous project.

This book is written in the fond memory of my late wife, Mridula Chatterjee, my constant companion and creative inspiration, for 43 years of our conjugal life, from 1967 to 2010.

Contents

Dedication . . . 3

Preface . . . 7

Acknowledgements . . . 9

About the Author . . . 11

PART I: THE DELHI KALEIDOSCOPE . . . 13

1. Geographic, Geological and Protohistoric Settlements Around Delhi . . . 15
2. The Early History of India – Emergence of Indus Valley Civilization and Vedic Civilization . . . 25
3. Early Invasions of India . . . 35
4. Historical Places and Archeological Sites and Settlements Around Delhi . . . 41
5. Cities and Rulers of Delhi Over the Centuries . . . 49
6. Unity of India Amid Diversity – As in Ancient Times . . . 57
7. The Early Inroads, of Islam in India . . . 63
8. Delhi the Cradle of Sufism . . . 67
9. Wars of Succession for the Mughal Throne . . . 75
10. Women Rulers of Prominence, from 1192 to 1857 CE . . . 81

11. The Darkest Period in the Annals of History of Delhi: The Battle of Plassey 85

12. Famous Battles of India 93

13. The Showdown Between the Marathas and the British 97

14. The Period of British Residency from 1803 to 1857 105

15. The Sepoy Mutiny 1857 113

16. Propagation of Christianity and Evangelical Activity 129

17. The Recovery & Realignments 137

18. Contribution of Railways in Bolstering Delhi's Claim as the Mercantile Capital of North India 151

19. Delhi, the New Capital of British India: Its Changing Face, Industrialisation and Modernisation 157

20. Post Independence Development of Delhi; Jagmohan's Delhi 163

PART II: SELECT ESSAYS ON DELHI AND BEYOND 179

1. Benevolent Despots 181

2. Emergence of Delhi as the New Capital of British India 193

3. Famines in Bengal and the Role of the British Government in India 227

4. India's Foreign Trade During British Rule: A Comprehensive Study. . . 235

5. The Loot of India 245

References 265

Preface

It is almost two decades after my retirement from services under the Government of India, that I started my journey as an author. My literary endeavour began with the thought of exploring the emergence of Delhi as the new capital of British India, shifting from the bustling city of Calcutta (now Kolkata).

The hours of dedicated research and study on Delhi- its origin and evolution over the centuries- inspired me to embark upon a lengthier journey. The result is this book: a history of the city of Delhi, since its earliest days, from Indraprastha, the capital city of the Pandavas, to the ninth city being the capital of modern India.

Also, as a permanent resident of Noida (Delhi National Capital Region), I felt the urge to delve into the sequence of dynasties and capitals since the founding of Delhi. There have been volumes upon volumes on the history of Delhi, penned by different scholars of eminence. This book is just a humble attempt to bring to the common man, the history of Delhi, the heart and soul of India, within an integrated narrative.

Acknowledgements

I thankfully acknowledge the encouragement and support that I received from family and friends. They were the ones to motivate me in my lows and to elbow me to action when I dozed off. Without their constant support, involvement and reassurance, this book would never see the light of day. My family provided the proper ambience so that the writer in me could persevere, braving ill health and advancing age.

I am truly grateful to Ms. Dipanwita Mukherjee for assisting me with reviewing, editing and proofreading the book to ensure a consistent narrative. Her efforts were instrumental in my completing the book and taking it to the publishing stage. I am also thankful to Sh. Sandesh Kumar Talwar for preparing the manuscript.

About the Author

The author was born on 19 September 1938, in the mica town of Giridih, in present day Jharkhand, India at a time when the dark clouds of World War II were hovering menacingly over the European skies. His father, Shri Bholanath Chatterjee, was the head of the British India Meteorological Department of Andaman & Nicobar Islands. His mother, Shrimati Shobhana Devi, was the niece of the famous Bengali novelist, Shri Sarat Chandra Chattopadhyay.

From 1945 till 1952, the author studied in Dinanath High School, Nagpur. Thereafter, following the transfer of his father to Allahabad, the author studied in Anglo Bengali Intermediate College from 1952–57. In 1960, he completed his Bachelor of Arts from Erving Christian College. After completing his master's in economics from Allahabad University in 1962, he joined Allahabad University and subsequently Saint Peter's College, Kolkata, as lecturer in Economics.

In 1965, he joined the Indian Civil Services of the Government of India and was attached to the Customs and Central Excise Department. He retired from active service in 1997. While in service, he along with his close friends, formed the Noida Bengali Cultural Association in 1983, now a reputed platform for Bengalis in Delhi NCR. He also held many positions in the organisation for a long time. He moved to Norway for around five years and there he organised the Durga Puja in the Bengali community. The author returned to India when his son was appointed the Accountant General, Jammu and Kashmir at Srinagar. During his stay at Jammu, the author established a Kali temple within the premises of Bharat

Sevashram Sangha there. He inspired Bharat Sevashram Sangha with his organisational skills and established various religious and cultural sections under different subcommittees. He donated a major chunk of his pension and savings for various philanthropic purposes.

PART 1

THE DELHI KALEIDOSCOPE

Chapter 1

Geographic, Geological and Protohistoric Settlements Around Delhi

It must be heartening to lovers of Delhi to know for a fact that the city of Delhi is integrally associated with the earliest days of the formation of the landmass of the earth. The rocks of Delhi boast of association with the earliest formation of the earth, some 250 million years ago when India, Malagasy, South Africa, South America, Australia and Antarctica were a consolidated and united landmass forming Gondwanaland. The Aravallis land constituted the backbone of the north eastern part of the continent where present day India exists. The present-day capital city of New Delhi and Delhi is situated entirely over the Aravallis which is the north-eastern portion of Gondwanaland Mass, which now stands disintegrated.

Apart from the Aravallis land mass which had been part of Gondwana land of early universe association, Delhi's geography and geology is inexorably linked with river Yamuna's Palaeochannels (Palaeontology is related to the study of fossils as a guide to the history of life on earth).

The river Yamuna's oscillatory nature in the Indo-Gangetic alluvial plains (composed of soil or earth left by rivers or floods) in Haryana and Uttar Pradesh is reflected in the various paleochannelic features. A section of the river was studied by Sharma and Bakliwal in 1980.

There had been tectonic upheavals from the early days of Gondwanaland which resulted in the raising of the land mass in Rajasthan, rendering this area into a desert. The rivers which were flowing from east and were emptying themselves in the Indus, changed their course toward the east. The Aravallis is the great Indian water system divide. It separates the river systems flowing towards the Arabian Sea and emptying themselves therein and the river system with River Ganga being the main river which empty themselves into the Bay of Bengal.

Geological history of the north of Vindhyas, so to say the Aravallis, is indicative of the fact that river Yamuna with rivers like Saraswati and Ghaggar which were once mighty rivers, used to flow possibly towards the south-west like the river Indus during 4000 BCE. During Alexander's invasion in India around 330 BCE, Indus used to flow south as of today. It is possible that western Rajasthan water flow of rivers belonged to the Indus River system in the Tertiary and Holocene periods of Indian Archaeology.

Due to subsidence in the Ganges delta and the later upliftment of Aravalli - Delhi Axis, the river Yamuna changed its course and started flowing towards the east. The occurrence of this phenomenon could be traced to the river courses and human settlement as late as the time of Alexander's invasion of 326 BCE.

The Rajputana desert formation is of recent origin within historic times. There is evidence that the region north of Kutch and south of Punjab was a fertile forested area and was inhabited as a regular human settlement. There is evidence of well populated cities even in 330 BCE, i.e. Alexander's invasion of 2500 years ago. It is also evident that the present eastern flowing rivers were south-west bound and emptied themselves into the Rann of Kutch.

Evidence shows that the basin of the Indus was not always separated from the Peninsula by the long stretch of sandy waste like desert as it is at present. The deposit of huge amounts of silt by the fast flowing rivers of the Himalayan origin had gradually raised the river bed.'The traces of ancient river beds testifies to the gradual desiccation of the once fertile region and throughout the deltaic region of the Indus may still be seen in old channels which conducted their waters to the Rann of Kutch giving life and prosperity to the port cities of delta, which have left no living records of the countless generations that once inhabited them'.

The much venerated, invisible river Saraswati of Hindu Shastra of Vedic times (second millennium BCE) flowed into the Arabian Sea through eastern Punjab and Rajputana by a channel that lost its identity in the desert of Bikaner. Saraswati river took an easterly course and finally merged with the confluence of Ganga and Yamuna at Prayag. It is worthwhile to refer to the Notes and References as in the Quarterly Journal Geological Society Vol XIX 1863. The above example illustrates, what in a general manner, was the behaviour of the majority of the rivers of this tract, including the Indus itself, which is supposed to have been originally in confluence with the Ganga.

It is observed that the river migration varied from 100 Kms in the north and west of Delhi to 40 Km in the area south of Delhi. The course of the Yamuna seems to have been more or less steady for a period of over 3500 years. The study of the relationship of the flow of Yamuna is important as it is inalienably linked with the topography of Delhi. It will be interesting to recount the journey of Yamuna in its north-easterly origin from the Himalayas to its flow in south westerly direction around 2000 BCE and discharging itself into the Arabian Sea. Yamuna shared its water with the river Saraswati, revered in the Hindu Shastras of Vedic period.

The changing of the course of Yamuna from original south-west direction to present north-east was effected around 4000 years back. The palaeochannels across the Aravallis and river Yamuna entering the plains had formed various lakes and ponds namely Najafgarh Jheel, Surajkund and Badkhal lakes. They are actually the remnants of earlier channels of the Yamuna, which got entrapped by the landmass due to the rise of the adjoining areas consequent to tectonic movements that ultimately resulted in changing the course of Yamuna. The desert conditions were accentuated with time. The water-action of the internal drainage of the country was too feeble to transport to the sea, the growing mass of sands.

Delhi, geographically, was very strategically positioned in South Asia. It was almost in the middle of the whole Indian subcontinent, that was before the partition of India, when Afghanistan was a part of the British Empire. Even today Delhi is at a gateway position between the Himalayan slopes and the Thar peninsula area. After the tectonic upheaval, a part of the land mass in the South-Central Punjab was converted to the Thar desert peninsula. The flow of invaders from western land of Iran and central Asia who had crossed the Indus and created the Indus Valley Civilization of Mohenjo-Daro, got its movement towards the east blocked because of the presence of the Thar desert area.

Even otherwise, the Indus Valley Civilisation which belonged to the third century BCE, was akin to ancient civilisations in the west, namely the ancient civilisations of Egypt, Assyria and Babylonia. These civilisations had emerged in the valley of the Nile for Egypt, the valley of the river Tigris in Assyria and that of Euphrates in Babylonia. The centre of Indus Civilization flourished in the plains of Larkana district of Pakistan, in a narrow strip of land between the main bed of river Indus in the west and western Nara canal. Due to its proximity to the River Indus, the area was washed away by huge flood waters of the Indus. There were inundations seven times when the whole settlement was abandoned. There was resettlement of the locality with a substantial gap of time period.

The Indus Valley Civilisation of Mohenjo-Daro, was finally abandoned after some five thousand years of the coming up of the settlement, which was nicknamed as Nakhlistan or the 'Garden of Sind'. The inroad of foreigners from Asia Minor and Iran was stopped in their route that they had followed for so long across Sind, by the river Indus. The new wave of invasion into India took the route through Hindukush, crossing the River Chenab, a tributary of the Indus, about 40 km downstream from Akhnoor.

Towards the end of the Indus Valley Civilization, in the second century BCE, there developed the early Vedic Civilization, when Indo-Aryan tribes migrated into Punjab from the lands around Central Asia. Around 1200–1000 BCE, Vedic Culture spread towards the east to the Indo-Gangetic plains and settled into an agricultural life there (later Vedic Period).

Some historians hold the view that the Indus Valley people were Sumerians. The other opinion is that the people of the Indus valley race were essentially Dravidians. This theory postulates that the Dravidian race was all pervasive in India, and abounded in all places in India including Punjab, Sindh and Balochistan. Their migration to Mesopotamia was a subsequent event. Incidentally the people of Balochistan (the Brahui people) still speak the Dravidian language. The argument that Indus valley people were Aryans, has a few takers. The general view is that the Indus

Valley Civilisation represented a separate race, distinctly different from the Vedic or Aryan race.

Incidentally, it is interesting to note that both the civilisations flourished in the area which now falls in Pakistan. The Indus Valley Civilisation thrived in the Larkana District in southern Sind while the Vedic Civilisation of Harappan era flourished in the Montgomery district of North West Frontier Province (now in Pakistan) and much later, spread towards the Indo-Gangetic plains.

This area comprises a concentrated part of north-western territory of Delhi and is akin to the adjoining area of Haryana in the west. A study of combing this zone systematically to bring out the whole range of ancient, deserted settlements along with their locational environments, size and cultural milieu will help ascertain the influence of nature, the decision of selection of site for human settlements and engaging in human activities. This research work enables us to understand the influence of nature on the choice of location by the dwellers and dissemination over the landscape of human activities.

Also, the pattern of human life that existed could be visualised with the help of the prevailing manner of use of land and ecological conditions along with the means of subsistence practiced by the settlers. This will provide the linkage of the interaction between men, their means of production and their subsistence as stated above.

In terms of physiography, this area is composed of two contrasting zones – one is the old alluvium (made of sand and earth left by rivers and floods- its soil deposits) and the new alluvium, separated almost in the north south direction by a narrow dividing line designated as the 'Western Margins of the Khadar', as was studied by Professor R.C Thukran. The old Alluvium, also known as 'Bangar', is situated in the western section. Overall, these plains do not slope towards the southwest direction as is the general pattern. These plains are undulating at different places, giving it a rocky look. The entire area however is a very rich composition of flat and low-lying patches promising a good subsistence activity according to the change in different seasons. There is around 30 feet difference from the low-lying flood prone area of Yamuna khadar in the east. In the absence of any perennial river system, the area is semi-arid. The subsoil water level is composed of brackish to saline water. The soil packets are composed of loam, clay and aeoline sandy soils. However, most of the area is rich in water retention, poor in percolation and aeration and the temperature fluctuates quickly depending on climatic vagaries. The soil is fertile, on availability of sufficient irrigation. So far as general vegetation is concerned it is generally poor and thin, mainly consisting of saline and drought resistant plants.

The New Alluvium is known as 'Khadar'. This low-lying area is situated to the east of the old alluvium Yamuna traverses through the Eastern section of the zone. While in full monsoon Yamuna normally touches almost all points on the western margin if allowed to flow without restrictions of man-made canals, raised tracks for railway movements and bunds etc. The plains run in north-south direction with a south-east sloping tendency. The soil in the zone is loam and is composed of clay, silt and sand particles. The soil has high water absorbing capacity and greater possibility of aeration. Salt content is less. Such soil is easily cultivable with ordinary implements and needs fewer rounds of tilling. Water table being generally high and its abundant availability helps maintain a moderate soil temperature. The process of growth, maturity and yield of crops is normal. Being the easternmost pocket of semi-arid region of northern India and the meeting point of western dry and eastern humid zone, the seasons of summer, rainy and winter are normal. However, vagaries of nature are also discernible and the unpredictable long summers, drought conditions and delayed rainy season did pose problems for the inhabitants from time to time.

In this background it is interesting to study the Protohistoric Settlements that flourished in this land. The excavation of the village "Qutubgarh Thali-Wale-Kheda" contains remains of the pre Harappan period with recovery of terracotta bangles, oval sling bath, thick red potsherds with finger lines on the exterior and the like. However, fertility of the area and its constant occupation and cultivation have destroyed all evidence of pre-Harappan era.

Incidentally, location of both pre-Harappan era and subsequent era demonstrate the same pattern. All settlements were located in the upland dry Bangar belt on the aeoline sandy raised pockets. This is a general trend with some variation here and there namely Alipur Garhi Khera, east of Bawana and South of Narela-Alipur road.

The Vedas and the Upanishads flourished in the land known to the Hindus as Bharata-Varsha or the land of Bharata, a famous and powerful king of Puranic tradition. According to the Buddhist scriptures of the third century BCE, this territory came to be reckoned as Jambu Dwipa, the territory not extending beyond the Himalayas. The great Mauryan dynasty held their sway over this land for a considerable period of time.

This land acquired two other names in the succeeding period. The name 'India' was a Greek coinage; the name is derived from the name of the great river 'Indus' or the river 'Sindhu', itself a derivative from the land of 'Sindh'. The people residing in the area around the river Sindhu came to be christened as Hindus. Its other derivatives are Sapta Sindhu and Hapta Hindu. All these terms are the appellations of the country of the Aryans, the race emerging from across the Hindukush Range. This race was distinctly different from the Dravidians, the local inhabitants of India. During the Muslim period, the terms 'Hind' or 'Hindustan' emerged from the term Hindus.

Geographically and topographically, the vast country of India can be divided into four distinct regions:

The first region is the Hill region. In the holy books known as the Puranas, this region comprised of the hill country foothills or 'Parvatasrayin', stretching from the Tarai jungles and swamps of the Himalayan foothills and also included the upland territories of Kashmir, Kulu, Kangra, Tehri, Kumaun, Nepal, Sikkim and Bhutan.

The second region consisted of the plains and fertile valleys of the river Indus and its tributaries, the sandy deserts of Sindh and Rajputana, towards the east, the huge fertile plains of the Ganga and its tributaries, mainly Yamuna and towards the north-east and east, the mighty Brahmaputra.

The third region consisted of the plateau of Central and South India and the Deccan, south of the Gangetic plains, shut in from the rest of India by the western Vindhya range (the Vedic equivalent being Paripatra) and the central Vindhyas, and enclosed between the Western Ghats and the Eastern Ghats, that is, between 'Sahyadri' and 'Mahendra' (as mentioned in the Puranas), respectively.

The fourth region is the long and narrow coastal plain between the Western and Eastern Ghats or mountain ranges and the seas- the Arabian Sea in the west and the Bay of Bengal in the east. These plains are the location of the famous ports in the Konkan and Malabar region on the west and Madras (Chennai) and Visakhapatnam on the Bay of Bengal in the east. This area has the benefit of fertile deltas of four rivers the Mahanadi, the Godavari, the Krishna and the Cauvery.

This four-pronged natural division is in slight variation with the traditional division as known in the Puranic tradition. In the Puranic brahmanical literature, the territorial division of the country is fivefold. The most prominent part was the Indo-Gangetic plain which was known as 'Madhya-desh', the central vista of which was the river Saraswati which flowed past Thanesar to Allahabad and Banaras towards the Rajmahal Hills. The Western part of Madhya-Desa was known as 'Brahmarshi-desh' and the entire region was equated to 'Aryavarta' as described in the Grammar of Patanjali. But the term 'Aryavarta' is also used to refer to the vast tract of land lying between the Himalayas in the north and the Vindhyas in the south and extending from sea to sea (west and east). To the north of Madhya-desh beyond Thanesar and Pehoa (Prithudaka), lay the land of north-west India called 'Uttarapatha' or 'Udichya' and to its west lay 'Pratichaya' (western India). In the east was the land of 'Prachaya', or Purva-desh.

The south was bifurcated: the territory up to the river Krishna was traditionally known as 'Dakshinapatha', while the area beyond the river Krishna was the Tamil land known as 'Tamilakam'. these were the five geographical regions of India, according to the Puranas. The two mountainous tracts, one for the Himalayas and the other for the Vindhya were recorded as 'Parvatasrayin'.

This whole country was the size of the continent of Europe minus Russia and came to be known as 'Bharat-Varsha' while the descendants of King Bharata came to be known as 'Bharat Santati'. The ancient scripture 'Vishnu Purana' is credited with the nomenclature of the land division. Several references are available of this land in the great epic, Mahabharata. A beautiful couplet in the Vishnu Purana states, "Uttaram yat Samdrayasya Himaddreschaiva dakshinam Varsham tad Bharatam Nama Bharati yatra santatih". (Meaning: 'The country that lies north of the ocean and south of the snowy mountains is called Bharata, there dwell the descendants of Bharata').

Evidently, India is not just a country but a subcontinent which also included Burma (which was separated under the government of India Act, 1935). India had an irregular quadrangular shape, having its south, west and east flanked by the Indian Ocean and the two seas, the north by the Himalayan range with high snow-capped ridges, north-east by the lesser hills like Chittagong Hills, Lushai Hills and north-west by the Sulaiman and Kirthar ranges. The distant hilly table land of Iran on the west and the valley of Irrawaddy in Burma in the east, protected India and demarcated it as a separate entity.

The whole large mass of land was called 'Jambudwip', the innermost concentric island continent, as conceived by ancient Hindu cosmographers. This designation had been forcefully projected by Buddhist cosmographers too from around the third millennium BCE.

The river Saraswati was once a mighty river. According to Rig Veda, river Saraswati in 3000 BCE used to flow from the Himalayas to the west and met at the confluence of Ganga and the Yamuna at Prayag (or Allahabad), finally emptying itself into the Arabian Sea. The river Saraswati has lost its identity now and is said to be flowing underground. Legendarily it is 'Antar-Sabila' or the underground stream. The river Saraswati flowed past Thanesar and Pehoa to as far as Allahabad, then Banaras to the Rajmahal hills as per the Buddhist records.

Yamuna, a tributary of the Ganga and the Sutlej, a tributary of the Indus, used to flow into the river Saraswati. Subsequently, over the centuries, the tectonic disturbance of underground oceanic plates, coupled with the declining rainfall led to the uplifting of the Rajputana plain, and rendering the plain into a desert, which in turn, changed the flow of Saraswati from north-west to north-east, and finally it emptied itself at the confluence of Ganga and Yamuna at Allahabad, as already stated. Also, it is interesting to note that the confluence which was close to Delhi, shifted eastward towards Allahabad.

* * *

Chapter 2

The Early History of India – Emergence of Indus Valley Civilization and Vedic Civilization

India boasts of a chequered and long history of developed civilisation. Leaving aside the pre-historic period for which not much conclusive information is available, there is fair chronological information about the Early Vedic period, highlighted by the early Aryan settlements, followed by the civilisation of the later Vedic Period, distinguished by the Magadha ascendency, the Persian and Macedonian invasions.

The Kabul River had been the centre of activity of the invaders to India as also the hill country on the valleys of the Kumrat and Swat rivers. This area was ruled by the clan known as Asvakas. This name is derived from the Sanskrit word Asva, meaning horse. So obviously horse-riding tribes of Greek origin did colonise the Gandhara area.

The river Indus had been the dividing line of Gandhara land. The land west of the divide was the kingdom of King Pushpakalavati. This kingdom corresponded to the modern district of Peshawar (Pakistan). The land to the east of the valley was the realm of Taxila (Takshasila in Sanskrit) and corresponded to the district of Rawalpindi (Pakistan). The locale of the capital city was Saraikala, about twenty miles north-west of present-day Rawalpindi. Even in those days, Taxila or Takshasila was known for its high degree of culture and sophistication. It was a seat of learning which attracted scholars from near and far away lands.

Taxila is fabled to be the town where the verses of Mahabharata were first recited. It was here that the four Vedas and the eighteen branches of knowledge were taught. Taxila was a very prosperous commerce centre, lying on the high road from Central Asia to the interior of India.

Taxila was also important because of its strategic location. It was the gateway to the adjoining mountainous kingdoms of Urusa (Hazara District) and Abhisara (Poonch and Nowshera). To the south east of Taxila, lay the kingdom of Pauravas, mentioned in the religious scriptures. The territory of the elder Paurava was the area between Jhelum & Chenab, and for younger Paurava, principality was between the rivers Chenab and the Ravi. There were other smaller independent principalities in and around, not in any way comparable to the Paurava lands as stated above. In the Indus delta lay the city of Pattala jointly ruled by two kings and a senate of nobles, similar to that of Sparta.

The most epoch-making event in the annals of Indian history was the advent of Alexander, the Achaemenian Emperor in the Indian Horizon. Alexander had already conquered Asia Minor along with Iran and Iraq. After he had inflicted the total annihilation upon the two great Persian kings, Darius and Xerxes in 330 BCE, in 327 BCE, Alexander set out on his mission to subjugate India whose fabulous wealth had become an eyesore for all in the west.

Alexander crossed the Hindukush Mountain range and invaded Sindh to recover the territories won during the reign of Bimbisara, the great king of Haryanka. This tradition started from sixth century BCE, which saw the growth of the formidable Samrajya or kingdoms of strong superior rulers who were capable of performing Ashwamedha Yajna, that is, the sacrifice of the unconquered royal horse let loose to traverse through independent kingdoms which remained unbridled over all the royal territories. The capture of the sacrificial horse invited war against the captor to decide the overall suzerainty over the challenging kingdom. The ushering in of the Magadhan ascendency saw the desire for a universal supreme king, capable of bringing the entire habitable area of the country under one umbrella, that is, from the foothills of Himalayan terrain in the north to the Satpura mountain range and river Narmada in the south, being the north-south axis.

The west-east axis was considered to be the territory from east of the Indus basin to the Rajmahal Chhota Nagpur mountain range, covering Rajagriha or Rajgir and Pataliputra on the banks of the Ganga. This included what came to be the middle country (madhyarna desh) stretching around the fast flowing mighty Saraswati river that is no longer in existence.

This was the land habitated by the Kurus, the Panchals and some other smaller tribes. It was the cradle of late Vedic, Brahmanical civilization. From this epicentre, another great kingdom spread its wing mainly in the eastern direction to the land of the Kosalas, to the birth place of Lord Rama, that is Ayodhya, located on the bank of the river Sarayu, stretching to the Videhas, on the east of river Gandak and Vidarbhas in the valley of Wardh, in the south.

Before discussing further about the Later Vedic Age, it is worthwhile to cast a glance at the Early Vedic Age and the Indus Valley Civilization preceding it. The name 'India' was a Greek coinage; as per the vedas, the name is derived from the river Indus or the Sindhu. The tribes frequenting the valley of the Sindhu were called Hindus and their habitat was named India from the name Indus. The tribes occupying the lower Indus valley had similarity with the people residing in Mesopotamia and were assigned by the archaeologists as belonging to the third millennium BCE.

One of the oldest and widespread civilizations of the world, the Indus Valley Civilization flourished in the third century BCE, along the basins of the river Indus. The main sites were Harappa, Mohenjo Daro, Dholavira and Rakhigiri, spanning what is today Pakistan and north-east Afghanistan. It was a Bronze Age Civilization, noted for their superb town planning, meticulously planned drainage and water supply systems, baked brick houses and large public buildings like granaries and baths. The Vedic civilization which came later, flourished in the second century BCE and belonged to the later Bronze Age and early Iron Age. This was the time when Vedic literature, including the four Vedas and the Upanishads were composed. The Vedic Civilization of the Indo-Aryan race is a civilization that is the source of subsequent civilizations of India. Hereditary caste system or the Hindu Varna Ashrama Dharma was an essential social construct of the later Vedic Aryans. In this way, the religion and social customs of the present-day Hindus have their source in the Vedic Culture.

It is worthwhile to do a comparative study of the two civilizations, that is, the Earlier Indus Valley Civilization and the Vedic Civilization which followed it. The two civilizations were totally dissimilar in nature. While the former was a developed city based one, the latter is largely rural and agricultural in its fundamental character. The Indus Valley Civilization belonged to the Bronze Age; the people were completely ignorant in the use of iron, using only copper and bronze. This is why this culture belonged to the Chalcolithic Age, where implements of both stone and copper were used. The later Vedic Age people knew the use of various metals. Initially, they used copper and gold but later on they used bronze, silver and also iron. There is evidence of the use of iron-based instruments and offensive and defensive armours made of iron. Again, while the use of horse and horse chariots was very much evident in the Vedic Period, there is no recognised evidence of the use of horse during the Indus Valley Civilization.

The religion, beliefs and forms of worship were distinctly different in the two periods. The Indus Valley people were worshippers of Mother Goddess and a male deity akin to Lord Shiva. They also worshipped Nature in many forms. So, it may be surmised that by and large, the inhabitants of the lower Indus basin were protagonists of the Hindu religion. While the Indus Valley people worshipped the bulls, the Vedic people had veneration for the cows. Worship of images was prevalent during Indus Valley Civilisation. While phallic worship was prevalent in the Indus Valley Civilization, it was condemned in the Vedic Age. Again, fire-worship or performance of yajna or religious rituals and animal sacrifice were not prevalent in the Indus Valley, but held a prominent place in the Vedic culture.

Coming to the people of the Vedic age, they were nature worshippers. These people pursued a religion which was normally 'aniconic', that is, where images played no part. They were the worshippers of supernatural powers who allowed the growth and sustenance of all living beings, including homo sapiens. Female deities had no place in their pantheon. There was a clear superiority of male deities. They were Indra, Varuna, Surya, Agni (fire), Prithvi and the like. The people who followed this system christened themselves Aryas or Aryans. The bedrock of Hindu civilization, that is, the caste system and the literature namely the Vedas and the Upanishad are the creation of the men of this period. The exact date of the emergence of these ancient texts is however, shrouded in mystery. The great German Indologist Max Muller placed the date of the origin of the Vedas as the second half of the second millennium B.C. Attempts to narrow down the exact year of their creation or compilation, based on the position of constellations or heavenly bodies, were also not reliable in this respect.

In view of some such fundamental differences, it is obvious to surmise that the two civilisations are distinct and very different from each other. While the period of Indus Valley Civilisation is considered to be of the Third millennium B.C, the Vedic one is considered to belong to the Second Millennium B.C. But some would place the sequence in reverse order. This issue has remained a contentious one.

Absence of iron in the Indus Valley civilization points to its periodic precedence over the Vedic Civilisation. It is sufficient to surmise as stated earlier, that the two are totally different from each other. Another view has also been projected, that the civilisations have different roots. As regards the race of the people during the two civilisations, the Indus Valley people were Dravidians while the Vedic people were Aryans.

In certain tablets of fourteen century BCE, discovered in Asia Minor region, there are references to kings bearing Indian or Aryan names and invoking the names of gods like Indra, Varuna, Mitra and Nasatyas, which retained early Vedic reference. These gods were not yet overshadowed by the Puranic Trimurti of Brahma, Vishnu and Maheshwar, - the creator, sustainer and the destroyer of the universe, which developed much later in the later Vedic Period. The aforesaid discovery clearly points out to the regular interaction or connection between two civilisations, that is, the Indian and the West Asian one, located in Asia Minor.

It is also interesting to read a passage of the Rig-Veda where a worshipper invokes from his pratnaokas or ancient abode, the god Indra whom his ancestors formerly invoked. We are also told that Yadu and Turvasa, two among the most famous Rig Vedic tribes, were brought by Indra from a distant land. In Vedic times, the people of Persia were referred to as ‘Pasu’ or ‘Parasu’. This confirms the link between India and Persia and even leads to another debatable point whether the Vedic tribes were brought from Persia (Iran) or vice-versa.

Before proceeding further, it is worthwhile to look into the origin, meaning and application of the terms Vedas and the Upanishads, the two bedrocks of Hinduism, for better understanding of the nuances of Hinduism and its ancient scriptures.

Before the close of the Vedic period or what is the later Vedic period, we can reasonably assume that the Kurus of Mahabharata fame appeared around 1500 BCE to 345 BCE, that is, before the advent of the Nanda dynasty. The word ‘Veda’ seems to appear during this aforesaid period. The word ‘Ved’ comes from the word ‘Vid’ which means ‘to know’. Thus ‘Veda’ means knowledge in general. This knowledge was transmitted through ‘Sruti’ which is a ‘divine revelation’. There was no written text as such.

The Vedas consist of four different classes of literary composition. The Mantra (saying, song or formula) is the oldest division, distributed in four ‘Samhitas’ namely the Rig, Sama, Yajur and Atharva. The Rig Veda is a collection of lyrics in praise of different gods recited by ‘hotri’ priests. Sam Veda is the book of chants incorporating the Rig Veda text except for seventy-five miscellaneous verses or ‘shlokas.

Yajurveda is the book of sacrificial prayers, containing stanzas from the Rig Veda, relating to the same, as also the prayers of inferior priests engaged in preparatory functions, ancillary to the act of actual sacrifice, that is, the preparation and cleaning of the sacrificial animal prior to the actual sacrifice.

The Atharva Veda related to the magic spells and incantations to ward off evil spirits in order to heal diseases, for exorcism of the evil spirits, and also to restore balance and annuity in the family. Thus, Atharva-Veda is the only stream of the Vedas which is intimately related to the common man’s daily life as against the other Vedas which invoke prayers to God the almighty through temple priests.

Kautilya’s Arthashastra, belonging to the Mauryan Period, is one of the most influential treatises on political science in the Indian Civilization. It deals with almost all aspects of monarchical government and governance, political and military strategy, economic policy, duties and nature of a king, statecraft, diplomacy and nature of government. The relation between the man and administration, including the arm of administration named the Municipality and other forms of local self-governments functioning under the overall jurisdiction or monitored by the government, had been explicitly enunciated in this magnum opus, The Arthashastra. Kautilya enumerated the seven organs or constituent elements of the state: Swami (the king or the ruler), Amatya (the ministers and councillors), Janapada (the territory along with its population), Durga (the fortified towns and cities), Kosha (the treasury or the wealth of the state), Danda (the forces of law and order, the army and defence) and Mitra (the allies).

The other great Hindu scripture, the Upanishad is sacred doctrine, understood only by the people of special acumen and special knowledge and esoteric as such. Literally, Upanishad means to sit down near the guru while receiving spiritual knowledge. It is a doctrine which enjoins people or disciples sitting before the master or Guru or the teacher, being a matter or knowledge of high philosophical character.

The study revolves around two concepts namely Brahman and Atman. The first being the Absolute soul and the latter, Individual soul. Generally, the Upanishad is considered to have originated before the advent of the Buddha, the enlightened one. Whereas, the Vedas are considered to be pure revelation or Sruti, the lesser authoritative text, handed down through memory or 'Smriti' by the learned ones, are considered to be Vedanga. Vedanga literally means the 'anga' or limb of the Vedas. They are less authoritative than the Sruti which are the revelations as handed down to the sages.

Vedanga are to be memorised and called 'Smriti'. They originated in the Vedic schools (Charanas). They are normally expressed in prose style intended for memorisation and are named as Sutra (thread, clue, guide, rule aphorism). Vedanga are six in number – namely - Shiksha (phonetics), Kalpa (Ritual), Vyakarana (Grammar), Nirukta (Etymology), Chandas (Metrics) and Jyotisha (Astronomy and Astrology). The most important for the common man is the Grihya Sutra, relating to the simple ceremonies of daily life in the Vedic times. There are other sutras relating to serious and complex sacrifice processes. Panini, Yaksha and Pingala, among others, were the great masters of the Verses.

Before Delhi became the cradle of mixed culture through the invasion of the Greeks, the Bactrians, the Parthians the Sakas, the Huns, the Kushavas, the Turks, the Turko-Mongols, and the Moghuls, the Vedas and the Vedangas ruled supreme.

During the later part of Vedic civilisation, India saw great changes in the mode of religious development. There had been a transition from deities, in praise of natural powers like Agni (fire), the Surya (Sun), Varuna (Water), Vayu (wind) and the beneficence of the earth goddess. Furthermore, the sacrificial part became more complex and was put in a separate compartment, as distinct from rituals to ward off daily common visitations like cholera, plagues, chicken pox, small pox etc. In addition, there were superstitions, beliefs in evil spirits, incantations, chantings to ward off evil spirits etc.

The monotheistic and monistic tendencies became more prominent towards the end of the Vedic period. The period saw the emergence of the cult of 'Avatars' like 'Varaha' or boar, tortoise or 'Kurma', 'Matsya' or fish etc. as divine incarnations.

The Theologians and the philosophers doubted the efficacy of the 'Avtarvad' and strove to achieve a goal of communion of individual or personal soul, that is, 'Atman' and the Universal soul of 'Paramatman'. Such a search for the absolute, was beyond the comprehension of the common mortals. So, there emerged a consequential desire to rediscover the deities known in the Vedas. This predilection led to the re-deitification of the known deities.

This led to the ushering in of the most crucial and understandably the bedrock of the Hindu religion, that is, the trinity of Brahma, the creator, Vishnu, the sustainer and Maheshwar, the destroyer. This is the kingpin of the supremacy of Hindu religion, in the comity of other world religions. The division of labour among the three deities is most logical and scientific. Lord Brahma presides over the birth or creation of all living and non-living beings which are discernible in the universe. Again, there must be one deity, who will oversee the growth and sustenance of all living animals (including the homo sapiens) and plants (the mute ones), till they reach the last day of natural (including unnatural) decay and final decimation which is termed as death. Vishnu presides over this phase. The final phase of all living beings is decay and death. Maheshwar is the presiding deity to oversee this last phase of life.

Right from the days of coming up of the living element, in the last phase of Hindu life, the forest, which is away from the din and bustle of activity, came to be known as the final destination. This phase was the 'Vanprastha' or the entering of the life of a hermit in the secluded forest life, where the final act of consummation of the individual soul with the universal soul will take place. The 'Atman' or the individual self will mingle and surrender its identity with 'Paramatman', the universal soul.

The cardinal principle of every living being suffering death and ending is absolutely essential, otherwise the earth's surface will be bereft of check and balance; the available living space will be rendered so overcrowded so as to create pandemonium. It will lead to fierce struggle among the living beings to extract living space from the existing land and sharing of the means of subsistence.

The Indra-worshipping tribes were divided into two. One belonged to the Srinjayas and their allies the Osharatas, both lauded by the priestly family of the Bharadvajas.

The other group belongs to Yadus, Turvadas, Annus, and Purus etc. who were close to the indigenous tribes, who were of Non-Aryan stocks and were known as 'Dasas' or 'Dasyus'. Apart from the two Indra-worshipping groups, there were the aboriginals also called the 'Dasyus' who were dark skinned, flat nosed cattle rearers, speaking a different language and also the worshippers of the Phallus and thus were the original inhabitants of the land of lower Indus Valley civilisation.

* * *

Chapter 3

Early Invasions of India

It was around 535 BCE that Cyrus, the founder of the Achaemenid Empire of Persia, started knocking at the gates of India. The invaders reached the area north-east of Kabul, at the junction of Ghorband and Panjshir after overrunning the then famous city of Kapisa. Cyrus the great (600 to 530 BCE) annexed the lands west of the river Indus and this marked the eastern border of his huge empire. It was his illustrious descendent, Darius the great (522 to 486 BCE), who further expanded the empire. Around 518 BCE, in a second round of conquest, King Darius crossed the Himalayas and entered India. He conquered the north-western regions of the Indian subcontinent by annexing regions up to the Jhelum river. He carried on expeditions of Sind, crossing the Indus and annexed the territory which today forms parts of Punjab, upto the desert of Rajputana. It was probably Darius, the illustrious successor of Cyrus, who named the conquered land as Gandhara.

The first documented invasion of India, dates back to the Greco – Scythian Invasion during 330–320 BCE. The king of the ancient Greek kingdom of Macedon, and an extremely strong military general, Alexander III, commonly known as Alexander the great, first conquered and annexed the powerful Achaemenid empire (Persian Empire) in the year 334 BCE, after inflicting crushing defeat on King Darius III and Xerxes, the existing kings.

In 330 BCE, Alexander set out for the conquest of the east, mainly India, which had the reputation of being the Golden land. In 327 BCE, he crossed the Hindukush mountain range and stormed into Kabul to subjugate it. The next year, he conquered the Swat and Kumar Valleys.

In 326 BCE, his marauding army crossed the mighty Indus, by boat bridge. He was amply assisted by the local chieftain Ambhi, who was also the King of Taxila. Alexander crossed the river Jhelum (Vitasta in Sanskrit and Hydaspes in Greek). The army marched along a road which was subsequently converted to the Grand Trunk Road, during the reign of Sher Shah Suri (1530–1540) who had dislodged Humayun, the son of Babur from the throne. The Grand Trunk Road, the most marvellous of Sher Shah Suri's achievements, ran for 1500 Km right from Sonargaon in East Bengal to the Indus. It still survives.

Alexander reached Multan, having crossed Jhelum through Nandan Pass. On the bank of Jhelum, Alexander was confronted by the ruling King Porus or Paurava, who was mortified to behold the abject surrender of his neighbour, the King of Taxila. Being the rainy season and the daunting prospect of facing the huge army of King Porus, Alexander made a tactical move to avoid Porus' army. He did so by moving about twenty miles upfront through dense forest on the bend of the River Jhelum. This was a heavily wooded but marshy land further inundated by flood water. The army of King Porus, was at reduced strength here, with 30,000 archers, without mount or elephant and fighting on foot, also rendered immobile because of the slush and slippery ground condition. The main battle formation of 300 elephants were attacked by archers of the enemy along with valiant and fierce desert horses. With master battlefield manoeuvrability, Alexander plunged in, attacking the Porus forces consisting of 300 chariots and 200 elephants in battle gear. The foot soldiers (archers) and mounts were completely devastated and defeated. The elephant of King Porus was severely injured by the arrows of Alexander's advanced mounted archers. It ran amuck with multiple injuries, trampling all underfoot, without discriminating between friends and foes.

King Porus was also severely wounded in this famous Battle of Hydaspes, but preferred to defend stoutly. He was finally defeated and captured and brought before Alexander. It was a well-known melodramatic verbal exchange between the victor and the vanquished, when Alexander asked Porus how he expected to be treated. The latter firmly replied 'like a King'. Alexander was so impressed with the indomitable spirit of Porus, that he forgave him and as a mark of goodwill, handed the kingdom back to Porus.

It was a master stroke by the Macedonian war veteran King Alexander, who realised the extreme difficulty in securing a permanent foothold in the unknown territory won by him in this distant unfamiliar land. Porus was granted the governorship of the conquered territory and for forging an alliance as a vassal state.

Alexander and his victorious troops were so exhausted with long and uninterrupted battle that Alexander had to give in to the overall feelings of his troops and decided not to proceed further to unfamiliar terrain towards the east. Rather, he fell back and decided to consolidate his conquests of the land of five rivers, Punjab and further west including Afghanistan.

On his retreat, Alexander crossed Chenab (Akesines in Greek) and Rabi (Hydraotes in Greek) and stormed Sangala, stronghold of Katharoi, situated probably in modern day Gurdaspur in Punjab. Too exhausted and drained of energy, Alexander crossed Indus and marched towards Babylonia in the intense summer heat but not before plundering the Rajput principalities on the way. He overran the territories of Malwa tribes and extracted huge gifts of precious metal, gems, draperies and also rare animals, tigers and lions. Trudging the way through the deserted and inhospitable land of Balochistan, he finally reached Babylon. However, physical injury sustained during the capture of Sindh added to prolonged bouts of diarrhoea led to his death in 323 BCE, just four years after he had embarked upon his conquest to the East.

Alexander was no temporary looter and plunderer. He chalked out a detailed administrative plan to permanently retain the territories he had won. He appointed permanent governors to administer the area, west of river Jhelum. Though the governors were Greeks, Indian chiefs like Sasigupta and chieftain of Taxila were assigned prominent responsibilities in the administrative setup.

The mighty Indus River was a natural divide of the Gandhara land, dating back to the days of the Mahabharata. To the West of the river lay the kingdom of Pushkalavati (present day district of Peshawar). On the east was the kingdom of Taxila (the present-day Rawalpindi district). Alexander laid stress on the creation of vassal kings who were administratively independent. The most important of such kings were the great and mighty Paurava and King Abhisara. Strategically new cities were built on river banks to facilitate trade through navigable waterways to take advantage of internal trade of Punjab which was known as the land of the five rivers. Alexander also secured the western borders of the newly acquired kingdom. Administration was assisted and watched over by Macedonian garrisons, stationed in the newly built cities.

After the invasion of Alexander around 326 BCE, the next invasion of India was carried out by the Sakas (Scythians). Greeks had renewed their incursion through their king Antiochus of Syria; they penetrated upto the Kabul River valley and defeated the Indian King Subhangasena. Subsequently, Demetrius, the Prince of Bactria and son-in-law of Antiochus III, conquered Punjab and the lower Indus Valley. Equally brilliant was king Mendhar of the same dynasty, who fought his way up to Patliputra.

This was the time when the great Mauryan Dynasty had reached its last stage of decay and had become too tyrannical and unbecoming of the ruler of Magadha. This dynasty was brought to an end by Pushyamitra Sunga, a general of the last Mauryan King, whom he dethroned. His rule extended from Sialkot (now in Pakistan) to Pataliputra. He performed double 'Ashwamedh Yajna', that is, the successful performance of two horse sacrifices and was hailed as a successful defender of 'Aryavarta'. His rule was for thirty six years 187–151 BCE.

He was succeeded by his son Agnimitra. His reign was marked by the presence of the great poet, Kalidasa. He had regular communication and trade with the Greeks in the borderlands of India. Vidisha in eastern Mahua, was a great centre of political and other activities. It was Vasumitra, son of Agnimitra, who defeated the Greeks, in the Indus valley area.

After the rule of the Sunga dynasty, where the name of the rulers ended with Mitra, came the Satavahanas, the Telugu speaking people of the Godavari-Krishna river basin, whose rule followed an undulating curve. They lost power to the marauding Scythian invaders. Subsequently, the Satavahanas' supremacy was restored by Gautamputra who assumed the mantle of being the destroyer of the Sakas (the Scythians), Yavanas (Greeks) and Pahlavas (Parthians).

Gautamputra's rule extended in a vast tract from Mahwa in the north to Canara in the south. In the reign of his son Vashistaputra, Puluyami, the areas of Vaijayanti (North Canara), and Amaravati (in Guntur) were added. Ten kings of this dynasty ruled for over three hundred years upto the middle of the third century CE.

After the glorious period of the great Mauryas there was a lull, before the renewed activity of the rebellious principalities, which had thrown away the yoke of the Syrian Empire under Seleukos, like Bactria swooped down upon India and subjugated areas like Punjab, Sind and parts of Afghanistan.

Demetrios, son of Euthydemus, king of Bactria was the main architect of this renewed Greek invasion. Menander, a successor of this dynasty had the most chequered history having extended his reign to Sakala, the modern Sialkot (now in Pakistan). Another king, Antialkids, ruled at Taxila (near Rawalpindi in Pakistan). It was in Gandhara district, also famous in history. The king and his tribe embraced Buddhism and became an integral part of the larger Indian society. The next tribe to command over the region were Pahlavas (the Parthians) around the second century BCE The last king was Itermaios, who had to make way for the Kushans (the Chinese name being Yue-chi). Sakas, as displaced by Kushans, migrated towards the south, to get relocated around River Kabul land. At the dawn of the Christian Era, they had settled in south Afghanistan. Their abode came to be known as Sakasthana, modern Sistan. Gradually, they extended their rule around the Indus Valley and western parts of India.

Around the second and first century BCE, the Parthians (Pahlavas) established their suzerainty over the Sakas whose dominance passed into oblivion, having been absorbed in the great Indian community, as stated earlier. The Saka-Pahlavas rulers were divided into five clans. The leaders of the clans were called "Kshatrapa" or Governors.

One of the Kshatrapa ruled in the Afghanistan itself, along the junction of Panjshir and Ghoraband rivers, the second at Taxila in western Punjab, the third at Mathura along the Yamuna, the fourth at the south, upper Deccan and the fifth at Ujjain. As independent rulers, all acquired great prosperity and fame. According to Ptolemy, the Greek geographer, Rudradaman, ruled between 130–150 CE and was one of the greatest Saka rulers.

Another important ruler of an earlier period who is famous in history was the Scythe Parthian king whose name is associated with the great Vikramaditya, who destroyed the Sakar and who was the initiator of Vikram Samvat, commencing from 58 BCE. The dates and events are greatly shrouded in mystery.

At this stage it will be interesting to recollect the observations of the famous Greek historian, Ptolemy of the second century CE. Few of his observations are historically very significant, serving as a beacon light to delve into this period. Ptolemy has given his testimony that during his time a historic tribe or clan with the name Pandus were the ruler of a portion of Punjab. Another contention of Ptolemy of equal significance was that the Satraps of Ujjain averred their descent from the Lord (Swamin) Chastana (or Jiastanes). The most famous descendant of this clan was Rudradaman, the grandson of Chastana, who ruled during 130–150 CE. or the second century CE. Interestingly, Ptolemy was aware of the names of important trading centres of Malaysian Peninsula, notably the big islands of Borneo and Sumatra, as well as islands such as Celebes, Madura, Banka etc. which were very much in the proximity to the big islands of Borneo and Sumatra.

* * *

Chapter 4

Historical Places and Archeological Sites and Settlements Around Delhi

No study of Delhi is worthwhile without a detailed accounting of the important historical places, whether it is from the Pre-British occupation or afterwards. It is through the careful study of these places that we piece together the past history of a city. Throughout the ages, many have made it their home, many have invaded it or plundered it. Many rulers have built their capital here; they have constructed forts and palaces and gardens in it. Subsequent rulers have built on the same ruins or have abandoned it and built their own capital around it. The ruins of these previous cities are all scattered here.

Delhi is an ancient city which never lost its prominence since the Mahabharata period. The earliest written reference of Delhi as a settlement dates back to the legendary city of Indraprastha as found in the Mahabharata. It was built by the Pandavas, an Aryan race on the Western bank of the river Yamuna. The Puranas (Padma Puran) refers to a huge forest known as Khandava Van on the west of river Yamuna, in modern day territory of Delhi It was burnt down completely and Khandavaprasth was created. This area later came to be known as Indraprastha.

The Adiparva of the Mahabharata refers to the existence of two known settlements (Janapanda) namely Uttara Kuru and Dakshin Kuru. This Janapada had three parts: Kuru Jangal or Khandava Van which was one of the parts, Kuru was another while the third was Kurukshetra. Kuru Jangal was a forested region of which Indraprastha or Delhi was a part.

Indraprastha was built in the cleared land from Khandava Van where a beautiful city was born with the help of Maya, a great artist and architect of the Asura dynasty, and as great an architect as Vishvakarma was among the Devas. This area, consisting of hills and forests and lying in desolation, was given to the Pandavas, by King Dhritarashtra to avoid any rift between his hundred sons, the Kauravas and the five sons of Pandu, the Pandavas.

To clear the forest, the pandavas set fire to it, killing all birds and beasts in it. In the huge inferno that blazed through the forest, Arjun, the third Pandav saved Maya. In gratitude for saving his life, Maya wanted to repay the debt. Maya wanted to construct something spectacular for Arjun. Initially, Arjuna was reluctant to receive anything from Maya. But Lord Krishna, all time mentor of the Pandavas was present and he insisted that Maya should build an assembly hall for Yudhisthir the King, a hall of such magnificence and brilliance that would put to shame all others, including the palace at Hastinapur. It would be a hall that the entire world of men, Asuras and Gods would find impossible to imitate. Maya was delighted at the prospect and agreed to build an assembly hall for the Pandavas that would resemble a palatial chariot of the Gods. It took him fourteen months to build the hall inside the walled city where the walls were as high as heaven and as white as silver. Maya with his gems, jewels, gold, silver and other precious stones created the celestial hall with solid golden pillars. Inside the hall was a peerless lotus pond filled with lilies and other water plants, covered with leaves and lotuses with gem studded stalks. The water was completely crystal clear and still so that the pool seemed to be empty.

Duryodhana, prince of Hastinapur and eldest son of blind King Dhrithrashtra, in his curiosity, came on a visit to Indraprastha to personally observe the beauty of the city. Maya's royal palace was full of illusions: he had created certain features with see-through marble, where water and solid stone were not distinguishable. Duryodhana, completely mesmerised and confused, wandered aimlessly, sometimes falling into pools of water and sometimes stumbling on the crystal-clear marble flooring. While walking down the step, he mistook it as an empty pond, could not maintain his balance and fell into the water, much to sarcastic criticism of Draupadi the Queen and her maids. Again, at another place while crossing a stream filled with fish and water lilies, Duryodhana stepped into it carefully expecting it to be water but stubbed his toe against the hard crystal ground that appeared like a rivulet.

Duryodhana was highly incensed and felt insulted as Bhima, the second Pandava joked and rubbed salt into the injury saying that Duryodhana looked like a young maiden dancing through puddles. Draupadi's flippant and caustic remark 'Duryodhana is really a blind king of a blind father', infuriated and insulted him further and he vowed to pay Draupadi back for her abject indolence.

In retaliation, Duryodhana challenged Yudhisthir, King of Indraprastha to a game of dice, an invitation that a Kshatriya king could not refuse. With the cunning advice of his maternal uncle Shakuni, the greatest master of the game of dice, Duryodhana won every round. As the stakes rose higher and higher with every round, Yudishtir lost whatever he had, first his kingdom, all his material possessions, including his own brothers and lastly his wife Draupadi who all became slaves of Duryodhana. At the height of shameless arrogance and audacity Duryodhana asked his brother Dushyasana to disrobe Draupadi, who had become his slave in the open court of Hastinapur, where all revered elders, including Pitamaha Bheeshma and Dronacharya, the warrior master, were present.

At this point, Krishana, the mentor and guardian of the Pandavas, entered the court and at Draupadi's prayer to save her modesty, created a 'Maya jal' with an unending supply of linen to Draupadi, while himself staying unseen. Dushyasana, in spite of all his efforts to disrobe and insult Draupadi in open court, failed in his mission and had to give up. However, this was enough to sound the bugle for the grand battle of Mahabharata at Kurukshetra, where after a long and fierce battle, the Pandavas emerged victorious and all the hundred sons of king Dhritarastra, the Kauravas, perished.

The triumphant Pandavas entered Hastinapur, as their newly conquered capital, leaving the reign of Indraprastha to Yadavas, the clan of lord Krishna. Hastinapur, which was situated at the Doaba region of river Yamuna, north east of present Delhi, was washed away by massive flooding of the river Yamuna. As Heavy flooding of Yamuna and Ganga caused the total destruction of Hastinapur, the capital had to be shifted to Kaushambi. The Yadavas who were given the city of Indraprastha after the battle of Kurukshetra, later shifted their capital to Mathura on the Banks of the Yamuna. The reason could be paucity of water. Indraprastha however, remained a city of significance. Most of the mention of the name of Indraprastha appears in early Buddhist literature, mainly the Jatakas.

The name of the city of Indraprastha was given by none other than King Indra himself. Indraprastha has been variously called Indapatt, Indapath, Indarapatha or Indrapattan. It was one of the most important settlements of Jambudvipa and as important as that of Mithila. It was the important Kurav country and a road ran straight from here to Varanasi.

Now, coming to the city of Delhi and its nomenclature, the name 'Delhi' emerges for the first time in the writings of the Greek geographer, Ptolemy, during the first century CE. Even before that, a geographer of the Greek invader Alexander the Great, names a place 'Daidala' near Indraprastha, in a map dating to the first and second centuries BCE. This is perhaps the first name resembling Delhi.

Firishta, the author of Tarikh-i- Firishta, stated that 'Delhi' comes from the name of the ancient King, Raja Dhilu. A stone inscription of the Pratihar king, Mahendrapal-I, mentions that a Tomar King ruled over the land of present-day Haryana and the name of its capital was 'Dhilhika'. Delhi was founded in 736 CE by the Tomars. The original settlement of Delhi on the Banks of the Yamuna was a village extending from Kotla of Firoz Shah to the Tomb of Humayun. The name of the village was also Indraprastha which existed as late as the time of construction of New Delhi after the 1912 Durbar.

In the course of time the name of the city took on different pronunciations, from 'Dhilli' to 'Dilli' and again from 'Dehli' to 'Delhi'. During the reign of Mohammad Bin Tughlaq (1325–1357 CE), the city was named as 'Dhilli' in a stone inscription in Nadayan village (modern day Naraina). Similarly, another inscription recovered from Palam village Baoli refers to 'Delhi' as lying in 'Haryanak', present-day Haryana.

The Tomar kings built their capital at Suraj Kund, an area protected by hills. An early landmark of Delhi is a pre tenth century temple fort and lake complex in and around present day Suraj kund. Sultan Garhi Suraj kund with its sun temple, the ruins of a dam and some fortifications in ruins all point to creations by Suraj Pal and Anang Pal of the Tomar Dynasty. Lal Kot was the creation of Anang Pal who brought the Iron Pillar now standing in Mehrauli Mosque. King Prithviraj of Rai Pithora fame reinforced the walls and ramparts of Lal Kot and named it as Qila Rai Pithora. The first floor of the Qutub Minar was also created during the reign of Prithviraj III of Rai Pithora fame. However, there is no conclusive evidence to that effect. The Jogmaya temple in the Palam Baoli owes its origin to the thirteenth century as discovered in the stone inscription of that period. Delhi was associated with neighbourhood cities like Mehrauli, Tughlaqabad, Siri, Firozabad and Jahanpanah to name a few. These cities belonged to the Turkish and Pathan Dynasty rules.

Purana Qila characterized a marked admixture of Pathan and Muslims construction designs. Shahjahanabad was the first capital which opted for the archaic fort of Mughal tradition. After Shanjahanabad, the British built the capital city of New Delhi in a meticulously planned way after demolishing a lot of well-known existing structures. Even the village named Indraprastha in the area between Kotla of Firoz Shah and Purana Qila was destroyed in the process of the construction of New Delhi.

The magnificence and gorgeousness of the capital city of Delhi claimed mention in various travellers who came to Delhi from time to time. The great Moorish traveller, Ibn Batuta who came to Delhi during the reign of Muhammad-bin Tughlaq and stayed in the city from 1334to 1342 CE profusely eulogised the beauty of the city with its spectacular edifices, dazzling habitats and inhabitants. Francois Bernier, who came in 1659, was also full of eulogy for the city.

In fact, the nodal position of Delhi, which geographically made the city the centre of attracting foreigners was well documented from days of yore. Extensive excavation carried out in 1969 to 1973 or even earlier brought clear continuous evidence of habitation of the site from Mauryan period 300 BCE to early Mughal period of 16th century.

Prehistoric evidence of stone tools found in the area around Suraj Kund is an indication of habitation even during the Stone Age. The mounds between the eastern and western bank of river Yamuna on excavation yielded Harappan cultural affinity. Modern day Nand Nagari Simbhaoli village and Timurpora Narela, Khera Kalan, Bhor Garh, Gharandan also are sites associated with Harappan culture 4000 years old. The sequence of Archeological cultures in the Indo-Gangetic Divide before Asokan times was as follows:

The Sequence of culture before Asokan times

Date (with ± 100 years)	**Culture**	**Stage**
on either side	Northern Block	Iron
600 BC – 200 BC	Polished Ware Culture	
1000 BC – 400 BC	Painted Grey Ware culture	
1800 BC – 1000 BC	Ochre Coloured Pottery Culture	
1900 BC – 1000 BC	Late Harappan Culture : Chalcolithic culture	
2500 BC – 1700 BC	Harappan Culture	Copper Bronze
3000 BC – 2000 BC	Proto-Harappan Culture (sometime Called 'Sothi-Kot Diji complex of The Pre-Harappan origin')	

Most of the weapons used during the War of Kurukshetra or the Mahabharata War were of Iron. It was mentioned as Krisna-ayasa i.e. Black metal or Iron occurring in Atharvaveda which belonged to the pre-Mahabharat period. However, according to the Archeological readings, it is to be safely summarized that the use of Iron technology entered into India around 1200 BCE – 800 BCE with a margin of ±100 years to 200 years.

It will be interesting to dwell on the archeological finds in present-day Delhi, of which the most prominent are the excavated evidences at Mandoli and Bhor. Excavations were carried out at Mandoli which is situated about 18 km from old Delhi Railway station towards the east. In his article, B.R. Mani focused on the finds of the Department of Archeology which carried out extensive excavations under the guidance of B.S.R. Babu who conducted the exercise during 1992–93 and 1993–94.

Even before this, there was a joint exploration by a team led by B.R. Mani and B.L.Suri of one of the mounds which revealed the existence of brick structures of the Kuṣhan period. Archeological evidence without doubt confirms the existence of Kushan rule in Delhi. The Kushanas had ruled vast tracts of land in the Yamuna valley upto Mathura, but actually the existence of Delhi can be traced back to a much earlier period. Asoka's Minor Rock edict at East of Kailash in Delhi is the earliest recorded evidence of Delhi.

Excavated Painted Gray Wares found in the Purana Quila area confirms habitation as early as the Mauryan era of 300 BCE. Nand Nagari and Simbhaoli villages have yielded red ware shards of jars with beaded ruins pointing out to the habitation in Delhi during late Harappan period at least around 600 BCE. Skipping over a couple of centuries, we come to the more modern city of Delhi where it is referred to as Dillika. Delhi as a capital city was founded by the Tomar Kings around 730 CE.

The Pehowa inscription in Kurukshetra of the Pratihara King, Mahendrapal-I indicates his rule over the Haryana area and Dhillika was its capital. Mahendra Pal-I, son of Pratihara King Bhoja-I, ruled over Kannauj in 836 CE and his power extended upto Pehowa in the north and Vindhyas in the south. Delhi, as the name of this city, dates back to first and second centuries CE on the maps of Ptolemy, the Greek. Various excavations and ancient literature like Rig Veda, Atharvaveda Puranas like Markandeya Purana, various Shastras and Sutras like

Samkhayan, Katyayam, Patanjali's Mahabhasya, Bhagwat Purana and the epics Ramayana and Mahabharata categorically describe the settlements in and around Delhi as well as the existence of River Yamuna which was the mother of all settlements around Delhi with Yamuna itself changing its course, moving more towards the east to finally to mingle with the Ganga.

* * *

Chapter 5

Cities and Rulers of Delhi Over the Centuries

Foreign Greek origin conquerors who invaded India and came to rule over north India and Afghanistan, were divided into three main groups, namely the Sakas, the Pratihars or Parthian and the Yuechi or Kushans. The Kushans were nomads of Central Asia, who were driven from their abode around 165 BCE. The most celebrated Kushan King, Kanishka, is credited with the foundation of the Saka era of 78 CE. They were first to take advantage of the decay of Parthian rule.

Earlier Sakas made inroads to the area around the tributaries of Kabul River which was in fact Afghanistan. The area in the southern part of Afghanistan came to be known as Sakasthana or modern Sistan. Gradually they extended their rule over the Indus basin and western India. Subsequently in the first century after Christ, a part of this territory fell in the hands of the Parthians. One of their earlier rulers was Maues or Moga. His suzerainty was acknowledged by the governor of Taxila near Rawalpindi, which is now in Pakistan and situated in the east of River Indus (Sindhu river). His successor Azes-I is credited to be the founder of Vikrama Samvat, around the year 58 BCE. The other view is that Vikrama Samvat is associated with the name of King Vikramaditya in post Gupta period who is credited as the destroyer of the Saka rule in India.

The Saka Pahlava kings ruled territories deep into India. One of the satraps or governors ruled in Afghanistan in the area of Ghorband and Panjshir in southern Afghanistan. Another governor family ruled over western Punjab (now Pakistan) province of Taxila (near Rawalpindi). Another clan went as far as Mathura in the Yamuna valley. One clan went to the Malwa region and established their rule in Ujjain. Another satrap or governor went down south to carve out a principality on the ruins of Satvahana kingdom. Rudradaman, one of the greatest Saka rulers ruled during 130 CE onwards. He is credited with the conquest of Konkan in the south and Marwar and Sind in the North. The rule of Saka Satrap ended in the fourth century AD with the advent of Samudragupta and Chandragupta-II.

From ancient times, Delhi has seen the rise and fall of kings and capitals. There have been many cities or capitals built on or around Delhi. Delhi has been under the rule of Hindu monarchs right from roughly 1500 BC to 1192 CE, after which it came under Muslim Rule.

The earliest Dynasty which can be reckoned was the Kurus (Pandavas) dynasty who ruled from 1500–345 BCE. Indraprasath was the legendary capital of the Pandavas. After fourteen years of exile, the Pandavas asked King Dhritarastra to hand over five villages namely Vrikaprasth – (Baghpat) Indraprath – Indrapat (now Delhi), Tilaparasth – Tilpat, Paniprasth – Panipat and Sonanaprasth or Sonipat.

The Hindu Rulers:

The Hindu kings who ruled over the city of Delhi were:

1. The Kurus (Pandavas) ruled during 1500–345 BCE. Capital city: **Indraprastha**
2. The Nandas from 345–320 BCE.
3. The Mauryas from 323 to 185 BCE.
4. The Indo Greek rulers from 185 to 50 BCE.
5. The Sakas & Kushanas from 50 BCE to 320 CE.
6. The Guptas from 320 CE to 500 CE.
7. The Huns from 500 to 600 CE.
8. The Pushyabhuti Dynasty from 606 to 647 CE

9. After this Delhi was deserted for some period, till the Gurjara-Pratihars came to rule during 836 CE – 1018 CE.
   During the intervening period, the capital shifted to Mathura. For a pretty long time there was a dip in Delhi's fortune. Some say that Delhi lost its prominence for almost 800 years, till the Tomar Rajputs founded their capital in the Surajkund area which was in the Aravali Hills, south of Delhi.

10. Tomars ruled around 1051 CE. Capital city: **Lal Kot,** the first city of Delhi
    King Surajpal built a big reservoir named Surajkund in the tenth century CE. A Sun temple was also built on the western side of the reservoir. The famous court-bard, Chand Bardai in his epic poem 'PrithviRaj Raso' mentioned that Delhi was built by Anangpal Tomar (1130 to 1145 CE). Lake Badkhal was also the creation of this period. The city built by Anangpal was called 'Lal Kot' which was the first fortified fort in the real sense. With proper defence fortification it became the first city of Delhi.
    Descendents of Raja Anangpal ruled over Delhi for several generations, extending over a period of 160 years, till the last king Paliraj, was defeated by Vishaldev Chauhan.

11. The Chauhans or the Chahamans 1151 to 1192 CE.

In the early 12th century, Ajay Raj established the Chauhan dynasty at the new city of Ajmer. Vishal Dev ruled from 1157 CE to 1164 CE. He was a great king who extended his rule over present day Hissar, Bhiwani, Gurgaon and also snatched Chittor from the Chalukyas. Prithvi Raj III, also known as Prithvi Raj Chauhan or the famous Rai Pithora, son of Someshvar ruled from 1178 to 1192 CE. In the second battle of Tarain of 1192 CE, he was defeated by Mohammad Ghori, having won the earlier battle of Tarain in 1191. After the capture and death of Prithvi Raj Chauhan, Mohammad Ghori was successful in capturing Delhi and Ajmer. This had far reaching effects on the establishment of Muslim rule in India, which continued till the advent of the British rule. Mohammad Ghori was the real founder of the Muslim rule in India. It was his successive invasions of India that led to the downfall of Hindu rulers, one by one, and opened the gates of India to other foreign invaders after him. After the capture of Delhi, the whole of India gradually came under the Muslim rule and Islam became the state religion.

Hindu rule in India was totally decimated due to internal dissensions, unnecessary benevolence and generosity towards enemies, along with lack of adventurism and ambition.

From 1193 to 1206 CE, Qutub- ud -Din Aibak, remained slave of Mohammad Ghori. After the death of Ghori in 1206 CE, Aibak declared himself the ruler of India. This started the reign of Muslim rulers, with Delhi or its neighbourhood city as the capital from 1193 CE to 1857 CE.

The Delhi Sultanate:

The dynasties of the Delhi Sultanate that ruled during this period were as follows –

1. Shamsabanis Muizuddin Mohammad Bin Sam 1193 – 1206 CE
2. House of Qutub-ud-din Aibak – 1206 to 1210 CE
   He founded the first of a succession of dynasties known as the Delhi Sultanate (1206 to 1526 CE) who were of Afghan and Turkish origin
3. House of Iltutmish – 1211–1266 CE
   It included rule of Begum Raziya, the only women ruler 1236–1240 CE
4. House of Balban – 1266–1290 CE
   Muiz-ud-Din Keiqubad founded the city of **Kilokari** in 1287 CE.
5. The House of Khiljis ruled during 1290–1320 CE.
   Ala-ud- din Khilji (1296 to 1316 CE) founded the city/fort of **Siri** in 1304 CE.

6. The House of Tughlaq ruled over the territory of Delhi during 1320–1414 CE.
   In the early days of reign, the city of **Tughlaqabad** was established in 1320 CE by Ghiyas-ud-din Tughlaq (1320 to 1324 CE). He is also known as Ghazi Malik.
   Next came Mohammad-bin-Tughlaq (1324 to 1351 CE) who founded the city of **Jahanpanah** (meaning, refuge of the world) during 1327 CE. Firoz-bin-Rajab or Firoz Shah Tughlaq of the same dynasty who ruled during 1351–1385 CE, built the city of **Firozabad** on the bank of river Yamuna, seven miles north-east of Jahanpanah.

7. The next dynasty to rule were the Sayyids who ruled during 1414–1451 CE.
   The first Sultan Khizr Khan actually captured Delhi in 1414 CE and founded the city of **Khizrabad** on the banks of river Yamuna, one mile south-east of Kilokari. After Khizr Khan's death, his son Muiz-ud-din Mubarak built a new city of **Mubarakbad** on the banks of the Yamuna in 1433 CE. But before the completion of the city, he was killed. This city is no longer in existence.

8. The Lodis came next, who ruled during 1451–1526 CE. However the Lodis shifted their capital to Agra. Ibrahim Lodi was the last of the line, who lost to Babur.

The Mughal Dynasty:

Mughal rule lasted in India for a reasonably long time, from 1526 to 1857. The Mughals were the descendants of two dynasties: on one hand they were successors of Genghis Khan, the Mongol ruler of China and Central Asia, and on the other hand they belonged to the family of Timur, the founder of the Timurid Empire and the ruler of Iran, Iraq and modern day Turkey.

The Mughal dynasty was established in India by Babur, a descendant of Timur, with the defeat of Ibrahim Lodhi in 1526 CE in the battlefield of Panipat. After the conquest of Delhi or India, Babar, the first Mughal King, had Agra as his capital. After the establishment of the Mughal dynasty in India, Delhi as the capital fell out of reckoning and Agra as capital took over.

The importance of Delhi as capital and seat of power was totally eclipsed with the victory of Babar over Ibrahim Lodi in the battle of Panipat in 1526 CE. In fact, even before that, the Lodis shifted their capital to Agra. So, after their defeat at the hands of Babar in 1526 CE, Agra automatically became the capital of Babar. The ascendency of Agra over Delhi continued till Shahab ud Din Shah Jahan decided to shift his capital to Delhi on the banks of Yamuna around 1640 CE.

Babur, with his capital at Agra, was on the throne for a short period, from 1526–1530 CE. He was succeeded by his son Humayun (Nazir-ud-din Humayun), who ruled from 1530–1538 CE. He constructed his new capital, '**Dinpanah**' on the ancient site of Indraprastha in 1533 CE.

Sher Shah Suri captured power after ousting Humayun and founded the Suri dynasty. He ruled briefly, from 1538 to 1545 CE. He expanded Humayun's Dinpanah and named it as '**Shergarh**'. In spite of his short rule, Sher Shah Suri was known as an able military and economic administrator; he organized the Indian postal system and is also credited with issuing the first 'Rupiya' from the previous 'Tanka'. The Suri Dynasty lasted from 1538 to 1555 CE. Mughals were restored to power in 1555 CE with Humayun as the head. However, he ruled for one year only, from 1555–1556 CE.

Jalal-ud-Din Akbar was the next ruler (1556–1605 CE). Akbar, the most prominent ruler of the Mughal Dynasty, had his first capital at Fatehpur Sikri, near the dargah of Salim Chisti. Nur-ud-Din Jahangir, was next to rule for the period (1605–1627 CE). After a short rule of one year by Dawar Bakhsh (1627–1628 CE), Shahab-ud-din Shah Jahan ascended the throne (1628–1657 CE). Shah Jahan's governor of Delhi, Khalilullah Khan in 1652–53 CE undertook the total reconstruction of Nizam ud Din Khanqah as it presently exists in the heart of Delhi.

In 1640 A.D, Shah Jahan decided to shift the capital back to Delhi from Agra. A new City with the Red Fort came up in 1648 CE on the banks of the river Yamuna, one mile north of Firozabad, which was named **Shahjahanabad**. It continued to be the capital of the Mughal Kingdom till the time of the Sepoy Mutiny of 1857. Bahadur Shah was the last of the Mughal Emperors of Delhi. After that, British rule started in India.

Chapter 6

Unity of India Amid Diversity – As in Ancient Times

The emergence of India as an integrated political entity is credited to the British conquerors of India according to the die-hard anglophiles. According to them the 'Pan Indian' identity, that is, recognising 'India' as one unified country is the gift of the 'British Coloniser'. It is no doubt a fact that during the two hundred years of British occupation, India was a conglomerated sub-continent of separate states. It was the British conquest that allowed the forging of separate disparate states / principalities into a union, politically called 'India'. It also presupposed that in the long history of the Indian subcontinent, the British colonists were the first to rule as supreme single authority, a trait not observed before in history.

This contention is factually wrong as borne out by the long history of India and if we care to delve into the history of ancient India. The very name "Bharata-Varsha" emphasises the fundamental unity of India. According to the Puranas, Bharata conquered the whole of the Indian subcontinent and then proceeded to rule over that land in peace and harmony. 'Vishnu Purana' was the first religious treatise to incorporate a Sanskrit shloka, which describes India as follows: 'The country that lies north of the ocean and south of the snowy mountains is called Bharata, there dwell the descendants of Bharata, the King'.

This is the unique sense of unity that pervades the whole community of people including political personalities, theologians, the poets and the common man. History of the days of yore bear testimony to the fact that the entire country from the Himalaya foothills to the sea in the south, had a single religion and a common language right from the third century BCE. First it was 'Prakrit' and later 'Sanskrit' which were both court languages as well as the language of the common literary people.

The concept of India as one single cultural and geographical unit was always recognized as an accepted fact in the minds of its political and cultural leaders as well as its conquerors. Even foreign invaders saw the land and its people as a unified whole. Coming in contact with the people of the Sindhu region or around the river Indus, different invaders at different times named the whole country as 'Hind', 'Hindustan' and 'India'.

The prime ancient epics – 'The Ramayana', based on life of Maryada Purushottam Sri Ram of Ayodhya and 'The Mahabharata', based on the great battle of Kurukshetra and incorporating the immortal messages of 'The Bhagavad Gita', the sacred text of the Hindus, command unique reverence and even today are recited with greatest devotion in the whole of India, albeit in the different languages in which they were translated. The old religion of the Vedas and Puranas still give solace to the teeming millions with the temples of Shiva and Vishnu drawing the same respect even today, as was the case thousands of years ago.

It is a credit to the catholicity of the Indian society that it has been continuously adopting and absorbing various traits be it social, cultural and even the religious traditions of the foreigners who initially came as invaders to grab the fabulous land riches of India, but finally settled down in this land after subjugating local rulers. In course of time, they became a part and parcel of Indian society.

The earlier invaders like the Sakas and the Huns, merged their identity within the people of the Indian society, and became Rajputs and Jat clans. The later rulers like the Turks, Pathans, Mongols, and Mughals, adopted India as the land of their settlements, however, retaining their exclusivity as the rulers, to distinguish themselves from the ruled subjects. This was pronounced because Islamic religious beliefs and practices, totally different from the Hindus, continued. However, over the years there were even exchanges of religious beliefs as exhibited in the adoption and spread of Sufism in India.

Delhi being uniquely placed as the capital and trading centre of India, received a chunk of such foreigners, who contributed to evolving a composite culture where different religions with their own ethos got a certain degree of amalgamation with the local majorly Hindu society.

Ancient India saw the birth of three major religions: Hinduism or Brahmanism, Jainism and Buddhism, which have, over time, interacted and intermingled with each other. A unique combination of the main traits of these three religions namely Hinduism, Buddhism and Jainism, which mutually coexisted, is expressed in their teachings, philosophy and literature. The Upanishads, Bhagavats, Puranas and the famous works of the Mauryan era, like the 'Arthashastra' by Kautilyaa, the 'Kalpasutra' of Bhadrabahu, the Grammar of Panini and the Buddhist 'Katha Vathi' are reckoned to be great works, traditionally related to the political personages of the time. These great works are based on a common philosophy and cultural milieu.

After Alexander's death, it was during the rule of Chandragupta Maurya, who founded the Mauryan Empire in 321 BCE, that for the first time, most of the Indian subcontinent was united under a single government, thus establishing one of the largest empires ever seen before in Indian history. He not only won over most of the fragmented and scattered small kingdoms in ancient India, but he also united them into a massive empire, boundaries of which extended to Afghanistan and almost to Persia in the west to Bengal in the east and from the Himalayas in the north to the Deccan Plateau in the south. After him, his grandson, Ashoka was one of the most important and influential rulers of ancient India who was responsible for further unifying the Indian subcontinent under one administration. India remained unified both politically as well as culturally, in spite of regional differences. A contemporary of Pushyamitra Sunga the founder of Sunga dynasty of late Mauryan dynasty originated from one of the sons of Ashoka, named Kunala. According to Kalhana, the historian and literary elite of this period, Jalauka was another son of Ashoka, who is associated with that branch of the Maurya dynasty, whose rule was confined to the Kashmir valley. The history of this period of the late imperial Mauryans is somehow shrouded in mystery.

Regarding political situation prevailing at the close of the third century BCE, a king named Subhangasena or Sophagasenas ruled over Kabul and Kapisa valley. The name was equated to the title 'King of the Indians'. This also suggests that Indus valley was under an Indian ruler. However, the area was far away from Pataliputra, the capital of the main Mauryan dynasty. Obviously, the ruler of Kabul valley was someone other than a Mauryan. The title Subhangasena was given by the Greeks. It also suggests that he was not merely the Governor/Viceroy of Taxila; in all probability he was Antiochos III, the Greek ruler of fame who ruled during 223–187 BC. He was the grandson of Antiochus II Jheos, a contemporary of Ashoka and great grandson of Seleukos I Nicator, a contemporary of Chandragupta Maurya. According to the Gargi Samhita, the Greeks had penetrated upto Pataliputra. India with its diversity of race, religion, customs, habits and financial conditions, already needed a very strong ruler to integrate this various diversity into unity. Ashoka was one such ruler who had the unique capacity to achieve a union of these diverse identities: social, political and cultural, which had not been possible before. He restricted the disrupting and opposing forces, both national and international, with strong hands and created his considerable empire. The Mauryan Empire (320 to 185 BCE) was the first major empire, including most of South Asia excluding extreme south India and developed as a result of state consolidation in northern India, centered in Magadha, now Bihar.

After the fall of the Mauryans, the most prominent empire was that of the Kushans (135 BCE to 375CE) who controlled over the Ganga valley and parts of Afghanistan and Central Asia. Kanishka extended the Kushan Empire well into Central India. This was followed by the Gupta Empire (320 to 550 CE) based mainly in northern India, extending upto Bengal. After the fall of the Guptas, north India was again divided into many small kingdoms. It was Harshavardhana (606 CE to 647 CE) who was able to unite many of these under his command, building a huge kingdom that extended from north and northwestern India till river Narmada in the south. The Gurjara Pratihara Empire (650 to 1036 CE), which arose after the fragmentation of the Gupta Empire, was in size and duration greater than many preceding it. They played a major role in uniting western, central and northern India. Setting up their capital in Kannauj, near Delhi, they developed fortifications throughout their empire, making them hard to conquer, and providing greater resistance to the later Islamic invasions.

The period 700 to 1001CE was a dark period of chaos in all fields whether defence, or finance or any other positive human activity. In the meantime, India was growing in riches, fabulously making it an object of envy to the invaders beyond the borders. The forays of the Crescent, from the distant lands of the west, i.e. Arabia started from 100 CE to 1200 CE. The valiant Rajputs resisted the Islamic invasions upto 1192 CE. The last Hindu emperor of Delhi, Prithviraj Chauhan was defeated and killed in the second battle of Tarain near Thaneswar by Mohammad Ghori. This ushered in the doom of Hindu rule from the annals of history of India. The establishment of the Islamic rule right upto 1857 CE was confirmed. There were successive rules of Turks, Afghans, then Mongols and finally the Mughals. The Timurid Dynasty started ruling India from 1526 CE, when Ibrahim Lodi, the Sultan of Delhi was defeated by the Mughal forces of Babur, the ruler of Kabulistan and sixth descendent of Timur. In spite of being a ruthless, marauding nomad and horse-mounted tribal of the Persian desert, Babur was a great patron of architecture; this being a trait of his character directly opposed to his harsh and ruthless warrior-like behaviour. He was partial to the art of building edifies and lavish gardens in India. Babur is said to have employed a retinue of 680 men working daily on his buildings at Agra and nearly 1500 men for buildings in Fatehpur Sikri, Dholpur, Biyana, Gwalior and the like. However, age and weather were responsible for destruction of the old edifices leaving comparatively smaller edifices like Kabuli Bagh mosque at Panipat, which was the victory site of the battle with Ibrahim Lodi in 1526 CE, and similar ones dotted all over north India and the Deccan.

Babur became the emperor of Delhi and founded the Mughal dynasty of northern India. Fighting off formidable foes on all sides, he set the foundation stone of a dynasty that was to rule over India for many years to come. The task of consolidating the empire however, was performed by his grandson, Akbar. Under Akbar (1556 to 1605 CE), the Mughal dynasty reached its pinnacle of glory; he expanded and consolidated the

Mughal Empire to include almost all of the Indian subcontinent. He should also be remembered for his inclusive vision for India, with his progressive views on communal harmony, religious tolerance and equal respect of all religions. He founded a new religion, Sulh-e-kul (universal peace), which was a confluence of the best tenets of Hinduism and Islamic ideals and based on peace, unity and tolerance. This served as the greatest unifying factor in bringing the subcontinent together under one centralised administration. Sulh-e-kul was further propagated by Dara Sikoh, son of Shah Jahan.

Chapter 7

The Early Inroads of Islam in India

The earliest inroad of Islam into India dates back to the tenth century CE, when Central Asia, Afghanistan and the eastern part of Persia, mainly Afghanistan came under the control of the Samanid Dynasty with Bukhara as the capital. Ghazni as capital was founded in 963 CE, by one of the slaves of the Samanid Dynasty Mohammad Bin Qasim who conquered Sindh. In 977 CE, Sabuktigin also a slave of the Samanid Dynasty like the one who founded Ghazni, fought a battle with the Hindu Raja, Raja of Waihind, Jaipal, who was defeated. He agreed to pay fifty lakh of Rupees, fifty elephants and territory upto Jalalabad. Jaipal however annulled the agreement on returning to the capital. Sabuktigin attacked Jaipal again and won the second battle whereupon he captured territory upto Peshawar and spread Islam there.

When Sabuktigin died in 997 CE, his eldest of four sons, Mahmud, succeeded him. But the authority of Ghazni was denied to him. Later on, he captured Ghazni, from his younger brother and forced the Samanid Caliph to accept his suzerainty over Balk, Herat, Tirmiz and Khurasan. Meanwhile Ilak Khan captured Bukhara, thereby ending the rule of the Samanid Dynasty.

Mahmud of Ghazni attacked Multan in 1006 CE and in 1008 CE, he defeated Ilak Khan. In the same year he again defeated Anand Pal, son of Jaipal and captured the Nagar Kot fort. In October 1014 CE Mahmud defeated Trilochanpal, son of Anand Pal, who died early and captured Thaneswar thereby winning over the entire area of Punjab. In September

1018 CE, Mahmud crossed the river Yamuna and reached Bulandshahar, where the Hindu ruler surrendered and even embraced Islam. By December of 1018 CE, he had completed the subjugation of the Hindu Kingdoms of Mathura and Kannauj. Towards the end of 1019 CE, he returned back to Ghazni, with a huge loot. In 1021 CE, he again invaded India and captured Gwalior and Kalinjar and returned to Ghazni in 1023 with an even larger booty.

After a lay off for a year, the fame of the Somnath temple and its fabled richness, lured Mahmud to attack Somnath in January 1025 CE. On the way, he inflicted defeat on the Hindu kingdom of Anhilwara in Rajputana. After two days of campaign, Mahmud decisively won the battle of Somnath. For 15 days, he vandalized the temple town, destroyed the Shiva Lingam and looted the untold treasures of Somnath, worth two million dinars. He returned to Ghazni in April 1026 CE. For this outstanding military victory, he received special accolades from the Caliph of Baghdad. He died because of Tuberculosis on 30 April 1030 AD. He had a chequered history of constant battle with little intermissions for thirty-three years and singularly eked out the complete subjugation of Hindu rule and establishment. He ensured the total domination of Islam. Nobody, more than him, can be credited for complete domination of Muslim rule in India. Sultan Mahmud never invaded Delhi. However, he severely destroyed the kingdoms in and around Delhi to break the backbone of Delhi's authority and defense. Delhi now lay morally and militarily exposed and weakened to the onslaughts of Islamic rulers henceforth.

In personal life, Mahmud of Ghazni was a great connoisseur of art and culture and established an academy at Ghazni with a collection of rare books and manuscripts. He patronised scholars like Firdausi, Farruki and Abu Raihan-al-Biruni, the author of Kitab-al-Hind. His victory tower in Ghazni was 144 feet high, and like the Qutub Minar in style. His son Masud ruled for twelve years, from 1030–1042 CE. He defeated his elder brother for the throne. He captured Hansi and Sonipat. His empire ranged from Iraq to the river plains of Ganga in India.

As can be observed, the ruthless exploits of Mahmud, led to the strong foundation of the rule of Islam in North India and which then percolated towards the south of the Vindhyas. It was consolidated by Qutab-ud-din Aibak, the most faithful Turkish commander of Md. Ghori and also by Ikhtiyar-ud-din Mohammad, a Turkish officer of Md. Ghori.

In 1191 CE, Muhammad of Ghor or Sultan Muhammad Ghori reached the Indian sub-continent, specifically Punjab, through the Khyber Pass. In the first Battle of Tarain (1191 CE), he lost to the army of the united Rajput Confederacy led by Prithvi Raj Chauhan but was ultimately victorious in the second Battle of Tarain in 1192 CE. His rule over India was short, but it is he who is credited to be the founder of the Muslim rule in the Indian sub-continent. Ghori returned to Ghazni appointing his slave and general, Qutub ud-Din Aibak as his regional governor in north India.

Aibak, was a slave in his childhood in Turkestan and was purchased by a merchant and sold to the Quazi Takhr-ud-din Abdul Aziz Kufi of Nishapur who imparted military and religious training to young Aibak. After the death of his father, Quazi's son sold Aibak to another merchant, who in turn sold him to the Ghurs of the Ghaznavi dynasty. Aibak, subsequently with his excellent military and religious acumen, became the most trusted officer of Ghur who handed over the governorship of subjugated territory to him.

He started what we know as the Slave Dynasty as the first three kings (Qutab-ud-din, Iltutmish and Balban) were Turkish slaves who were manumitted by their masters. Qutab-ud-din received a letter of manumission from the successor of Mohd. Ghori, Sultan Ghiyas-ud-din the nephew and successor of Md. Ghori and was therefore elevated to the throne as the Sultan of Delhi. Similarly, Iltutmish received his manumission from his master.

The third namely, Balban was in league with forty selected Turkish slaves of Iltutmish, who gave him his freedom. Incidentally, all the kings were 'Turkish' and not 'Pathans' or 'Afghans' as commonly believed. This is according to historian Zia-ul-Barni (Tarik-i-Firuz Shah).

With Qutb al-Din Aibak, we have the beginning of the vast and powerful Delhi Sultanate, comprising the Mamluk dynasty, the Khilji dynasty, the Tughlaq dynasty, the Sayyid dynasty and finally the Lodi dynasty, after which it was replaced in 1526 CE, by the Mughal Dynasty led by Babur.

Chapter 8

Delhi the Cradle of Sufism

Right from the Prehistoric days of Indraprastha, the capital of the Aryan race of the Pandavas, close relations of the ruling clan of the Kauravas with their temporal capital at Hastinapur, Delhi has been the cradle of spiritual and religious dispensation.

The regular rule of the Muslims in India commenced with the victory of Mohammad Ghori over Prithviraj Chauhan of Rai Pithora fame in the second battle ofTerrain in 1192, thereby laying down the strong foundations of Muslim rule in India which continued till its culmination in1857, with defeat of Bahadur Shah Zafar, his capture by the British in Delhi.

It may be mentioned that in Islam, there is no dichotomy between the temporal and the spiritual authority. It is a religious political system. This system had flourished during the Delhi Sultanate (1206–1526 AD). A part of this period accommodated the Chishtiya School of Sufism. A major portion of this period saw the rule of Turco-Muslim Dynasty with Delhi or its outskirts remaining the capital. Shaikhs, Mashaikh, Pir and Murshids had been the different masters of the Sufi clan. It is essential to delve into the basic tenets and characters of Sufi mendicants, who spearheaded the mystical Islamic movements which were popularised through their personal deeds. For the mystically minded Muslims, irrespective of their standing, whether educated or illiterate, talented, powerful or affluent, everybody accepts the temporal and spiritual authority of the Shaikh. This acceptance of total supremacy is manifested in the oath of allegiance or even kissing of the feet of the Shaikh. The Shaikh is considered to be a man in direct communion with God and who can lead an uninitiated common man in acquiring blessings of the divine will through the directed path of meditation. He is venerated as the perfect man whose human infallibilities like greed, craving for material comfort, sin etc., are incompatible with the flawless nature of the divine.

As a stepping stone to achieve perfection in life, it is worth recalling the daily routine or conduct of the Prophet Muhammad as penned down by Sharafad-din maneri, the outstanding Firdauji master of the fourteen century who lived in Bihar. His testament is worth reproducing in verbatim – "He himself used to arrange the fodder for his own mount. He used to go home and light the lamp himself. When the strap of his sandal broke, he himself repaired it. He used to mend his own torn garments with his very own hand. He helps the servants in the house. If someone asked him to do some foolish thing, he never declined. If a stranger was aggrieved with him, he did not punish him. Never at all were such things a cursing, imprecation, abuse or vile language found upon his tongue. He was always smiling with no laughter or frivolity. Coupled with these admirable traits of self-reliance, malleability and sobriety were acts of charity and solicitude, uncommon egalitarianism, voluntary poverty, prayerful responsiveness and grandfatherly forbearance." The same letter speaks elaborately and eloquently of the extraordinary piety and benevolence for his friends and his servants. The same letter further eulogises his absolutely frugal way of living and not craving for even minimal comforts like sleeping on a base mat without any mattress or covers. There is no end to such examples of piety, self-abstinence from all comforts, total frugality even in respect to minimum intake of food and foregoing minimum necessities, without compromising the steadfast devotion of praying in isolation to seek spiritual communion with God.

There is a close link between the development of Sufism and the contribution of Delhi, an urban city towards the same objective. One thing is clear, Sufism is basically a phenomenon associated with urbanism. It did not find its base in the rural environment. A Sufi saint need be wellborn in a good Muslim family, yet he should be motivated to seek the path of divinity as ordained by the Sufi master, to improve the quality of Islamic faith, through severe fasting and prolonged meditation as guided by his Sufi master. The person seeking Sufism needs to remain in isolation yet help his fellow Muslims in the hour of their need.

There is no bar even for the married person striving to imbibe Sufism. But once initiated to Sufism, it is essential that he practise celibacy in temperament and disposition in daily life while being enthralled by music and verse. Along with music in the company of others, he must abide by his obligatory basic duties as a Muslim.

He should avoid the company of rich city dwellers, merchants, soldiers, government officials including kings and court nobles; yet he would live in their proximity, in a city in a Khanaq (Monastery) and be in communication through his murids (the disciples).

It is relevant here to discuss the association of the city of Delhi with the Chistiya Silsila of Sufism during the period 1192 to 1526, that is, the period of the Delhi Sultanate. This was the period of great influence of the religious leaders over Delhi. Sufi saints were a special class of Muslim mystics who were believed to have been directly selected by god to guide men on the right course of truth and preserve the moral, spiritual and cultural character of the people. The Chistiya Silsila of Sufism was one such silsila of sufism in India, founded by Khwaja Muin-ud-Din Hassan Chishti Sanjari (born 1141 CDE), a descendant of the great Prophet Mohammad. He came to India to preach the gospel of universal truth and brotherhood through Sufism. While discussing the 'Silsila', certain concrete traits are discernible. Chistiya Silsila is an urban phenomenon. All the great Chistiya Shaikhs, including Nizam-ud-din Auliya (the fourth Shaikh), had all their activities centred around Delhi. Of all the Sufi saints, two names that stand out as most popular and outstanding. They were Hazrat Khwaja Nizam-ud-Din Aulia and Hazrat Khwaja Nasir-ud-din Mahmud Chirag of Delhi, who was the spiritual successor of Nizam-ud-din Aulia.

With the fall of the prime Sufi seat of Baghdad in 1258 CE at the hands of Hulagu and thereafter the establishment of the Mongol Empire, a large number of Muslim refugees and holy men sought asylum in north India. From the eleventh to the sixteen century, Muslims, through military consolidation and conquest, had a firm foothold in India, with strong political religious base and through the consolidated Muslim Sultanate.

Their strength and political power further increased through the conversion of low class and a few high class Hindus into Islam. From the beginning of the eleventh century, Muslim political influence was extending through military expansion and their religious influence was spreading through their religious leaders, the Sufi saints.

1290 CE saw the liquidation of the Slave dynasty by the Khiljis. During this period, the spiritual activities of the Sufis suffered a setback. The Sufi saints of Delhi region acquired huge popularity and following at the cost of the wrath of the Delhi Kings. One such was Hazrat Khawaja Nizam ud Din Aulia. In 1265 CE, Nizam-ud-Din Aulia moved to the outskirts of Delhi and established his Khanqah or monastery in Ghyaspur, then a small village in proximity to Delhi, away from the din and bustle of the capital. The monastery (Khanqah) was built by his favourite disciple Maulana-Zia-ud-Din. With passage of time, this Khanqah became an integral part of the Nizam-ud-din basti, adjacent to the Nizam-ud-din railway station in Delhi. The saint lived in the same place from 1265 to 1351 CE. He was witness to the reigns of eight Delhi Sultans. The first was Ghiyas-ud-din Balban (1266–87). Then came Kaiqubad (1287–90), who was the grandson of Balban, his only son, Burga Khan, having refused to take up the responsibility. Kaiqubad shifted the capital from Mehrauli to Kilokhari near present day Humayun's Tomb. Because of his ill health, he could not continue as Sultan and his only son being a minor, the Khilji nobles of the court, placed Jalal-ud-Din Firoz Khilji (1290–06) to the throne. He ruled for sixteen years. The Khilji rule continued for thirty years (1290–1320 AD). After Jalal-ud-Din, the next Sultan was Ala-ud-Din Khilji (1296–1316 AD). Next was Mubarak Khilji (1316–1320 AD). Khusru Khan (1320) ruled for a short period of four months. The next Sultan to occupy the throne was Ghiyas-ud-din Tughlaq (1320–5 CE), who at the request of court nobles ascended the throne in September 1320. After him came Mohammad Bin Tughlaq (1325–51).

On the side-lines, a little of Ala-ud-Din Khilji's time needs special mention. The period of his rule was marked by peace and tranquility all around as never witnessed before. The trade was flourishing and goods in general were very cheap, especially food. The Sultan never displayed his religious bearings. He never came in close proximity to Nizam-ud-Din Aulia, neither did he interfere in his religious affairs, in sharp contrast to Mubarak Khilji (1316–20 AD) and Ghiyas-ud-Din Tughlaq (1320–25 AD) who were jealous of the extreme popularity of Aulia. With mass support, a total of three Sufi Silsilas emerged, namely Chistiya, Suhrawardi and Firdausi, in India. Nizam-ud-Din was severely troubled during the reign of the two aforementioned Khiljis. But he was extremely fortunate in having his mother who was a very pious lady and who mentored him in his spiritual life, prayed for him and gave him solace to tide over his problems. Her grave or dargah is in Adhchini village, a part of Mehrauli. Nizam-ud-Din was also offered the job of Qazi but was advised not to accept it by his guide Sheikh Najib-ud-Din Mutvakil.

Nizam-ud-Din, is also credited with his immortal prophecy – 'Hanuz Dilli Door Ast'. 'Dilli is yet far off'. The incident occurred during the reign of Ghyas-ud-Din Tughlaq who missed no opportunity to make his life miserable. He had ordered the Aulia to leave Delhi, before he made a triumphant entry into the capital after annihilating and looting Lakhnauti (Bengal) in 1325 CE. What happened next was surprising; the Sultan himself perished before entering the capital. Aulia's favourite was the great court poet, Amir Khusrau.

Just before his death, in 1325 CE, he handed over the traditional sacred relics to Hazrat Khwaja Nasir-ud-Din Chirag (of Chirag Delhi fame) and distributed his worldly possessions to Khalifas, murids and common disciples. Undoubtedly, he was the doyen of all Sufi saints.

Some of his own philosophy of life and his impact on the society is penned by the famous historian of the period, Zia-ud-Din Barni in his 'Tarikh-i-Firoz Shahi'. Nizam-ud-din Aulia received his spiritual initiation from his Pir, Sheikh Farid-ud-Din Ganj-i-Shakar, who mistrusted any proximity to the king and nobles, and warned that every Darvesh who makes friends with kings and nobles will end badly. (from Barni's Tarikh-i-Firoz Shahi).

The motto of Nizam-ud-Din was spelt in his own words: "The main object of Man's creation is the love of the Supreme being. The love of God implied love of humanity". To quote the concept and aim of life as propagated by him, "A Muslim must abstain from doing harm of any kind to anybody, he must also abstain from every sin and should protect his eyes, tongue and hands from an undesirable act, he should direct his eyes and tongue towards the truth and keep glorifying Allah, steering clear of every doubt that might develop in his mind... the heart is a mirror which is in itself clear; but sins cover it with dust which can only be removed by repeating the names of Allah and his Prophet Mohammad" (Dara Shikoh – Safinat-ul-Aulia). [Delhi: Biography of a city, Ram Avtar Sharma and Madhukar Tiwari, Aakar publications]

The saint impacted the society greatly through his noble character. Zia-ud-Din Barni eulogizes his contribution in moral uplifting of the society: 'All people, believing in him, tried to emulate him in devotion and virtue. Men and Women, young and old, low and mean servants and slaves and even small boys had began to offer their prayers regularly. Rich and benevolent persons had constructed in several pleasant spots between the city and Ghyaspur, terraces with thatched roofs and had wells dug there. The terraces were supplied with large jugs full of water, clay jugs and mats, and keepers and reciters were posted there so that people coming from or going to the monastery of the Sheikh may not feel inconvenient in making their ablutions at prayer times. In each of these terraces one saw crowds of people offering prayers. Perpetration or talk of crime had declined among the people, and they talked mostly of religious things.... There was no quarter in the city where after twenty days or a month there was no gathering of the pious listening to Sufi music and weeping in ecstasy. Sultan Ala-ud-Din himself, with all his family, had great faith in the Sheikh and the hearts of all classes of people were inclined towards virtue and piety. Never did the name of wine and women, crime and sin, gambling or other such practices, profane the lips of people during the latter portion of Ala-ud-Din's reign. Most of the students, nobles and great men who attended upon the Sheikh were seen to be busy in the study of books on Sufism or the Islamic law'.

After his death the funeral was performed by Hazrat Sheikh Abul Fatha Rukh-ud-din, grandson of Hazrat Khwaja Baha-ud-Din Zakaria Suhrawardi of Multan. Sultan Mohammad bin Tughlaq built a tomb on his grave. The shrine of Sheikh Nizam-ud-Din Aulia is a revered place of visit by Muslims and Hindus alike depicting a unique feature of Indo-Muslim piety. All Mughal rulers paid their obeisance at the Dargah. Timur, Babur, Humayun, Akbar, Jahangir, Aurangzeb and later Mughal kings paid respects to this Dargah and donated land and money. Aulia had himself built a bawri (pond) before his death at the place of his burial. The grave of the great poet Amir Khasrau, his favourite disciple, Jahan Ara Begum, Shah Jahan's daughter and other famous personalities also had their graves in and around the Dargah.

Another such saint of this period that needs to be remembered was Hazrat Khawaja Nasir-ud-Din Mahmud 'Chirag' of Delhi. He was appointed the spiritual successor of Hazrat Nizam-ud-Din Aulia with the order that he 'had to stay in Delhi and suffer the persecution of the people', an order that he followed quite dutifully.

Nasir-ud-Din was a descendant of Hazrat Imam Hussain. Another theory is that he was from the family of Hazrat Umar-Bin-Khatab, the second Khalifa. The Sufi saint shifted to 'Chirag Dilli' after his initial abode at Awadh (Faizabad Oudh). His Mazaar or tomb stands in Chirag Delhi, a bustling locality of Delhi. He was one of the leading Darvesh of the Chistiya mission of Sufi saints. He was severely persecuted by Sultan Mohammad Bin Tughlaq who hated the Sufis for their indomitable spirit and belief in the gospels of Sufism. Unfortunately, he was killed in 1356 CE at Jalalabad by an anti Sufi fakir. With his death, the Chishtiya Silsila of Sufism collapsed.

In his memory several memorials were erected which still dot Delhi's skyline. Mainly a Dargah was erected by Firoz Shah in 1378 CE. At present as stated earlier there is the fully developed city (Chirag Delhi) around the Dargah which is near Kalkaji. With the burial of Hazrat Nasir-ud-Din, all the relics of his Silsila were buried with him. This was because the saint did not nominate his successor.

The influence of Sufism and the 300 years old Chistiya mission suffered a serious setback during the rule of Mohammad Bin Tughlaq who ascended the throne in 1327 CE. His total dislike for Sufis and execution of innocent Sufis and mendicants brought a curtain on Chistiya Silsila which finally collapsed after the death of Hazrat Nasir-ud-Din 'Chirag' Delhi in 1356 CE, as he had not appointed his successor.

Shahjahanabad has been a centre of spiritual and educational activity, giving a free hand to Sufis for their religious activities. This peaceful pursuit of spiritual activity continued till the attack and devastation of Delhi by Nadir Shah in 1739 CE. After Nadir Shah, Ahmad Shah Abdali invaded Delhi a number of times for forcible extortion and looting the wealth of Delhi's residents. He invaded Delhi nine times. Many Sufi saints were forced to abandon Delhi at this time. Thereafter, Surajmal plundered Delhi in 1753 CE. It was followed by the plundering of Delhi by the Rohillas under the leadership of Ghulam Qadir. Marathas were the next plunderers and their activity continued till 1803 CE, when they finally faced defeat at the hands of the British.

Chapter 9

Wars of Succession for the Mughal Throne

The Mughal rule over India spanned generations: starting from Babur (1526) to Bahadur Shah Zafar (1857). Though this was a time of comparative political stability for India, there were many internal wars of succession that took place during this time. To understand why this happened so often, it is essential to understand that the Mughals did not follow the 'rule of primogeniture', according to which the father's property or empire was inherited by the eldest son. Rather, they followed the Mughal and Timurid custom of 'coparcenary inheritance', in which the kingdom or empire was divided equally among the male heirs.

Naturally, this led to perpetual tension among the male heirs of the emperor. The princely contenders for the throne maintained a network of allies and supporters and regularly spied on each other. The princes, therefore, often went into war against their own brothers, uncles, cousins and even against their own father, to become the emperor.

The Mughal empire witnessed many such wars of succession for the throne. Bloody wars of succession became almost a family tradition with the Mughals. Humayun, Akbar, Jahangir, Shah Jahan and Aurangzeb, all had to fight their brothers and rivals to the throne.

There was a revolt by Humayun's brothers (1540–53) ten long years after the death of Babur. Humayun had to fight his rebellious half brother, Kamran Mirza to secure the Mughal throne. Then there was the rebellion of Mirza Hakim against Akbar in the 1560s. There was a showdown between Prince Salim and Akbar (1599 to 1604). During the last days of Akbar, Salim (Jahangir), was pitted against his own son Khusrau (1605–06). However, towards the end, Akbar chose Salim (Jahangir) as his successor, instead of Khusrau. Prince Khurram (later known as Shah Jahan) too rebelled against his brothers and against his father, Jahangir (1622 to 27) for succession.

According to general perception, the reign of Shah Jahan was the golden period of Mughal rule in India. Complete tranquility prevailed during his reign. His accession to the throne was, however, marked with internecine clannish battle, as had been the usual feature of the Mughal dynasty.

Shah Jahan was in the Deccan when Jahangir died in October of 1627. Of three brothers who were aspirants for the throne, two brothers Khusrau and Parvez had already expired. The only surviving prince who could lay claim to the throne was Shahryar Mirza. He was supported by his mother-in-law Nur Jahan. So, Shahryar ascended the throne in Lahore. In Shah Jahan's support was Asaf Khan, father of Mumtaz Mahal. With the intention of buying time till the arrival of Shah Jahan from the Deccan, Asaf Khan installed Prince Dawar Baksh, son of late Prince Khusrau on the throne. After Shah Jahan arrived, Asaf Khan stormed Lahore, defeated Shahryar, imprisoned him and blinded him as per practice.

Shah Jahan came to Agra (the then Capital) and was proclaimed as emperor in February of 1628. He assumed the title of Abul Muzaffar Shihab-ud-din Muhammad Sahib-i-qiran II Shah Jahan Badshah Ghazi. Prince Dawar Baksh, abdicated and went to Persia, as a state pensioner.

Ironically, Shah Jahan, in the concluding period of his life, had to witness a similar war of succession among his own sons. His favourite and oldest son, Dara Shikoh, lost to Aurangzeb only to be executed by him later. Same was the fate of his other son Murad, while Shuja was driven out of the country.

Incidentally all the four sons of Shah Jahan had military acumen and were quite experienced and mature in the handling of state affairs, having served as governors of different promises. Dara was the Governor of Punjab, Murad was the Governor of Gujarat, Aurangzeb was Governor of the Deccan while Shuja was the Governor of Bengal. When Shah Jahan fell severely ill in September 1657, the war of succession showed its most ugly head, with the claimants being Dara Shikoh aged 43, Shuja aged 41, Aurangzeb 39 and Murad 33. Of the two daughters, Jahan Ara, the favourite of Shah Jahan, sided with Dara Shikoh and younger daughter Roshan Ara, sided with Aurangzeb.

Dara was at Agra, at the time of Shah Jahan's illness. The other brothers were the governors of territories south of Agra. All the brothers rushed to Agra with their troops, anticipating some foul play and machination of Dara, and also due to the alleged apprehension that Shah Jehan was already dead. The fierce battles among the brothers followed. There were no qualms about cheating. While all the brothers had sufficient governance and military skills, there was a wide chasm in their various traits of head and heart. To take the case of Dara Shikoh, he was the eldest son of Shah Jahan, whom he trusted the most, the frontrunner to ascend the throne and Shah Jahan's favourite. Dara Shikoh was a man of 'eclectic views, liberal disposition and a scholar by instinct'.

Dara Shikoh was a healthy and ardent supporter of the religious doctrines and dogmas of different faiths, be it the Hindu Vedanta, the Christian New Testament or the Sufi Silsila. He is also credited with the translation of the Vedas (Atharvaveda) and the Upanishads, two of the most iconic religious works of the Hindus, into the Persian language, with the help of Hindu Scholars of the court who were equally conversant with Persian, the count language. (Advanced History of India, Jahangir and Shah Jahan by R.C.Majumdar, Raj Chaudhary, K.K.Datta, Macmillan ibid]

Dara never discarded the essential tenets of his faith. He only disliked the dogmatic rigidity of various Islamic schools. Dara Shikoh was liberal in his approach towards religion, never wanting in his appreciation of Christian Church doctrines as well as Hindu religious philosophy.

But such catholicity of thinking of Dara Shikoh was the greatest cause of contempt by zealous and bigoted followers of Sunni Islam like Aurangzeb, and was also the cause of his undoing. The excessive and faithful bonding between Shah Jahan and his eldest offspring, Dara, his constant presence in court and close proximity to his father Shah Jahan, did not work in his favour as he could not develop the shrewd and schematic acumen and the guiles of stagecraft so essential for political success as were exhibited by his brother Aurangzeb. Also, the ruthless capability of a brave and successful military general was lacking in him. Instead, a sense of pride and contempt of the advice of court nobles, had been his disastrous undoing.

On a side note, it is worthwhile to briefly mention the private lives of the Mughals. In spite of all the failings of the Mughal princes and their polygamous habit of maintaining large harems, some of them they exhibited exemplary conjugal life with one main queen. Dr. Vincent Smith showed eloquent praise on the conjugal life of Dara Shikoh, the eldest son of Shah Jahan, with his queen Begum Nadira, whom Dara considered as his dearest and nearest friend. In fact, the premature death of Begum Nadira, due to a prolonged bout of diarrhoea and non-availability of proper medicines, practically drained out his joy for life and his desire to live.

Shuja, the second son of Shah Jahan and two years younger to Dara, was a brave and intelligent soldier. But all his positive qualities were overshadowed by his nature and his reputation as a pleasure-loving prince; his lack of sincerity and indolence to combat the intrigues rendered him incapable of handling both the internal and external threats against him.

The youngest brother Murad who was ten years junior to Dara, and only three years to Aurangzeb, did not lack in valour but was too much of a simpleton and too liberal minded to shield himself from the evil designs of his brother Aurangzeb, who took advantage of his simplicity and duped him. Murad who was away at Gujarat, as Governor, crowned himself king at Ahmedabad on 5 December 1657. Murad then formed an alliance with Aurangzeb at Malwa. He agreed to join Aurangzeb and vowed to partition the kingdom in the name of Allah and the Prophet Mohammad. In the event of successful conquest of Hindustan, Murad would be given the reign of the bordering state/territory of Sindh, Punjab, Kashmir and Afghanistan where he would be proclaimed as King with the usual powers and authority of King like minting of coins in his own name.

The combined troops marched towards Ujjain. The troops sent by the Emperor to check them, confronted the combined army of Aurangzeb and Murad in the vicinity of Ujjain, fourteen miles south-west, at a place called Dharmat. The Imperial army under the command of Raja Jaswant Singh of Jodhpur along with Quasim Khan, suffered total rout and fled the battlefield. Inferior battle field strategy, inadequate fire power and the religious divide of the Rajput Rathore soldiers of Raja Jaswant Singh and Muslim soldiers under Quasim Khan, ultimately led to their downfall. The two groups became antagonistic towards each other, so much so that the latter started playing the role of a mute spectator at the time of engagement in the battle field.

The chivalrous and valiant Rathore Rajputs were wont to display 'do or die' policy in the battle field, but without any support from the Muslim army under Quasim Khan, ultimately suffered terrible losses before the superior skill, battle field strategy and generalship of Aurangzeb. The great Indian historian Sir Jadunath Sarkar observed, 'The hero of Deccan wars and the victor of Dharmat faced the world not only without loss but with his military reputation rendered absolutely unrivalled in India'.

Crossing the Chambal, the victorious combination of Aurangzeb and Murad, hurried to reach the outskirts of Agra Fort (Samugarh plains, eight miles west of Agra). By the end of May 1658, Dara Shikoh confronted the advancing combined army of Aurangzeb and Murad.

Numerically, the Imperial Army of Dara Shikoh was a formidable army of 50,000 soldiers, but in reality, it was a random combination of hastily assembled individuals and classes without proper coordination, motivation and forward vision as is essential for any well drilled, battle ready army. There were separate battle formations of Aurangzeb & Murad. The Rathore Rajputs of the Imperial army clashed head on, against Murad's well entrenched division, only to be annihilated. Misfortune loomed large in the battle field, when the elephant with royal howdah and the master, Dara Shikoh on top accidentally received a severe wound from a stray arrow and started behaving capriciously, forcing Dara Shikoh to disembark and mount a horse. The sight of the empty royal howdah of Dara's battle elephant, sent a chill of obvious despair among the troops who started hurriedly fleeing the battlefield.

Dara had no option but to abandon the battlefield and ran for his life towards Agra, leaving a huge array of guns and other armament as a triumphant catch for the combined army of his brothers. The army was completely defeated and disgraced. Dara was completely devastated, both physically and mentally. His life energy completely sapped out. Thus the battle of Samugarh settled the issue of war of succession among Shah Jahan's sons, with Aurangzeb emerging victorious and ascending the Mughal throne after defeating his brothers.

Another war of succession took place after the death of Aurangzeb in 1707. As Aurangzeb died without declaring his successor to the throne, his three sons, Bahadur Shah I, Muhammad Azam Shah and Muhammad Kam Bakhsh fought each other for the crown. After a series of bloody encounters, Bahadur Shah I defeated his two brothers and ascended the throne.

* * *

Chapter 10

Women Rulers of Prominence, from 1192 to 1857 CE

A very rare and minor role has been assigned to the womenfolk in the long history of Turco-Islamic rule and subsequent Mughal rule, spanning a long period from 1192 CE to 1857 CE. There were very few women who have had the fortune to occupy the throne of Delhi. The only Muslim lady to have become the Sultan of Delhi was Raziya Sultana, the daughter of Iltutmish, who was nominated as an heiress at the time of his death from his death bed. His eldest son, Nasir-ud-Din Mahum died in April 1229 CE while serving as Governor of Bengal. The other sons of Iltutmish were found incapable of becoming the sultan. Rukh-ud-Din Firuz had served Badaun, a very prosperous city at that time before being elevated as Governor of Lahore, even before the death of Iltutmish. He was absolutely ill equipped to assume the Sultan ship being a thoroughly incompetent ruler. He was given to low tastes and prone to unnecessary extravaganza at the cost of the state exchequer. There was chaos and confusion in the major cities of the kingdom like Badaun, Lahore, Multan and Bengal. The Queen mother was held responsible for this and put to prison. Firuz fled to Kilokheri, was imprisoned there and died in November 1236 CE. Raziya, being the only choice left, ascended the throne in spite of the strong disapproval by Mohd. Zunaidi, the Wazir. Iltutmish at his death, had nominated his daughter Raziya as his heir, much to the chagrin of the overwhelming majority of the conservative court nobles who were averse to the idea of being ruled by a woman. They plotted to put the late Sultan's surviving son Rukh-ud-din Firuz, the Governor of Badaun and later of Lahore to the throne. However, his mother Shah Turkan seized all power while her son was immersed in all sorts of frivolities, resulting in the total breakdown of law and order and inflating severe strain on the state exchequer. As discontentment was spreading in different parts of the kingdom, the court nobles imprisoned the Queen mother. Her son Firuz fled to Kilokheri, where he died in November 1236. Raziya ascended the throne. She was however constantly bothered by the Wazir of the kingdom. Raziya with her astute diplomacy and boldness overpowered her opponents and established her supremacy over Delhi and Punjab. Raziya possessed remarkable talents. She was beautiful, educated and trained. She was well versed in all matters of state. She wore men's clothes and led her army to war. She suppressed the rebellion of Nur-ud-din the Turk, leader of a different sect, with great valour. However, her undue closeness to Jalal-ud-Din Yakut, the Abyssinian slave was disliked by the powerful lobby of court nobles. They rose up in rebellion, killed Yakut and imprisoned Raziya. She married Ikhtiyar-ud-din Altuniya under whose charge she was placed after being dethroned. Meanwhile, her brother Muiz-ud-din Bahram Shah was proclaimed as the Sultan.

Raziya had already married her captor Altuniya, the governor of Bhatinda (Punjab). Raziya with her husband marched towards Delhi, to retrieve her throne but on the way in Kaithal where due to treachery of the followers of Altuniya, Raziya along with her husband was imprisoned and put to death on 14 October 1240, thus terminating the rule of the only woman ruler of Delhi in whole history of India, starting from the introduction of Turkish rule and final culmination of Timurid Dynasty with defeat of Bahadur Shah II Zaffar in 1847 revolt.

Apart from Raziya, there were only three women rulers (all Hindus) in the long period from 1237 to 1847 CE. The first was the Hindu queen Durgawati, a Rajput of exquisite beauty and valour, who ruled north of Central Province (present day Jabalpur district) during the period of Akbar. The kingdom at that time was known as Garha Katanga eastern province also known as Gordowana. Durgawati ruled in the name of her minor son Bir Narayan. Durgawati resisted the army of the Muslim Emperor, Akbar, led by Asaf Khan, the governor of Kara. She was however defeated and she committed suicide by self-immolation in true Rajput style. Young Bir Narayan fought the invaders until he lost his life. This was in 1564 CE, just two years after Akbar had proclaimed himself the Sultan after throwing off the tutelage of Bairam Khan and Adam Khan.

The next Hindu queen of note was Ahaliya Bai Holkar, the purest and most religious lady who headed the Maratha confederacy during 'Pitt's India Act' of 1784. She became the ruler of Indore in 1767, after the deaths of her husband and then, her son. Her reign lasted for thirty years. According to Sir John Malcohm, the success of Ahaliya Bai in the matters of internal administration displayed her unique ability and organization skills, her empathy with her people and her military skills. Ahaliya Bai expired in 1795 and the government of Indore passed into the hands of Tukoji Raj Holkar I, her commander-in-chief.

The third and the last Hindu queen was none other than Rani Lakshmi Bai of Jhansi. Her bravery and indomitable courage has been a matter of evergreen folklore. The Rani, attired in a male outfit as a sawar atop a horse and dauntingly striding the battlefield with open sword, received unstinted accolades from even her opponents. She was one of the most prominent leaders of the Revolt of 1857. She attempted to heroically defend Jhansi from the British. However, she was defeated and died on the battlefield on 17th June, 1858. Sir Hugh Rose, the British Commander, checked the activities of Tantia Tope, the Maratha Brahmin with his mutinous Gwalior contingent, and defeated him. Tantia Tope was captured in early 1859 by Man Singh, a feudatory of Scindia and handed over to the British to be hanged in April 1859.

* * *

Chapter 11

The Darkest Period in the Annals of History of Delhi: The Battle of Plassey

The saddest period of India's political history had its origin in the emergence of the British power which was alien to India in all respects. The invaders to India right from the eleventh century were the seekers of the rich and wealthy land of India along with the plethora of precious jewels and valuable metals accumulated in the temples of India over centuries through the munificence of the kings/rulers.

After capture of the lands and riches, the invaders settled down permanently in the newly acquired land of conquest. With the passage of time, the early invaders, the Sakas and the Huns, through socialising with the original inhabitants and also through slow but steady participation of the locals in the state administration, helped in the reduction of the chasm between the victors and the vanquished. It paved the way for social, cultural and administrative integration. The Sakas and Huns were completely integrated with the originals of the land and surrendered their separate identity and constituted different clans of Rajputs and Jats of northern India.

The later invaders namely the Pathans, Mongols and Mughals followed suit to get intermingled with locals who were basically the larger community of the Hindus. However, they retained their religion and related customs, cultural heritage and their language which was totally different from that of the Hindus. This enabled them to stay on a higher pedestal as the rulers, as distinct from the ruled subjects. Hindus and Muslims never lost their separate identities, beliefs and cultures. Even during the reign of Emperors like Akbar, with their religious catholicity, toleration and liberation, this fundamental divisiveness was stark.

As against the ethos of the previous rulers of India, as mentioned above, the British came to India, not to stay permanently. They came as hordes of traders only to swell their coffers with whatever loot they could muster. Their aim was commerce, as seen by the establishment of the East India Company which was basically a trading company. That the traders, through crafts, legal and illegal became rulers of India, is a long and different story. With this ambition and mind-set in view, the British tred a crafty, often illegal and unscrupulous path and were able to establish a strong and firm foothold in the political landscape of India.

In securing the firman from Jahangir in early 1613 to establish a factory permanently in Surat, a firm beginning of business was set up by English Company in India. Even before 1613 CE, Captain William Hawkins had made an appeal to Jahangir's court to establish a factory in India. However, he was not successful in his mission.

There was strong opposition from local Surat merchants supported by the Portuguese, which foiled his bid to manage concessions from the Mughal Emperor. This led to military intervention by the English. Under order of King James I of England, Captain Best under command of the British fleet of Sir Henry Middleton, defeated the Portuguese. Sir Thomas Roe, was sent by the king of England as the accredited Ambassador, to the court of Emperor Jahangir in the year 1615 CE.

Even before that, Emperor Jahangir had issued a firman to the British, permitting establishment of the permanent factory in Surat as already stated. To extract further trade concessions from the Emperor, Sir Roe came to the Mughal court in the year 1615 and he stayed back at the Mughal court till the end of 1618. Though he could not conclude any definite commercial treaty in favour of Great Britain, he managed in securing several economic privileges like the establishment of several permanent factories in Surat, Ahmedabad, Broach, Baroda and Agra, in west and central India.

He ensured unbridled trade with Red Sea ports. A stroke of luck, in the form of a matrimonial alliance between England's King Charles II and the Portuguese Princess Catherine of Braganza, saw the English King receiving the gift of Bombay in 1668 CE as a marriage dowry. East India Company, in turn acquired trading rights from Bombay port, on a small annual rent.

In course of time, the locational advantage of Bombay Port made the trading from western India and north India subservient to Bombay Port trading. It also included trading of Indigo through Bombay. By 1687 CE, Bombay Port started to rule the roost, in respect of foreign trade, and replaced Surat, as the prime trade centre of the west coast. The manoeuvrability displayed by the British in the Mughal court in wresting various trade concessions was the trend setter for the rest of the country especially in Bengal and eastern Indian states after British victory in the battle of Plassey in the late Eighteenth century in 1757. During this period, British wrested political ascendancy by all sorts of intrigue and dubious means.

Much before this, the growth of British influence and politics and the steady inroads in the sphere of trade and commerce were affected. As early as in 1633 CE, factories were started in Orissa's Balasore and Mahanadi delta area. In 1651 CE, the trade in the settlements of Bengal, Bihar and Orissa, mainly of silk, cotton, sugar and saltpetre grew haphazardly. All trade in these settlements were placed under control of Fort Saint George in Madras (Chennai).

The period between 1658 and 1688 CE, was one of chaos and confusion. The first half of the seventeenth century was especially set with utter confusion. 1657 CE saw the revival of trade as a consequence of the trade charter granted by Oliver Cromwell during his short regime in England. The period of restoration in 1660 CE, gave further impetus to trade activities. Both Charles II and James II, continued the active and liberal policy as initiated by Cromwell.

The next thirty years saw a growth of prosperity in trade. This period also witnessed the establishment of a Joint Stock Company of permanent nature which greatly ameliorated the company's financial uncertainty and instability. This changing scenario brought out a tremendous change in the overall climate, through political intervention and expansion and through the charters of both Charles II and James II, who restored the old privileges of the company thereby making it possible for the company to dabble in the political affairs of the native states.

The company's initial policy had been only trading; this underwent an unexpected transformation. By fishing in the troubled waters of political uncertainty, it transformed itself into a power hungry entity, eager to establish and consolidate its position through territorial acquisitions and a firm political base. This was the precursor to the company's ultimate ambition of subjugating territories politically and consolidating its firm foothold administratively and militarily. The focus of trading activity shifted from the south. In Job Charnock, the British found a manifestation of its ultimate aim in monopolising trade and extracting various trade concessions from the Mughal Emperor at Delhi and the local Governors appointed by the Delhi throne.

This started with the annexation of Bengal, following the defeat of Siraj-ud-Daulah, the Nawab of Bengal in the Battle of Plassey of 1757. There was further consolidation of political authority and subjugation of territories of Bengal because of the abject treachery of the Nawab's general Mir Jaffar.

The Battle of Plassey 1757 CE occupies a pristine position in Indian history. However, one thing may be noted that, there was no battle worth the name at all. It was nothing more than a skirmish. The army commanders of Siraj-ud-Daulah the Nawab, remained mere spectators throughout, having treacherously plotted the defeat of the Nawab. The main culprit was the supreme commander Mir Jafar and associate Rai Durlabh, who were stationed behind the mango grove on the banks of the river, from where the British troops under the command of Clive were operating. Only a small part of the Nawab's army under Mohan Lal along with Mir Kasim was engaged with the army of Clive with infantry attacks of mainly bullets and a few cannons.

At this moment, the traitor, Mir Jaffar ordered Mohan Lal to retreat. The bewildered Nawab entreated Mir Jaffar personally to actively intervene instead of retreating, but without any success. This sealed the fate of the

Nawab, forcing him to abandon the battlefield. This ultimately led to the capture of the Nawab and his assassination.

Mir Jaffar ascended the throne with the support of the rich banker Jagat Seth after Siraj-ud-Daulah was killed in the battle of Plassey. Clive was awarded the Zamindari of 24 Parganas, including that of Calcutta by the new Nawab, Mir Jaffar, apart from huge loot in cash and kind. It also enabled Clive to take actual political control over the conquered capital of Murshidabad, reducing Mir Jaffar to the level of a mere puppet in the hands of the British, who consented to keep a Resident at the Nawab's court.

In June 1758, Robert Clive was formally appointed the Governor of Bengal Presidency by the Company. Mir Jaffar, as the new Nawab, had a torrid time being constantly tormented and harassed by Clive's blatant interference in his administrative decisions. He was so frustrated that the Nawab, Mir Jaffar secretly courted the Dutch, the other European trade interest in Bengal's territory of Chinsurah. The Dutch through the embellishment of troops from their settlement confronted the British.

However, they were squarely defeated by British troops at Bedar in November 1759, much to the dismay of Mir Jaffar. Earlier, Clive had thwarted the efforts of Mir Jaffar in dismissing Rai Durlabh, the Diwan and the co-conspirator with Mir Jaffar at the battle of Plassey. Also, the Governor of Bihar, Ram Narayan, a devout Hindu, was protected by Clive. During the same period, the Emperor Shah Alam II marched with troops towards Patna to occupy Bengal and Bihar and laid a siege of Patna.

With the help of Clive, Mir Jaffar could manage to deflect Shah Alam II off the hook through diplomatic manoeuvre, thus confirming that Mir Jaffar could not survive without the wholehearted support of Clive. The relation between the British and Mir Jaffar started showing cracks over the disputes of payments of transit taxes by the traders and interpretation of trade firman as available as also certain dues which the company owed from the Nawab.

Another issue came up about the successor of Mir Jaffar. His son and heir apparent, Miran, had expired in early March 1760. Around the same time, Clive departed from India. On the issue of appointment of the heir apparent, there were differences of opinion among the top British officials.

Finally, Mir Kasim, the son-in-law of Mir Jaffar was appointed the Deputy Subedar with guarantee of succession to the throne but trouble started brewing over the relations between the Nawab Mir Kasim and the British which culminated in differences over inland trade policy. The British were demanding preferential treatment, not only for the Company as per the firman but also similar concessions for private British traders including members of the East India Company who wanted to trade privately.

It created so much bad blood that the chief of the Patna factory went up in violent protest against the Nawab who had shifted his capital to Monghyr. The final climax came when Mir Kasim put his foot down against the flagrant violation by the officials the East India Company in unauthorised appropriation of concessions, granted by firman of the Rulers of both Delhi and Bengal, authorising trade concessions only to the trade conducted by the Company and not by the officials of the company.

The servants of the company started appropriating concessions for themselves. When Mir Kasim's petition to the Company's Supreme Council in Calcutta, fell on deaf ears, the exasperated Nawab, withdrew the special concessions and abolished the duties totally, thus removing all discrimination. Faced with the disadvantages over traders of all other hues, the chief of the British factory at Patna went into armed revolt along with the British Governor stationed at Patna. The revolt was however, suppressed. But it ultimately led to the war between the British and Mir Kasim in the battlefield of Buxar in 1764 CE when British troops inflicted major defeat on the confederation of Nawab Prince Shuja and Emperor Shah Alam II along with Mir Kasim.

Though not given due importance, the Battle of Buxar (1764) was truly a watershed moment in the annals of Indian History. Mir Kasim was replaced by Mir Jaffar as the Nawab of Bengal. Moreover, in 1765, the Mughal Emperor appointed the East India Company as the Diwan of the provinces of Bengal. This had heavy implications: this meant that from then on, the Company had Diwani rights over Bengal and could use the vast revenue resources of Bengal for their own purposes. Revenues from

India (Bengal) would be used to finance Company expenses and maintain Company troops.

The Battle of Plassey was hardly more than a mere skirmish but its result was more important than many of the greatest battles of the world. It paved the way for the British conquest of Bengal and eventually of the whole of India. Because of the wide military and political ramifications of the Battle of Plassey towards the conquest of the Bengal Presidency and of India by the British, this event of 23 June 1757, has been highlighted. It also, naturally, commands a mention in the categorisation of the Dark Period of Delhi, the capital and throne of India.

Chapter 12

Famous Battles of India

Wars and battles have always defined the ethos and identity of any country: not only its political and social identity but also its cultural and linguistic distinctiveness. The Indian subcontinent has also seen its fair share of conquests and wars that have defined and moulded India to be the nation that we know today.

The first Battle of Tarain (1191) was fought between the Ghurids led by Sultan Mohammad Ghori and the Rajputs led by Prithviraj Chauhan. Though Ghori was unsuccessful, he returned a year later, better prepared and with prior knowledge of his enemy's strengths and weaknesses. The second battle of Tarain (near Thaneswar) was fought in the year 1192, between Mohammad Ghori and Prithviraj Chauhan, with Ghori emerging as victor. This battle has a lot of significance in history because this initiated the Muslim reign in India.

The next battle which calls for recollection in the same vein, was the First battle of Panipat. (1526–27) which marks Babur's victory over Ibrahim Lodi. This battle laid the foundation of the Mughal Dynasty in India and put an end to the Delhi Sultanate.

Next, it was the Battle of Khanwa (West of Agra) in 1527, between the forces of Rana Sanga and Babur. Rana Sanga led a combined army of the rulers of Marwar, Ambar, Gwalior, Ajmer and Chander and Sultan Mahmud Lodi (another son of Sultan Sikandar Lodi, whom Rana Sanga acknowledged as Sultan of Delhi). In this battle, Babur defeated Rana Sanga. Rana Sangha's combined army on paper, appeared to be the most brutal. Numerically also, it was much superior to Babur's army. Rana Sanga, the leader of Rajput national revival led the force of 120 chiefs of various Rajput clans. He had mustered 80000 war horses and 500 war elephants.

Faced with such mighty Rajput adversaries, who were otherwise known for their indomitable 'Do or Die' spirit, oozing strong nationalism and chivalry, and fond of face-to-face combat and bloodshed, Babur's small army fell into insignificance and was awfully terror struck. Beholding utter panic among his troops, Babur took a master step. He stirred the sagging morale of his soldiers by infusing fresh courage and determination into them. He openly vowed in the name of Allah and the Prophet to give up all pleasure and fun, broke all the bottles and casks of hard drinks and vowed never to touch the same in the future. His stirring calls to save Islam with his swearing in the name of the Holy Quran, revived the spirits of his army. The showdown took place on the battlefield of Khanwa, adjacent to Agra, on 16 March 1527. Despite all the desperate valour, traditionally associated with the Rajputs, they suffered an ignominious defeat, with Rana Sanga leaving the battlefield completely defeated, devastated and heartbroken. He escaped to Chittor, but within two years he expired, and with his death, set the bright sun of the Rajput revival. Quickly, Babur crossed the Yamuna River and stormed the Rajput citadel of the fortress of Chanderi, (1528), thus leaving his adversaries in total disarray. It took almost thirty years for the Rajputs to regroup into battle fitness. Sir L.F. Rushbrook Williams, the great historian, had observed that this became the key note of Babur's activities for the remainder of his life. It marked the significance of his new career, of cementing his power and presence in India, of keeping the throne unopposed and free of all rebels and opponents and laying the firm foundations of Timurid Rule in India.

In 1529, there was another war, the Battle of Ghaghra, where Babur defeated the Afghans. This was the third important battle fought by Babur, after which the Mughal rule was even more firmly established in India.

The battle of Chausa (1539) also deserves a mention here. This battle took place between the forces of Sher Shah Suri and those of Humayun. Humayun was defeated and he had to escape to save his life and recuperate, thus breaking the continuity of the Mughal rule in India (1540 to 1555).

In the following battle of Kanauj (1540), Sher Shah defeated Humayun for the second time.

In 1556, Akbar the Great defeated Hemu in the Second Battle of Panipat. The famous battle of Haldighati took place in 1576, between the forces of the Mughal Emperor Akbar, led by Raja Man Singh and the army of Maharana Pratap of Mewar. Though the Mughals were victorious, they could not capture the valiant Rana Pratap, who fought bravely.

The next most significant battle was that of the Battle of Plassey in Bengal, year 1757. The battle broke out in the early morning of 23rd June. This was fought between the East India Company's army led by Robert Clive on one side and the Nawab of Bengal, Nawab Siraj-ud-Daulah, at Plassey. The Nawab lost the battle, mainly due to the treachery of one of his military commanders, Mir Jaffar, who, after Siraj-ud-Daulah's death, was made the next Nawab of Bengsal.

The Battle of Plassey is considered to be the most prominent watershed in the annals of India's history as it was the first major victory won by the British in India. It laid down the foundation of British rule in India with the conquest of Bengal by the British invaders under the leadership of Lord Clive. In 1760, the British defeated the French in India, again important in cementing the British foothold in India.

The next important battle was the Battle of Buxar (1764), fought between Mir Kasim and the East India Company. Though apparently not as significant as the Battle of Plassey, this victory made the British masters of Bengal, Bihar and Orissa. The Mughal Emperor granted the Company Diwani rights over the Bengal Province, and this in turn paved the way for British rule in India.

Chapter 13

The Showdown Between the Marathas and the British

The British Raj in India formally began with this defeat of the Marathas who were protecting Shah Alam II, at the war of Patparganj and the British Residency system was started. The rule or control of Delhi actually started by Mahadaji Shinde in the year 1789. At that time Shah Alam II lived in Allahabad as a British pensioner having lost to the British at the Battle of Buxar. Shah Alam II resided in Allahabad for six years, upto January 1772, at a pension of Rupees 26 Lakhs. He was only a dignified royal pensioner without any iota of administrative power of royalty. Lord Clive had installed Shuja-ud-din Dawlah as Chief Minister having removed Shah Alam's own son as Wazir.

In 1765, Shah Alam II planned to go back to Delhi to reclaim his title. With the assistance of Najib-ad-Dawlah, Amir al-Umra, the Regent of Delhi on behalf of the British, Shah Alam II went up to Fatehpur, on the bank of the Yamuna, intending to march to Delhi with the help of the Marathas. This effort was foiled by the British and he had to return to Allahabad. After a lot of machinations and political intrigues and astute manoeuvrability, the Marathas captured Delhi. Next, the Marathas with help of Najib-ud-Dawlah's son, Zabita Khan entered Delhi and in January of 1772, Shah Alam entered Delhi again. It was Zabita Khan who conferred the jagir of Sardhana to Walter Reinhardt, the German, more known for his wife Begum Samru, who became a very well-known political figure of Delhi and adjacent areas.

The Anglo-Maratha relations which were getting strained ultimately resulted in the First Anglo- Maratha war in the January of 1779 CE. British troops suffered a humiliating defeat in the Western Ghats and were forced to sign a humiliating convention at Wadgaon. This treaty was however repudiated by Governor General Lord Hastings, who ordered a strong army from Bengal under the leadership of Colonel Goddard to march across Central India to capture Ahmedabad in February 1780. They captured Bassein in December 1780.

Captain Popham in the meantime captured the Fort of Gwalior in 1781 August, while General Camac, defeated Mahadaji Scindia in the battle of Shivpuri in February 1781, thus inflicting a severe blow to his prestige and his ambition to become the de-facto ruler of Delhi as the Reagent of Jalal-ud-din Shah Alam II (1759–1806 CE).

In the meantime, a war of succession was being enacted at the seat of the Peshwa at Poona. Peshwa Madhav Rao 1 had expired untimely in 1772 CE. The Peshwa's uncle Raghunath Rao (Raghova), an extremely ambitious person, wanted to be the Peshwa. Narayana Rao, Madhava Rao's brother and successor, was murdered at the behest of Rahava Rao, his own uncle.

Raghav Rao became the Peshwa. But he was confronted by the nominee of the Poona Confederate namely Nana Fadnavis. The wife of Madhav Rao I, Ganga Bai, gave birth to a posthumous child, named 'Sawai' Madhavrao, who was proclaimed as the rightful Peshwa. Sensing his deposition as Peshwa and driven out of Poona, Raghunath sought help and intervention from the English at Bombay, who were otherwise on good terms with the Maratha confederacy of Poona. This allowed the British the opportunity to meddle in the affairs of the Maratha Confederacy. Raghunath Rao was able to come to an agreement with the British of Bombay and concluded the Treaty of Surat on 6th March, 1775. The combined troops of Raghunath Rao and the British Army under Colonel Keating defeated the Poona Government troops near the town of Anand in May 1775.

Another drama unfolded in the meantime: Raghunath Rao was planning to establish his superiority over Delhi following the Treaty of Surat which was concluded by the Bombay Government of Britain. However, this treaty was repudiated by the Council at Calcutta, even overruling Governor General Warren Hastings, by a majority verdict. The Calcutta council condemned Bombay council's action as 'impolite, dangerous, unauthorised and unjust'.

The Calcutta Council sent Colonel Upton to Poona to negotiate a peace treaty with the Poona Supreme Maratha authority. Treaty of Surat was rescinded, and the English renounced the cause of Raghunath Rao, who was signed off to Korargaon in Gujarat on a monthly pension of Rs. 25000 from the Peshwa's Government. This measure led to the emergence of Mahadaji Scindia. After an intervening period when, overruling the Calcutta Council's decision, Hastings ordered a strong army under Colonel Goddard to restore the prestige of the British by occupying Ahmedabad in February 1780 and Bassein in the same year.

After Gwalior fell into the hands of the British, Mahadaji Scindia adopted a policy of aligning with the British, promising to broker a truce between the Poona Maratha Government and the British. As a result, the Treaty of Salbai was signed on 17 May 1782. It gave the British twenty years of truce with the Marathas which allowed them to gain ascendancy in the south. This treaty marked the end of the first Anglo -Maratha war. The treaty also recognized Mahadaji Scindia as an independent prince so far the British were concerned and his hold over Delhi Sultan was rendered powerful over the British and the Marathas. By 1792, Mahadaji Scindia established his ascendency over the Rajputs and the Jats and his power in Northern India reached its meridian splendor.

Next, on the pretext of paying respect to the Peshwa, young Madhav Rao II, Mahadaji Scindia decided to visit Poona, to test his hold at Poona against Nana Fadnavis, an astute politician. Mahadaji Scindia had been recognized as an independent prince by the British, and consolidated his position in Northern India including Delhi. He organized a proper fighting army with Rajputs and Mohammedans under French Military expert Benoit de Boigne, with other Europeans of different hues and classes as his commanders. He obtained from the Emperor the title of Wakil- i- Mutluq for his nominal master the Peshwa and himself became the Peshwa's naib or deputy. This enabled him to hold sway over Shah Alam, the titular

Emperor of Delhi. However, while he was maneuvering to establish and enhance his credibility with the Poona Government, he unfortunately died of fever on 12 February 1794, at the age of sixty-five. His death had a huge impact on the throne of Delhi. In his absence from Delhi, Tukaji Holkar, challenged his authority. However he suffered a humiliating defeat at the hands of Benaoid-De Boigne, Mahadaji's trusted Commander-in-chief at Ajmer. Tukoji Holkar was handed over the throne of Indore after the death of Ahalya Bai, a distinguished and pious lady who ruled over Indore.

After the death of Mahadaji, his vast possession was inherited by his thirteen year old nephew and adopted son Daulat Rao Scindia. Mahadaji's death had created a real vacuum in the political atmosphere of Delhi. The young Daulat Rao Scindia could hardly wield the same influence over Delhi, leaving a wide space for the rival British in taking commanding positions in the affairs of Delhi.

Actually, it sealed the fate of the Maratha influence in Delhi. Though Section 34 of Pitt's India Act of 1784 asked the British to refrain from their policy of war and conquest, yet the British continued to rule the roost in handling the affairs at Delhi vis-à-vis the King. From 1749, there was a severe deterioration in the administrative set up of the Mughal Court.

The doyen of Indian History Jadunath Sarkar recorded the following observations in his treatise: 'Delhi during the Anarchy 1749–88 as told in contemporary records, Indian Historical Records Commission proceedings':

> *'From 1749 to 1788 is a sad period in our history. It was a period marked by frequent bloody fights between rival nobles claiming the supreme control over the state, street brawls by soldiers mutinying for arrears of pay or between soldiers of different races who had quarrelled in the Bazar. The emperor is timid and imbecile defeating the efforts of his best friends by listening to base flattered and corrupt ministers for his pleasures and vanity trying to recover his power by means of low and cowardly intrigues such as creating a new Wazir or setting up his Commander in Chief (Bakshi) against his Chancellor (Wazir) of the Empire. The heir of the mighty Timur had fallen very low indeed when he could not think of achieving his own emancipation by manly*

exertion or manlier death. Delhi during these forty years in a sickening and monotonous tale of sack by Afghans and Marathas, Sikhs and Jats, even Gujjars and Pindaris, frequent panic among the citizens whenever such attack was expected, the flight of the rich, closing of the shops, the looting of the unprotected house by the ruffians of the city population who took advantage of the public alarm and confusion, the utter spoliation of the peasantry and ruin of the surrounding villages by organized hands of brigands or soldiers out forging and consequent famine prices in the capital, the incurable intrigue, inefficiency and moral decay of the imperial courts, culminating in the crowning agony of Ghulam Qadir's capture of the palace, outrage of Emperors family and blinding of Shah Alam II. The peasantries were so exasperated by their sufferings and the failure of the state to protect their life and property that they naturally regarded all strangers and even the forces of the crown as their enemy'

A manuscript which Jadunath Sarkar obtained from Patna narrates the actual incidents in corroboration of the aforesaid statement: 'On 14th, March 1753, there was a tumult in the fort, on 17th March there was a tumult in the daytime. On 6 May 1753, the Jats and other people plunder the inhabitants of the old city in the neighbourhood of Lal Darwaza at the instigation of Safdar Jung. On 12 June, the role of Wazir was conferred on Intizam-ud-daulah who replaced Safdar Jung for one prahar. There was a fight between Safdar Jung and Bakshi-ul-Mulk leading to the looting of Faridabad. Afghan troops burnt Faridabad, cut off six to seven hundred poor people and brought them before Ahmad Shah Abdali, representing them to be heads of Marathas killed in the battle. For each head, Abdali paid a reward of Rs. 8.

The Mughal army comprised of soldiers of various races which included Jats, North Indian Muslims, Purbias of Awadhi Hindus, Rajputs, men of Central Asia known as Badakhasis, Rohillas, Mughals of Persian origin, drilled and orderly sepoys trained by the Europeans including the French. Such a diversity in the races of the Imperial army made the matter worse.

On February 13, of 1754, soldiers blockaded the roads of the capital demanding their pay and arrears.In April 1754, the Badkhashis (of Central Asian origin) revolted against the Emperor and wanted to capture him after destroying the wholesale markets of Delhi namely Khari Baoli and Khas Bazar. They were repulsed by the Wazir, who used the guns of the fort against them. There was a heavy battle in Lahori Gate area where over one hundred men were slain. Even the Empire's favourite paltan of Bhawani Singh and Gangaram along with Majid-ud-Daulah, the Emperor's favourite Wazir, were kept confined in the mosque of Ruhan-ud-Daulah for two days for want of salary and arrears.

In 1757, the Emperor was left without any conveyance or horse to go to the mosque from his harem. In 1759, the Marathas looted the Dargah of Nizam-ud-din Auliya and adjacent houses and seized the men of the area for ransom. At that time the Emperor did not have a well regulated royal army of his own.

Next began the wave of attacks by the Sikhs in 1765, when the residents of Delhi were confined to the city and the temple of Kalka Devi was closed. The next attack of Sikhs came in 1773 CE where they seized Shahdara and decamped with a huge booty of 50 bags of goods. In 1782, Sikhs from Aligarh encamped at Burari and set fire to the Subzi Mandi and Malka Ganj and put to sword the people of Mughalpura. The terrorized people of Delhi, sought asylum at the fort. Next year, the Jats looted Faridabad and the adjoining area, killing over 2000 people. The Sikh chiefs encamped with their force near Shalimar Bagh and demolished a mosque at Rakabganj and at the Gurdwara of the Rakabganj, as the remains of Guru Tegh Bahadur, slain by Aurangzeb, were found in a pot. At this spot, Lakhi Shah Banjara had bought the remains from Kotwali. Bangla Sahib Gurudwara was built in the area of Raja Jai Singh, where the Seventh and Eighth Guru stayed.

Around this period, Delhi and the rest of the country faced a terrible famine. It resulted in a total loss of revenue apart from other issues like illness and premature death due to unhygienic conditions and pestilence. The water supply through the Persian wheel system, initiated by Ali Mardan Khan, had fallen into disuse due to lack of proper maintenance.

Royal coffers were entirely empty and even the Emperor's Privy Purse fell into arrears.

So was the case of Princesses, the begums and all others entitled to royal allowances. British stopped the payment of revenue due from Bengal including Bihar and Orissa as was required to be paid for their rights to trade as conferred to them by the Emperor's edict, Shah Alam had to write to King George III of England to demand payment of Rupees one crore and sixty-eight lakh of tribute from Bengal, which had fallen due. This is an indication of the pathetic condition of the empire's economy and political instability. As there was a total economic and political breakdown, the British were waiting in the wings to unleash their evil plans to fish in the troubled waters.

Chapter 14

The Period of British Residency from 1803 to 1857

The expected war to wrest power from the Marathas who were in control of Delhi finally broke out in the year 1803. This was during the rule of Shah Alam, the emperor of a decaying and weakening Mughal Empire, actually holding only nominal suzerainty over the kingdom. The Scindias were the Vakil-i-Mutlaq or the Regent of Shah Alam. Accordingly, Shah Alam had to choose between the two contending parties, the British and the Marathas, claiming suzerainty over Delhi Masnad.

The declared objective of Lord Wellesley, who arrived as Governor General in April 1798, was to aggressively expand British domination to the west of Bengal, having given up the policy of non-intervention, hitherto, being adopted by the British Government in Bengal. The declared objective of Lord Wellesley was to annex Delhi and the adjoining Yamuna Doab land. Possessing a vast knowledge of Indian political affairs as the Commissioner of the Board of Control in the East India company, Wellesley came to guide the destiny of the Company in India, at a time when the political situation in the country was extremely critical. The Company was suffering politically largely due to Sir John Shore's policy of non-intervention and neutrality.

In the tussle of hegemony over Delhi Masnad, Shah Alam, obviously had to side with his Maratha regent, treating the East India company and the British as rebellious vassals. However, Shah Alam was in an acute dilemma. He could not forget the seven years of succour the British had given him when he was virtually the Royal Pensioner at Allahabad, a sort of asylum against the rule of Ghulam Quadir at Delhi. Subsequently however, the Marathas had rescued him from the clutches of Ghulam Quadir, to restore him to the Mughal throne. Shah Alam had substantial gratitude. At the same time, he had many grievances too. By nature, the Marathas were disrespectful towards him. The British also did not give him liberty of action and had thwarted his attempts at reasserting his authority as the Emperor of Delhi. Further, the British had stopped paying him the Bengal tribute as decided by the treaty of 1765. They also did not pay heed to his request for military and financial help to restore his legal authority over Delhi. It was the period which saw the hostility between Britain and France in Europe over the domination and annexation of colonies in Asia and Africa. French officials in the capacity of military experts and military advisors had made forays in the Indian States. However, they were not numerically strong enough to dominate the Indian States on their own, as the British did with the establishment of Regencies in the native states.

The seeds of British dominance had been planted in 1613 by Jahangir, when British were granted permission to establish a factory at Surat permanently under the East India Company. This was the path breaking moment in bringing the Mughal Rulers of Delhi into the vortex of British domination. The late seventeenth and eighteenth centuries saw the decay of strong Mughal rule of Delhi, due to a long line of inept and incompetent Mughal Badshahs who came in succession as the Mughal Rulers of India. It was the devising period Delhi witnessed, with slow but steady establishments of European style buildings, which intercepted the traditional Mughal architecture, including Hindu architecture. European style townhouses, bungalows, cemeteries and churches became more and more visible.

The British Regency System started after defeating the Marathas in 1803 and the British became the de-facto rulers of India. It will be worthwhile to dive deeper into the background of the British victory of September of 1803 under the command of General Gerard Lake at the conclusive battle of Patparganj in Delhi where the combined Maratha force of Scindias and Bhonsales were trounced by Lake. This was the Second Anglo-Maratha war (1803–1805). There was a long history of feuds, internal intrigues and backstabbing at the centre of Maratha power in Poona. The Maratha army that faced General Lake in Patparganj in Delhi in September 1803 was the last effort at a semblance of consolidated Maratha power of the Scindias and Bhonsales. The internal dissent and intrigues at Poona, the Supreme seat of Marathas had started earlier. Before the Second Anglo Maratha war, the Marathas had scored a spectacular victory when a combined Maratha force under Nana Fadnavis had defeated the British force at Kharla. It was here that the Marathas assembled unitedly under the banner of the Central Poona authority of Nana Fadnavis, to defeat the British.

Nana Fadnavis started acting like a dictator, much to the annoyance of the young Peshwa Madhava Rao Narayan, who in a fit of despair committed suicide on the 25th October, 1795. The next Peshwa was Baji Rao II, son of Raghoba, who was a bitter foe of Nana Fadnavis. However, the differences between the two were reconciled with Baji Rao II becoming the Peshwa and Nana Fadnavis his Prime Minister on 4th December 1796. This internal strife at Poona court emboldened the British to recover territories lost during the battle of Kharda. Baji Rao II who ascended as Peshwa, lacked the wisdom and military acumen worthy of a Peshwa. To add to this, tragedy befell the Maratha nation when great stalwarts like Mahadaji Scindia, Malhar Rao Holkar and Tukoji Holkar left the world in quick succession, thus creating a deep void in the united Maratha front. Their descendants Daulat Rao Scindia, nephew of Mahadaji Scindia and Jaswant Rao Holkar, son of Tukoji Holkar were absolutely no match for the departed leaders.

Marquess Wellelesley who became Governor General on the 26th April 1798, was quick to take advantage of the situation. With his experience of Indian affairs as Commissioner in the East India Company Board, he decided to jump into the fray ignoring the Company's guideline of non-interference in Indian state affairs. He once again started indulging in the policy of Subsidiary Alliance with the Indian states, debarred from entering into any military coalition with foreign armies namely the French, who were then at war with Britain in Europe. The Company was involved in a tense and intriguing tussle for power with Hyder Ali in Mysore and the Nizam had alienated himself from the British to forge an alliance with the French. The Raja of Malabar region had apprehensions of an attack by Zaman Shah, ruler of Kabul. Further, Napoleon's march to Egypt, with a view to threaten India, all added to the anxiety of Wellesley to secure the Company's position desperately. He pushed the policy of Subsidiary alliance with the Indian states, which meant that the Indian states were to make no wars or to carry on no negotiations with any other states whatsoever, without the consent of the British Government. In return, the British Government undertook to protect them against their enemies of every sort and kind. The obligation on the part of the Indian States was that they would be maintaining, at their own cost, a regiment of Indian soldiers under the command of the British officers. The British would be paramount and have complete suzerainty to collect revenue and financial tributes to meet their expenses. The conditions of this agreement were most derogatory and against the self-respect and pride of Indian States. As long as Nana Fadnavis was the Prime Minister and de-facto central authority at the seat of the Marathas at Poona, he resisted all efforts of Wellesley to breach the solidarity of Maratha confederacy with profound wisdom and statesmanship. However, tragedy befell the Marathas with the sudden death of Nana Fadnavis at Poona on 13 March, 1800. With him, remarked Colonel Palmer, the British Resident at Poona, 'departed all the wisdom and moderation of the Maratha Government'. Nana Fadnavis' death immediately brought acute bitterness and animosity among two Maratha Chieftains namely Daulat Rao Scindia and Jaswant Rao Holkar regarding their struggle for supremacy at Poona. The matter was further complicated by the weak handling of the situation by the then Peshwa, Baji Rao II.

In the immediate battle for supremacy, Scindia was initially successful. However, when he was engaged with Holkar's troops at Malwa, the Peshwa murdered Vithalji Holkar, brother of Jaswant Rao Holkar. This highly incensed Jaswant Rao Holkar and he defeated the combined army of the Peshwa and Scindia at Poona and captured the capital. Peshwa Baji Rao II ran for his life and safety and had to accept British supremacy. He accepted Wellesley's Subsidiary Alliance at the Treaty of Bassein on the 31st December 1802. In Poona, Jaswant Rao Holkar put young Vinayak Rao, the adopted son of Raghoba, on the Peshwa Masnad.

As per the Treaty of Bassein, a trained troop of not less than 6000 regular Infantry and an equal number of British Artillery soldiers were posted in perpetuity in the Peshwa's territory with cessation of some territory which would yield revenue worth twenty-six lakh of Rupees. Further Baji Rao II was debarred from entering into agreement and seeking help from any nation which was hostile to the British. This ensured that there were to be no French troops and advisors to protect Baji Rao II.

A British force under Arthur Wellesley, brother of Lord Wellesley, inducted Baji Rao to the Poona Masnad on 13 May, 1803. This allowed the company to have control over the Maratha confederacy of Poona. This treaty had a negative side too, since it drew the British into the endless vortex of the complicated and turbulent Maratha politics of the times. The abject surrender of the Peshwa, aroused the passion of Maratha nationalism among other powerful Maratha leaders, who, abandoning their mutual jealousies, forged a united front against the British. Daulat Rao Scindia and Raghunathji II of Berar at once combined. They sought the active intervention of Holkar to enter into the alliance. Holkar however retired to Malwa with his troops. Gaikwad of Baroda remained neutral. The final showdown was ready around August 1803. The total strength of the Maratha Army was 2,50,000 and 40,000 troops, trained and commanded by Frenchmen. The British forces, with Wellesley at the helm, were adequately prepared. Gaekwad of Baroda and King of Oudh were neutral, as per their treaty with the British. Help from Mysore and Surat enabled the British to attack the Maratha confederacy at all fronts. Finally, the D-day arrived when the British army under the command of General Lake took the final initiative. On September 11, 1803, in the middle of the monsoons, General Lake ordered a rapid advance from Kanpur and Fateh Garh to capture Aligarh and reached the village of Patparganj in Delhi on 14th September, 1803. Two regiments of Native Cavalry and seven regiments of Native Infantry under the British command and 4900 soldiers, in a swift action between 3.00 am to 7.00 pm completely routed the Marathas. General Lake entered Delhi on 14th September, 1803, after annihilating the Marathas in this battle of Patparganj, and the Regency of the British was established in Delhi. General Lake received the Insignia of the Second Noble of the decaying Mughal Emperor, the first being given to Daulat Rao Scindia.

The British Residency at Delhi having been set up in 1803, it's important duty at that time was the management of British relations with the Mughal Emperor. The post of Resident was considered to be the richest and prized post in a public servant's career, in India. He was provided with a splendid princely mansion and his yearly remuneration was £5,000 to £10,000 a year, depending on the status of the state. As the representative of the Governor General at Calcutta, he took ceremonial precedence over everyone except the king or Maharaja or Sultan as the case may be. His office was decorated with most distinguished civil servants and most decorated defence personnel.

Col (later Sir) David Ochterlony was the first Resident in Delhi and held the post from 1803–1806. Next was Alexander Seton (1806–10). He was followed by C.T. Metcalfe (from 1810–18). Again, Sir David Ochterlony became the Resident, from 1818–21.

CT Metcalfe had the distinction of having control over Rajputana, the largest conglomerate of Indian States, and the authority to conduct foreign relations with Lahore and Kabul. During the early days of Ochterlony, Jaswant Rao Holkar made a valiant attempt to wrest power from the then resident Ochterlony, which was however, repulsed after nine days of fierce battle. In 1805, it was settled that Shah Alam would receive a monthly allowance from the East India Company of 60 thousand rupees and his other relatives, a sum of 30 thousand rupees per month. Rupees 10 thousand was also granted to all as festival allowance. No death sentence was to be passed without the sanction of the King. Sentences of mutilations were to be carried out only under orders of the King. Commutation for crime would be restricted to five years imprisonment in lieu of severance of one limb. In another major change, Marquis (later Lord) Cornwallis was sent as Governor General in Calcutta in place of Lord Wellesley with specific orders to stop the war which Lord Lake was pursuing against Holkar. This Lord Lake refused to agree to. Lord Cornwallis died around the same time and Sir George Barlow came in his place. On 7th January, a treaty was signed between Lord Lake and Holkar in Amritsar. Soon Shah Alam died and was buried near the shrine of Bakhtiyar Kaki at Mehrauli.

Akbar Shah II, succeeded Shah Alam with many of his powers curtailed. In 1808, his son Mirza Jahangir fired a pistol at Seton and was removed to Allahabad. In 1809, the monthly allowance of Bahadur Shah II and his family was increased to Rupees One lakh after doubts about his sanity were cleared. In 1811 Charles Metcalfe had put certain restrictions but coins still continued to be struck in his name. The period between 1803 to 1857 (except for last years) passed off without major political upheaval. Mirza Jahangir who was banished to Allahabad, was allowed to stay at Delhi fort. His mother went to the Dargah of Bakhtiar Kaki and from there launched the famous Phool Walon ki Sair. It was a journey from Bakhtiar Kaki's mausoleum to the temple of Yog Maya. David Ochterlony's Muslim wife Mubarak Begum built a famous mosque at Chawri Bazar known as Masjid Mubarak Begum.

The Third and final Anglo-Maratha War (1817 to 1810) was fought between the British East India Company, led by Governor General Hastings, and the Marathas under Peshwa Baji Rao II, supported by Bhonsle of Nagpur and the Holkar of Indore. The Maratha army was thoroughly defeated, leading to the loss of Maratha independence and the breakdown of the Maratha Empire. The Maratha kingdoms of Holkar and Bhonsle were annexed by the British, and became princely states under British suzerainty. The Peshwa was captured and his territory was annexed to become a part of the Bombay Presidency. This war had far reaching consequences, as it led to the Company gaining control over most of India.

* * *

Chapter 15

The Sepoy Mutiny 1857

The famous Indian Revolt of 1857–59, was a great landmark, rather a watershed in the history of India as it was the first time we see an outburst of nationalistic spirit from various parts of India. It was also the first collective attempt, however erratic, to overthrow the ever-growing British domination over India. Popularly known as the Sepoy Mutiny, it was nonetheless a valiant effort of Indian soldiers to challenge the entrenched might of the ever-expanding British rule in India. The Sepoy Mutiny started in June of 1857, exactly a hundred years after Robert Clive had defeated the Nawab of Bengal, Siraj-ud-Daulah, at the Battle of Plassey. There were many immediate causes of the revolt of 1857: apart from the political and economic dominance of the East India Company over the whole of India, the administrative changes brought out by the British were much to the annoyance of the Indian people, peasants, traders, nobles and rulers.

It also saw the ushering of the interference in the mode of living of the populace to which they were accustomed to through the ages. There was tumult, sometimes small, sometimes large, in the age-old placid way of Indian life. Commotions had started surfacing in different societies across the wide expanse of India.

There was a rising in Bareilly as early as 1816. There were a series of small uprisings in the tribal belt of Chotanagpur, notably the Kol outbreak of 1831–32. There was a muslim Ferrazi disturbance in Barasat in Bengal in 1831, under leadership of Syed Ahmed and his disciple Tittoo Mir. Later on, there was an uprising in Faridpur (East Bengal), under Deedoo Mir.

There was a long chain of Moplah uprising during the period 1849 to 1855. There was the Santhal revolt of 1857–1859. These upheavals were certainly shocking to the British might. Then came the crucial revolt of 1857.

The immediate cause of the revolt was the arbitrary introduction of land management policy, namely, Lord Dalhousie's policy of annexation of principalities through the infamous Doctrine of Lapse. This caused consternation in the minds of old ruling families, both Muslims and Hindus. Muslim sentiments were wounded because of the illegal annexation of Oudh. There was also a lot of public indignation because of the insults inflicted on the Begum of Oudh. In addition, the refusal of the British to continue the pension of the ex-peshwa Baji Rao II's adopted son, Nana Saheb of Bithoor. Some of the other prominent rulers, influential and rich zamindars saw through the British game of political deceit. Among them were as stated above Nana Saheb, Nana's nephew Rao Saheb, his aide Tantia Tope, a Brahman warrior, the Rani of Jhansi, Kunwar Singh, the Rajput Chief of Jagadishpur, Bihar, Azim Ullah Khan and Firoz Shah, a descendant of Mughal Emperor Bahadur Shah, to name a few.

The first spark of the rebellion can be traced to the introduction of the Enfield Rifle, the cartridges for which were greased with animal fat. The fat used were those of cows and pigs. One was a taboo for the Hindus and the other, for Muslims. It was indeed an ill-conceived measure. It brought immediate discontent among both Hindu and Muslim sepoys as the greased paper used in the cartridge had to be removed by teeth. They felt that this was a ploy of the British to make them lose their faith.

This led to a rebellion among sepoys in Barrackpore and Berhampore in Bengal, leading to a revolt by Mangal Pandey in Barrackpore, who was hanged for attacking the regiment's British officers. Though rebellion was quickly suppressed as it was localised, the fire quickly spread to Meerut, a major cantonment town in west U.P. Sepoys broke out in open revolt in Meerut on 10 May 1857. There was heavy fighting by the rebel troops in Meerut followed by Delhi.

The sepoys swarmed into the prison, freed their imprisoned colleagues, murdered the European officers and set fire to their houses. General Hewitt, in spite of having 2200 European troops under him, failed to tackle the revolt. The sepoys strode to Delhi the very next morning, crossed the boat bridge over Yamuna and roused the sepoys of the cantonments in Agra Fort. The old king Bahadur Shah ordered the closure of the palace gates. However, Indian guards soon joined the sepoys. They murdered the English Commander and the chaplain who happened to be staying at the palace. The bewildered octogenarian Bahadur Shah, the Mughal emperor, was forced to accept nominal leadership of the revolting sepoys. Soldiers treated him with due respect. However his age and antecedents made it impossible for him to give leadership worth the name, even if he had wished so. The Europeans in Daryaganj were rapidly exterminated. Their womenfolk and children met a violent end for refusing to abjure Christianity. Some however took shelter in Indian families who endured great risk to avoid the wrath of the marauding sepoys.

Next came an important phase in the sepoy mutiny. Indian troops were brought down from the cantonments to take up positions along the guard house of Kashmiri Gate. There a handful of desperate defenders, mainly Indians, were instrumental in blowing up the Magazine tower near the General Post Office, thus depriving the mutineer of a huge stock of bullets and gunpowder, so vital for carrying out the battle. The male folk having been thus eliminated while guarding the magazine, the hapless English women and Children collected at the flagstaff tower at the end of the Ridge, eagerly awaiting the arrival of reinforcements from Ambala.

Though the rebellion had started on the 11th of May 1857, there was little military activity till 8th June, when the British won their first victory at Badli-ki-Sarai. After this victory, British moved their headquarters to the Ridge, which was bare, hot and rocky.

It was not before 8 June that the Ambala contingent under command of Sir Harry Bernard could arrive, after battling their way to the besieged ridge. Their attempt to recapture Delhi was unsuccessful and they had to endure the long summer wait in the extreme heat and accompanied sickness, until full enforcement could reach from Lahore on 11 September. With heavy bombardment, the city was finally captured in the week of 14th to 20th September 1857. It was indeed a ferocious battle. With Hindu Rao House (now Hindu Rao hospital) at the central citadel, flanked by Metcalfe House on the left, flagstaff house nearby and golf course main camp on the old Viceregal lodge, it was truly a formidable fortification.

On the city side, it was days of scorching summer heat, scarcity and deprivation due to siege. Coupled with it, was the lack of real leadership among the mutineers with the Mogul Commander in chief, Mirza Mogul, who proved unfit to provide proper leadership.

Amongst the overall chaos and confusion all around, there was a havildar of the Bareilly force, named Mohammad Bakhtawar Khan, who emerged as a leader. However, though he was a valiant soldier, he could not enforce order and discipline amongst the disorderly troops who were suffering severe deprivation due to non-payment of salaries, shortage of supply of provisions due to high prices and were in a state of acute distress. They went on a rampage, threatening the common citizens and resorting to plundering and loot.

The Hindu bankers and traders were not forthcoming to render real assistance. Periodically, the palace asked for loans from the bankers, who were Hindus. With passage of time, the amount of loan, to the Palace from the bankers, started dwindling. The lives of the peace loving citizens of Delhi, started getting more and more miserable day by day.

However, after a violent battle, the better organised and militarily equipped British won the day. The mutiny had been successfully suppressed. There were heavy casualties on both sides due to the severe summer heat, lack of proper planning and resources and irregular and insufficient food supply leading to outbreak of cholera and dysentery.

Also, the King hardly mustered proper support for the mutineers. As already stated there was a dwindling supply of food and ammunition like assault weapons, bullets, gunpowder. The gullible Indian soldiers were caught at a disadvantage because of the espionage of British agents and their planting of mutual suspicion among sepoys of different communities. The British also had superior military leadership, planning and strategy and better supplies of food and ammunition.

The British, now in a commanding position, started their retaliation and ushered in an era of trigger hunting revengers, who would not distinguish between peace loving ordinary citizens and fugitive sepoys. Both became canon fodder of the reneging British soldiers.

In addition to this, there were Gujjar villagers out to plunder any insecure house. Delhi witnessed a week of terrible assault and revenge as stated earlier. After the fall of Kashmere Gate, there was intermittent fighting in the lanes and bylanes where the British were not always the winners. The heat was terribly sickening and the ordinary non combatant citizens of Delhi yearned for peace and respite from the unending violence.

The ground reality swung distinctly in favour of the British, with the arrival of the well equipped brigade of John Nicholson on 7 August. By 24 August, the British won the decisive battle of Ludlow castle and Najafgarh. Nicholson himself died of a bullet wound during the assault, but not before the capture of Mori Gate and Kabuli Gate. After capturing Kashmere Gate, advancing troops advanced upto Jama Masjid. On 20 September, the fort of Salimgarh was captured and the next day, the Red Fort. On 21 September, King Bahadur Shah was captured from the Humayun tomb area.

Around the 20th of September, the British could restore some semblance of authority. Mohd. Bakhtawar Khan fled from Delhi, leaving the octogenarian Emperor Bahadur Shah alone. Bahadur Shah surrendered to the British under the condition that his life and that of his family would be spared. He was captured by Hodson on the 21st of September along with his retainer from Humayun's tomb, where he had taken refuge. However, Hodson mercilessly killed the three beloved sons of the Emperor at Kabuli Gate which came to be known as Khooni Darwaza for posterity. However, as the rebellion ended, the city of Delhi saw a holocaust of revenge by the British as an aftermath of the mutiny. British authority within the city of Delhi was restored by September 20, 1857.

Then ushered in the period of revenge. Captured rebel soldiers were routinely executed before Kotwali Police Station at Chandni Chowk. There was a sham of a trial by the Military courts. In all, 3000 captive rebels were tried and out of them, 1000 were mercilessly executed by the Military courts.

King Bahadur Shah himself got a reprieve from death, but was however banished to Rangoon where he spent the last of his pathetic days, his death dropping the final curtain to centuries old Mughal Rule in India.

However, putting an end to the Mutiny was not that simple. Elsewhere, in the vast stretches of north India, the flame of the mutiny kept on burning, where valiant battles at various places of upper Gangetic plains and central India broke out. The main centres were Bareilly in Rohilkhand, Cawnpore (Kanpur), Lucknow, Banaras Oudh and Nasirabad in Rajputana.

The brave Rajput hero of Jagdishpur of Bihar, Kunwar Singh unleashed a ferocious battle on the British. Even though subdued by Commissioner of Patna division at Arrah and Major Vincent Eyre of the Bengal Artillery in August 1857, the valiant Rajput hero continued his battles outside Jagadishpur till his death on 23rd April 1858. Kunwar Singh's brother Amar Singh tried his best to carry out the unfinished struggle of his illustrious brother.

The valiant battle of Banaras was put down by Colonel Neill, of the Madras Fusiliers. A grim and terrible revenge followed and martial law was promulgated by the Governor General; mutineers all around, including young boys, were mercilessly massacred. Colonel Neill captured the fort of Allahabad on June 11, 1857. The mutiny at Kanpur was led by Nana Saheb of Bithur, a suburb of Kanpur. The British Commander, Sir Hugh Taylor, already seventy five years old, failed to defend. Skirmishes went on from 8th to 26 June when the Kanpur Garrison surrendered on the condition they be given safe passage to Allahabad.

However, there was betrayal on part of the rebels, who, throwing all norms of decency and humanity aside, engaged in widespread massacre. This came to be known as the Siege of Cawnpore (Kanpur). In a rare bout of carnage, the sepoys put to death all the English men, except for four who were able to flee. Next, an even more pathetic thing happened: the British women and children were not spared. They were mercilessly put to death at Bibighar, near Allahabad, by Nana's troops, and their bodies were thrown down a well, with the intention of burying the evidence.

This killing came to be known as the Bibighar Massacre. Nana was not personally involved, however, this was not accepted by the British, as a plea of Nana's innocence. Following the massacre, the enraged Company forces engaged in revenge and brutal retaliation against the captured sepoys, not even sparing the innocent civilians. They felt that the Indians were not reliable: they had no decency, no decorum, no humanity and no respect for the values of life.

The indomitable heroics of Rani Laxmibai of Jhansi, is worth recalling. When the British refused to acknowledge her adopted son as the legitimate heir to the throne, she joined the revolt. The way she attired in male battle uniform, mounted on a horse, with an open sword in hand and fought valiantly till her death at the battlefield, evoked praise from friends and foes alike. It became an enduring subject of folklore for ages to remember. The fleeing Tantia Tope was caught in the Nepal Jungle by Man Singh, a vassal of the Scindias and handed over to the British to be hanged.

Nana also fled to the jungles of Nepal, where his last days are shrouded in mystery. Finally, the total betrayal of Sikh community led by Sikh Chief Gulab Singh of Kashmir sounded the death knell of the rebel cause. Jang Bahadur, the Nepal ruler, Scindia and his prime minister Dinkar Rao, Salar Jung ruler Nizam of Hyderabad, openly sided with the British. Sir Colin Campbell (later on Lord Clyde), the Commander in Chief of the British army, broke the long siege of the Lucknow garrison, which was hitherto valiantly defended by Outram Havelock. Sir Colin Campbell is also credited with the annihilation of Nana Saheb at the battle of Kalpi on the 6th December 1857. Sir Hugh Ross, with his base at Mhow, battled his way against Tantia Tope, stated above, defeating him in February 1858, in the Betwa area.

The departure of Nana Saheb under mysterious circumstances, was considered as the culmination of the Sepoy Mutiny by Governor General Lord Canning. Lord Canning, also derided by the British as 'Clemency Canning', handled the post mutiny affairs with deft statesmanship and a wise and expedient policy with no feelings of revenge, strictly going by prudence and judgement.

The revolt of 1857 resulted in some very significant events. Most importantly, there was a transfer of power from the East India Company to the British Crown. Equally significant was the trial of Bahadur Shah Zafar, the last Mughal emperor of Delhi, leading to his exile and death. The trial of Bahadur Shah was mostly symbolic; it was a grand show of colonial power, a tool used by the British to eliminate their political adversary and quell their opposition. At the time of the trial, Bahadur Shah was an old man of 82, infirm and powerless, a mere shadow of what his mighty ancestors had been.

It must be kept in mind that Bahadur Shah had been an unwilling participant in the Sepoy Mutiny of 1857. The mutiny was not of his making. As a matter of fact, when the rebellious sepoys from Meerut cantonment marched into the Mughal capital and reached the Red Fort, Bahadur Shah refused to take over the command of the rebellious sepoys. He was however persuaded to give in to their demand and agreed to be their commander. But even though he was forced to take over as their leader, Bahadur Shah never entered the battlefield in person against the British army. He was just a nominal head of the mutiny which was primarily that of sepoys. There was no reason to implicate him in the battle unleashed by the sepoys to overthrow British rule in India. However, after his surrender, he became the target of the revengeful fury of the British. His arrest followed by his exile and the murder of his sons and legitimate heirs, finally extinguished any hope of recreating the rule of the Mughal Empire.

Bahadur Shah had been taken to Humayun's Tomb by his aides and advisors, possibly to evade imminent arrest by the advancing British army. The idea was to delay his arrest, which would bring down the last Mughal Emperor of India and sound the death knell of the Mughal Dynasty. However, he could not escape the ultimate arrest, nor could he flee from Humayun's Tomb to some place safe, away from Delhi. When the British army finally caught up with him, he did not heed the advice of his generals and surrendered, mainly to avoid a massacre. His surrender came with a clause, that his life, that of his queens and those of his sons, would be spared. As Bahadur Shah was taken into custody by General Hodson, on the 21st of September, he was assured by the head of the British army that no physical harm would be inflicted on him or on his family.

However, on 22nd of September, in spite of assurances and ignoring all human values, the beloved sons of Bahadur Shah, namely, Mirza Mughal and Mirza Khizr Sultan and his grandson, Mirza Abu Bakht, were killed in cold blood by Colonel William Hodson, the very man who was charged with their protection. As the royal princes were being transferred from Humayun's Tomb to the Red Fort in a bullock cart, they were ordered to disembark midway and strip, and then were mercilessly shot to death at point blank range. Their bodies were taken to Agra and presented to Bahadur Shah, who was so shocked and saddened that he could not show much reaction. The gate where they were shot to death, Kabuli Darwaza, came to be known as Khooni Darwaza or Lal Darwaza.

The killing of the three sons of Bahadur Shah was highly symbolic: it ended the progeny of Bahadur Shah and marked the end of the age-old Mughal rule in India. It heralded the complete victory of the British over the last Emperor of India. All the political opposition to the British had been eliminated.

Bahadur Shah himself was treated with great indignity after his arrest. He was displayed to the general public 'like a beast in a cage'. He was placed before the military court in 1858, which was formed to debate on the crimes committed by him. He became the primary accused for the rebellion of 1857. He was charged with waging a war against the British government, aiding and abetting the mutineers and sedition. The military court had only British members and was a total farce. The trial of Bahadur Shah went on for 40 days; it began on 27 January and ended on 9 March, 1858. Ironically, the trial was held in the Diwan-e-Khas of the Red Fort, a hallowed hall where so many of his ancestors had held court. There was no sense of propriety and no fair play. The British judges did not bother to heed the protestations of Bahadur Shah, nor did they listen to any arguments advanced by him in his favour, to exonerate him of the charges levelled against him. The emperor himself was a pitiful sight: he was old and infirm, and often appeared lost and unfocused. Though he pleaded 'not guilty' to all the charges levelled against him and accused the British of negating the terms of their agreement with him and total dishonesty in their dealings with him, he seemed browbeaten and resigned to his inevitable fate.

This was a sham of a trial, and also an invalid one, according to the international law of the time. Even so, in final analysis, the military court found him guilty of rebellion, treason and murder, and sentenced him to life imprisonment and banishment from Delhi, the home of his ancestors. Bahadur Shah Zafar, along with his queens, his still surviving sons and other members of his household were exiled to far away Rangoon in Burma (present day Myanmar). His life was spared because of an assurance extracted by the Maharaja of Patiala. Bahadur Shah was however, put under severe torture as he was ferried to Allahabad, the port of departure, in the peak of summer in a bullock cart. Later he was put on a boat to be ferried to Calcutta and thereafter, to Rangoon, which was his ultimate destination, and where he died as a prisoner in a small cell on the banks of the river Irravadi. His death, in October of 1862, aged 87, finally put an end to the Mughal Dynasty in India which had commenced in 1526, after the eventful victory of Babur over Ibrahim Lodi.

The revolt of 1857 ended in the conclusive victory of the British and the total annihilation of the rebels, both Hindus and Muslims, irrespective of their actual participation in the battle against the British. A region of terror, by the marauding British troops, was let loose. Any iota of justice and fair play had gone to the winds. Any able-bodied native, irrespective of their involvement in the skirmish against the British, was gunned down.

The massacre continued till 18 January, 1858, when Delhi was handed over to the civil authority. Delhi remained under the total control of military troops upto 24 February, 1858. All Hindus and Muslims were ejected from Delhi. Things had come to such a pass that there was a clamour for the demolition of the palace of the Red Fort. Subsequently, the whole area from the foreground of the Fort to Jama Masjid. (that is, the area west of Lothian Road, upto Roman Catholic church), was demolished in order to place guns and cannons overlooking the fort.

This happened despite the moderate policy of Lord Canning and his sincere effort to reestablish the rule of law. Canning's moderate policies earned him the nickname of 'Clemency Canning' from his British peers.

Apart from the indiscriminate massacre of Indians of all faiths and religions by the trigger-happy British troops, according to official records, 392 rebels were hanged and numerous others were shot dead. Bahadur Shah's sons and grandson were shot down at Khooni Darwaza, the emperor himself was tried by the Military Court at Diwan-i-Aam and was banished at Rangoon where he breathed his last. In october of 1857, two more sons of the king, Mirza Bakhtawar Shah and Mirza Mahndu were found guilty and shot dead. There was also the quick summary trial and execution of some important personalities who were believed to be involved in the mutiny, like Raja Nahar Singh of Ballabgarh and Nawab Abdul Rahman Khan.

There cannot be a more pathetic account of the British revenge post the 1857 mutiny than the wailing letter written by Mirza Ghalib to his friend Mirza Hatim Ali: "Thousands of my friends died. Whom should I remember and to whom should I complain! Perhaps none is left even to shed tears on my death. Sometimes innocent people are killed along with the sinners. This is what happened after the Mutiny. The English soldiers began to shoot whomsoever they met on the way. Among the men who stayed in the city, there were some whose equal has never been born nor shall be born. Mian Mohammad Amin Panjakush, an excellent writer, Maulvi Imam Baksh along with his two sons, Mir Niaz Ali and the persons of Kucha Chelan (It is said they were fourteen hundred in number), were arrested and taken to Raj Ghat Gate. They were shot dead and their dead bodies were thrown into the Yamuna. As for the women, they came out of their houses along with their children and killed themselves by jumping into the wells. All the wells of the Kucha Chelan were filled with dead bodies. My pen does not write more."

This was just the tip of the iceberg. The massacre and butchery that followed knew no limits and no bounds. Mirza Ghalib, who was the eyewitness to the butchery, wrote many letters to his brethren and contemporary literati. They were later compiled and published in 1869 as 'Urdu-i-Mulla' and 'Dastanbu'. Ghalib was arrested on October 5 1857, only to be released through the intervention of his friend Colonel Brown.

At the height of their revenge, the triumphant British forces drove the entire population of the walled city, men, women and children, out of their homes, irrespective of caste, creed and distinction, to consign them to a life without an address, without a shed over their heads. Their homes were raided and ransacked. This went on for two years. The huge population of the evicted natives had to scramble to get a foothold in the Mehrauli complex. After some time, the Hindus were allowed to return, as they were considered less hostile to the British during the Mutiny. The British held the Muslims more responsible for the mutiny, hence they had to face stricter scrutiny before they could be allowed to return.

Next came the destruction and desecration of Muslim religious places. The Jama Masjid was captured by the British soldiers, who kept using it for various purposes other than religion for six long years. Fatehpuri Masjid was sold to Lala Chunnamal only to be restored later. Same was the fate of Sunehri Masjid and Ghata Masjid, which was used as bakeries; this was a mighty blow to the Muslim sentiment.

The rule of the East India Company ended and the administration of India came directly under the British Crown. The Secretary of State for India was now responsible for formulating policies for the governance of India. This put an end to the mindless greed and profiteering as displayed by the Company officials. Religious tolerance was promoted and there was inclusion of Indians into the civil services. In the regiments, the ratio of British soldiers to Indian sepoys was increased and artillery was kept only in British hands.

The Indian Mutiny of 1857, though unsuccessful, was the first widespread and collected effort against British rule in India. This rebellion has been variously called the sepoy mutiny or even the first war of independence. Indeed, the revolt was started by the sepoys in Barrackpore and then Meerut, but as it gained momentum, many rulers, local leaders, peasants, artisans, zamindars, land owners and village chiefs joined them. From Meerut, the rebellion spread to many parts of north India, like Delhi, Kanpur, Lucknow, Gwalior, Jhansi,Bareilly, Benaras and Faizabad, to name a few. There is no second opinion that the events of 1857 were a violent resistance to British power and authority. The revolt of 1857 also commemorates hundred years of the famous Battle of Plassey of 1757.

The British were also attacking the social and cultural fabric of India. The Hindu society felt increasingly threatened by the introduction of new western ideas and reforms. Many Christian missionaries came to India at this time, and they posed a challenge to the religious and cultural beliefs of the Hindus. People started believing that the British wanted to break down the age- old caste system as well as the social and religious customs of the Hindus. The Brahmans were dissatisfied as they were losing their hold over society. New inventions like the railways and the telegraph and the spread of western education, were looked upon with suspicion. The Religious Disabilities Act of 1856 granted that all those who converted from Hinduism to Christianity would be able to inherit the property of their father. The common people felt that the British wanted to convert them to Christianity. Lord Dalhousie worked for the emancipation of women. Social practices like female infanticide and the sati system- the practice of immolation of the widow on the funeral pyre of her husband, were abolished. Many women centric reforms were introduced; polygamy and dowry system were banned. Widow remarriage was encouraged (by Hindu Widow Remarriage Act of 1857) and women's education was widely promoted. Sister Nibedita (Margaret Elizabeth Nobel) was a pioneer of Hindu women through education.

The zamindar class too were dissatisfied with the oppressive British rule. In the Indian countryside, the poor peasants and the property owners, that is the landlords and the zamindars, were reeling under excessive taxes and a rigid revenue system. Indian trade and crafts were also suffering, hence artisans, craftsmen and traders were also disgruntled. They too wanted to throw off the yoke of British rule and they all plunged into an armed struggle against the British.

Thus we see that though the revolt started off as a military outbreak, it certainly was more than just an uprising or mutiny of disgruntled soldiers. No doubt, it was for the Sepoys to take up arms against the British, but it is necessary to recognise the bigger spirit behind the revolt. The revolt of 1857 did end with the conclusive victory of the British and total annihilation of the rebels. The uprising was not properly planned and lacked military organisation. Further, lack of resources, modern weapons and lack of a central leadership- all led to the failure of the revolt. Still, it marks a very important step in India's fight against a foreign power.

Some prominent Indian nationalists and historians have called the revolt the first war of Indian independence. Veer Savarkar (Vinayak Damodar Savarkar) in his book 'The History of the War of Indian Independence" (1909), written originally in Marathi, calls the mutiny the 'Indian war of Independence', a war that was fought by Indians for their 'swadharma', one's own religion and 'swaraj', one's own land. This revolt was definitely different in character to earlier smaller and localised uprisings in different parts of India. This was the first directed and collective attack on the British.

The revolt did start off as a sepoy mutiny against British Officials, but soon it turned into a popular uprising where a large number of common people, peasants, artisans, zamindars, local chiefs, maulvis, rulers and even women joined, making it wide spread.

It is also true that different sections of society had different reasons and motives for joining the rebellion. Not all could see the bigger picture; that was gaining independence for the whole of India, as a nation. The spirit of nationalism was missing. The concept of India as one nation was also missing. It took fifty years for the British to annex the South of Vindhyas and the whole of Sind and North West frontier province upto the Indo. Afghan border and upto Burma border in the east to recognise it as Indian nation,

The revolt of 1857 was not a pan-Indian effort. It was largely localised to the fight of the sepoys in the payroll of the indigenous Indian rulers who were being deprived of their hereditary lordship over their land and properties.

Geographically too, the rebellion remained restricted. The north and some central parts of India had participated in the revolt, but there were many parts of India that were not affected at all. Many local rulers did not participate in the revolt and many provided active support to the British. The provinces south of the river Narmada remained untouched by the uprising. The Scindias of Gwalior, the Holkar of Indore, the Nizam of Hyderabad, the Nawab of Bhopal, the Raja of Jodhpur, the Rana of Nepal and rulers of Patiala and Kashmir did not participate in the revolt at all. Sindh did not participate, while Rajputana was loyal to the British. Except for the Mughal emperor Bahadur Shah Zafar and his sons and Nana Sahib, the adopted son of Peshwa Baji Rao II, none of the prominent Indian princes joined the revolt.

The modern educated class of Indians also did not support or participate in the revolt. They felt that the British were required for the development of India, and they approved of the social reforms brought in by the British. They were also supporters of the western education system. There was no participation from the intellectual capital of India, that is Bengal. Other than providing the initial spark, the rebellion had not cast any shadow on Calcutta, which was the capital of the British empire.

Because of these reasons, many writers and historians have branded it as a 'sepoy mutiny', a purely military outbreak. Almost all British and European historians brand it as a mere 'mutiny' of disgruntled and undisciplined sepoys. Many prominent Indian historians like Dr. R.C.Majumdar, Dr. S.N. Sen, Dr. Jadunath Sarkar and Abul Kalam Azad have also called it a sepoy mutiny and not a national war of independence. It must, however, be kept in mind that they were shaped under Macaulay's system of education and hence their opinions were moulded and influenced by the British point of view.

In conclusion, it can be said that the revolt of 1857 was not a national war of independence. It was not a national movement in the true sense, lacking a pan-India appeal. But, it would be wrong to totally dismiss it as just a sepoy mutiny. It was the first great and direct challenge to British rule in India on an extensive scale. It sowed the seeds of nationalism in the minds of the people and shook the very foundations of British dominance in India. It can be safely said that though the revolt of 1857 was not the first national war of independence, it was far more than a mere sepoy mutiny; it was a popular people's uprising, the first targeted and collected attempt of the Indians to throw off the yoke of British rule in India.

Chapter 16

Propagation of Christianity and Evangelical Activity

No history of Delhi during 1803 onwards would be complete without a mention of the pioneering zeal of the Christian missionaries who came to India during this time. They could well visualise that the total conquest of India would not be possible without converting the Indians comprising mainly Hindus and Muslims into Christianity, the religion of the British conquerors.

A catalogue of events involving Christian Missionaries with memorable events is worth focussing on, as it leads to the permanent inroads of colonial British into the mind and soul of India. The earliest church in India was the Syrian Church developed by the branch of Nestorian community in Malabar. The community came to India in the fifth century CE. Their descendants could be well over 2 lakhs today. It was in the fourteenth century that Roman Catholic activity entered the field of evangelization in India.

Vasco da Gama discovered a sea route to India in 1498 and on 25 November 1510, Alfonso de Albuquerque, another Portuguese, conquered Goa. This allowed the various priestly orders namely Jesuits, Franciscans, Augustinians and the Dominicans to arrive in India. With the arrival of Francis Xavier in 1542, the mass conversion in Kerala received a momentous fillip. However, they could not make much inroads in North India. In tribal areas like Bastar and Chota Nagpur adivasi belts as also areas like Dadra Nagar Haveli, the Christian Missionaries started preaching in local language.

During the famine of 1597, in the Kashmir Valley, a lot of famished children were baptized by Christian priests. During the rule of Jehangir, Sir Thomas Roe came to his durbar. But nothing remarkable emerged as Jehangir and his son Shah Jehan never trusted the foreigners. During the reign of Aurangzeb, Jizya Tax was reimposed on Non-Muslims. Furthermore, during the last days of Aurangzeb, the leash of Mughal order started declining with the political instability and the emergence of the open Mughal-Maratha conflict.

In Mysore, Tipu Sultan was a stumbling block against the activities of Christian Missionaries. He forcibly converted Christians into Islam around 1784. In the Mughal Kingdom, the roots of Christianity were planted by Myriam Begum, one of the wives of Akbar who was Portuguese by birth.

It was not until acquisition of Bombay by the East India Company in 1668, that the Carmelites started their religious activities. English merchants of the south, acquired a small village namely Madras on the seashore of Marina in 1675 and built their first church there.The seventeenth century saw a lot of upheaval with European colonial powers vying amongst themselves to acquire a permanent foothold in the coastal towns of India. The Dutch expelled the Portuguese from the Malabar coast except Goa. The French established themselves in Pondicherry in the south, and Chandannagar and Srirampur in Bengal.

The Protestant Missions in India developed in the Eighteenth Century under the Royal patronage of King Frederick of Denmark. Although the British were the first to land in India through the East India Company in 1600, it was not until 1681 that the first church could be built by the British. The services of Chaplains & school masters were put on regular footings in the British Church. The Society for Propagation of Christian knowledge was established by Dr. Thomas Bray in 1698 at Madras, and 1720 at Cuddalore, Calcutta, Trichinopoly and Tanjore.

In 1793, the Baptist Mission Society reached Calcutta (Kolkata). After 1813, even countries which did not have any colonial roots in India started sending their missionaries. Among them were American Quakers, Methodists, Presbyterian, Freewill Baptists, German Lutherans, American

Lutherans and Canadian Baptists. These were all voluntary societies with enthusiastic missionary zeal.

Returning to Delhi, it may be recalled that General Lake defeated the Marathas at Aligarh and finally at Patparganj. The Marathas were under command of Bourquein, the French General. A treaty was formalised in 1805, which gave the British authority over revenue administration, establishment of an Agent (Resident) in the Mughal Court, reducing the King to a simple British pensioner and retention of their monopoly with the use of force. The perpetuation of the British hegemony over the Emperor caused great heartburn in the Mughal durbar. There was an apparent lull in their strained relationship till the Sepoy Mutiny of 1857, when Bahadur Shah was completely defeated and his favourite sons were murdered by Colonel Hudson, at Delhi Gate which came to be known as Khooni Darwaza. Bahadur Shah was captured and deported to far off Rangoon in Burma, to remain in exile till his death. Post the Sepoy Mutiny of 1857, Delhi was in for a quick transformation.

The British entrenched in the North and South of the Red Fort. The Kashmiri Gate area came into prominence with a bazaar, a hospital and quartering of two battalions of soldiers in Daryaganj area. Also, accommodation was made for stables and ammunition. Qamar-al-din's mansion at Ajmeri Gate was converted to Custom House. A chapel was established in the military area of Red Fort. Even after the mutiny, the relationship between the Christian Church, under the Church Missionary Society led by Dr. Pfander and the Maulanas of Jama Masjid holding Wahabi faith like Shah Mohammad Ismail, had not become strained.

The Baptist Mission was formed in 1818 and the society for Propagation of Gospel in 1852. In 1852, two Hindus namely Ram Chander of Panipat and Chaman Lal, a Sub Assistant Surgeon were baptized. Ram Chander (1821–1880) was educated at the Govt college and was a teacher of Mathematics. Both were baptized on 11 July 1852, at St. James Church by Chaplain John Jennigs. The conversion of Master Ram Chander and Dr. Chaman Lal led to the alienation in maintenance of composite culture. The conversion of Master Ram Chander had the most salutary effect. He was the editor of two influential Urdu newspapers published from

Delhi namely, The Fawaid-ul-Nazarin and the Krian-us-Sadain. He also translated Macaulay's works for the advancement of English literature and culture.

Bishop Huber, a prominent personality of the Anglican order, first came to Agra in January, 1825. Akbar Shah, the then nominal Mughal Ruler, was highly impressed by Bishop Huber. In 1828, the British shifted their cantonment and offices, store rooms and Parade grounds into a fifteen hundred acre land (now the site of Delhi University and its periphery).

The north wall of the city, with the Ridge and the river Yamuna bed forming a low lying triangle, became the houses of government officers and agents. In 1854, Metcalf built his castle off the bank of Yamuna, after uprooting the village of Chandrawal. During the period 1830–57, there was hectic construction activity with Rajpura Cemetery (now Reids Line) coming up. The famous St. James Church, also known as Skinner's Church, came up at Kashmiri Gate in November, 1836. After the mutiny, the British Army took over possession of Jama Masjid, Ghata Masjid and Zinat-ul-Masjid.

In 1854, two missionaries of Society for the Propagation of Gospel (S.P.G), J.S. Jackson and A.R. Hubbard, both educated at Coirs College, Cambridge, arrived in India with their wives. The Indian Christians used to assemble on every Sunday at St. James Church and were addressed by Mr. Steward, who was a teacher in Delhi College. Mr. J.S. Jackson had the unique privilege of delivering sermons in Urdu.

They started a school and embarked upon a project for establishment of a college. The Delhi Mission started progressing and prospering under the missionary, Daniel Carey Sandy from Bishop College. At 22, the young missionary took over charge of Mission School, whose strength grew to 170 students. In 1852, Jackson left India and was replaced by L.Koch from Bishop College.

The prominent churches and Mission Houses that dotted Delhi's sky before the mutiny were Mission Hall, Daryaganj Central Baptist Church, Chandni Chowk, Nickolson cemetery, where Master Ram Chander was buried, Rajput Cemetery (now housing Patel Chest clinic nearby), Saint Stephen' Church, Fatehpur, Baptist Mission Church Malka Ganj,

Cambridge Mission House, Trinity Church, Turkman Gate, Armenian church, chapel & cemetery KishanGanj Church & Cemetery – Rajpura, Saint Thomas Church at Panchkuian Road, Saint Anthony Church, Gol Dakhana, Saint John's Church at Mehrauli founded in 1927 by Bishop S.S. Allnutt, boasting of composite Hindu, Islamic & Christian architecture and Saint Mary's Church, at Khari Baoli.

From 1757 to 1857, the East India Company had slowly expanded their political tentacles and pursued their policy of political expansion and annexation of Indian territory. The draconic policy of Lord Dalhousie in annexing native states through his policy of Doctrine of Lapse was instrumental in annexing the state of Sind in 1843 and Punjab in 1849. Even the enmity with the independent Kingdom of Jhansi fermented due to this policy of Doctrine of Lapse, where authority vested with ruler of the state passed on to the British in the absence of kingdom begetting or legal heir to the throne and not through adoption.

The English authorities in the meantime were gradually becoming more arrogant and started interfering in the basic ways of living of the people, their century old culture and traditional beliefs, norms and values. The social reforms of evil social practices such as immolation of widows, practice of sati and female infanticides, even though spearheaded by great Hindu reformers like Raja Ram Mohan Roy of Bengal, started to be considered as direct interference of the British, on the practices of the Hindu Religion.

Then came another very vexing law through the Act XXI of 1850, which enabled converts to have rights over ancestral property. This led the people to think that the British Government was hell bent upon large scale conversion of upper caste Hindus to Christianity. Even otherwise, the conversion to Christianity of lower-class Hindus and Muslims was going on unabated.

It is worthwhile to note that the structural composition of the social fabric of the British Society in England was structurally a feudalistic aristocratic society with little or no space for socialism as such. The hereditary upper caste aristocrats enjoying social privilege through birth were prevalent. The post of covenanted officers whether in defence services or civil services were strictly earmarked for aristocrats by birth, who also because of their proximity to royalty by birth, were entitled to the House of Lords. There is a buffer class, who by virtue of their various scholarly acumen, were entitled to occupy this strata. They were the snobs, which would mean that they were below the level of the nobles or who were yet to occupy the status of nobles in the social structure.

The Anglo Indian Community in India emanated through the marriage of British or Anglo Saxon men and Indian women or in a broader sense, European men and Indian women; they came to be known as Anglo Indians. The British Administration had earmarked a specified category of employment for this class. These were the Railways, the riverine activities mainly Customs, Ports Commissioners (later on Port Trust), Licensed Measurers being the main source. However, the most effective source of spread of Christianity in India could be attributed to the aftermath of the construction of E.I.R or Eastern Indian Railway from Calcutta (Howrah) to Old Delhi around 1866.

By the Act of 1857, the East India Company was abolished, and the Authority of the Government of India was transferred to the British crown. The Directors of East India Company were not supportive of the work of the Christian Missionaries working in India. However, Queen Victoria, in her declaration considered all communities equal and indicated that she herself was a Christian. The educational policy of 1854, of Lord Macaulay, outlined a national system of education with English language being the kingpin. English was made the common language of the elite class. English literature and history, with emphasis on British History and western philosophy provided an opportunity to develop Christian content at the expense of the vernacular or Indian content of thoughts. With the coming up of the Railways, other public works such as Bridges, Canals, Irrigation and Water works saw an influx of Englishman, Anglo Indians and Indian Christians who had expertise in these kinds of works.

In 1866, East Indian Railway entered into an agreement with the Society for Propagation of Gospel (S.P.G) by which S.P.G became a shareholder of Indian Railways with £7000, to provide service of clergies along the railway establishment from Calcutta to Delhi. Government provided additional remuneration of £180 a year to each clergy.

So, there came about the Anglo-Indian Railway colony, Railway Chaplain & Railway Parish, Railway School and Railway Institute. The foundation stone of the Indian congregational church was laid by Bishop Cotton in 1865, in whose name an Anglo-Indian School was established in Nagpur.

The St.Stephens Church was consecrated on 17 October 1867, by Bishop Milman. Some communities, namely Missionary Brotherhood of England, started evangelical work in Delhi around this time. Original Indian converts were mainly poor and from the low caste of Hindu Society.

St. Stephens College, the hallmark of Christian education was established in 1882 and was affiliated to the New University of Punjab. St. Stephens College acquired a new building in 1890 designed by Sir Swinton Jacob. This was at Kashmiri Gate. In 1886, Sushil Kumar Rudra, a Bengali Christian whose father was a Missionary in Burdwan, Bengal, joined St. Stephens College. He rose to be the first Indian Christian Principal of the college in 1907 and continued till 1923, as Principal till his resignation due to ill health. Indian Christians who used to assemble in St. James Church, where Mr. Steward Jackson started the service in Urdu. Bishop Lefroy, who was the Bishop of Lahore, wielded great influence in Delhi, along with the blind Maulvi, Ahmad Masih.

Study of Christianity and education in India will be incomplete without a reference to Charles Freer Andrews (1871–1940). His father was a Minister of Catholic Apostolic Church. He had a mystical faith in Christ. But that did not impact his liberal outlook, whether in cultivating lifelong friendships with great Indian leaders or in his pursuit of educational experience and actual impact of classroom education. He was a brilliant product of Pembroke college, Cambridge. With Basil West Colt (died 1900 in Delhi) he joined Cambridge Brotherhood.

In 1907, after coming to India, he joined St. Stephen's College, Delhi, befriended S.K. Rudra, Sundar Singh, met Rabindranath Tagore and taught at Santiniketan. He met Gandhiji in 1914 in South Africa, and again in 1931, in the second Round Table Conference in London.

In 1936, he drew more towards evangelical activity, attending the Holy Communion at St. James Church, Delhi. He died in Calcutta on 5 April 1940 and was buried at the famous Lower Circular Road cemetery, at Calcutta.

A new Diocese was formed in Delhi in 1947, with the first Bishop being Aurobindo Nath Mukherjee, a Bengali, who was the Principal of Delhi United Christian School. Lord Irwin, the Viceroy, built the Church of Redemption, near Central Secretariat, New Delhi, which was consecrated in 1931.

Chapter 17

The Recovery & Realignments

Post the sepoy mutiny of 1857, the city of Delhi suffered a terrible depredation because it was reduced to the status of a provincial town under the jurisdiction of the Punjab Government. The fall of its status, from the royal capital to just a provincial town, was both a physical and a psychological blow.

This was a period of ignominy for the city of Delhi. The High Court had disappeared. The prestigious Delhi College was closed. The Jama Masjid, the monument of pride for the muslims of Delhi, was closed for worship for six long years. The British military's presence and occupation had desecrated the Masjid. The other iconic religious landmark, the Fatehpuri Masjid was sold to Lala Chunna Mal, only to be retrieved after the intervention of Lord Lytton after seventeen years and given back to the Muslims. Zinat -ul-Masjid suffered the ignominy of being used as a bakery.

Following the handing over of the administration to the military post the British victory of 1857, the British Government immediately flung into action to ensure measures for their own security. It decided to ensure a shooting range of 500 yards (later reduced to 450 yards) between the palace or the fort and its vicinity, so as to prevent any possible attack on the fort. As mentioned earlier, the area around the Red Fort was cleared and many structures were demolished. Some of the notable edifices destroyed were the palaces of the Nawabs of Jhajjar, Ballabhgarh, Bahadurgarh and Farrukhnagar which were vulnerable towards the safety of the Palace. Many ancient structures of aesthetic beauty were ruthlessly demolished, as also a part of Dariba Kalan. Also, the aristocratic localities of Kucha Bulaqi Begum and Akbarabadi Masjid were destroyed. Ghalib estimated that there was overall destruction of over thirty lakhs worth of property. Hindu temples were however spared from destruction.

Its most important and expensive work was the maintenance of the Municipal Police to oversee law and order within the city. The next important work was related to conservancy. Thereafter would come education, health and other local requirements. The enacting of Punjab Municipal Act of 1867 defined the activities and jurisdiction of the Municipalities.

Viceroy Lord Lawrence was mainly instrumental in bringing in a new horizon for the Municipality in 1864. A committee was also formed to restore Jama Masjid to its pristine glory. The first major step towards the recovery and restoration, post the sepoy mutiny and consequential retribution and revenge era, was the construction of the Town Hall which was the central ethos to Victorian civic life.

Even before the mutiny, the construction of a Town Hall along with a Municipality was very much in the air. However, post the mutiny, during 1860, the actual construction of the Town Hall started, rather than waiting for the Imperial grant. It was started with the voluntary contributions of Hindu and Muslim businessmen who had been loyal to the British during the revolt. Also, the funds were made available from the provincial government. There were contributions of individuals of which the main donor was Lala Mahesh Das, whose individual contribution was Rs. 25000/-. The Town Hall came up as the centre of local government. Strategically it came up at the ideal location: it was easily approachable from the Delhi Railway Station. Also, the havelis of many affluent Khatri and Marwari families were in close proximity to the Town Hall and the Railway Station. The richest family of Delhi, the Khatri businessmen of Delhi, the Chunna Mal family built their haveli there.

The road running across Chandni Chowk came up, of course drastically reduced in width, having different causeways, one for carriages and another smaller one for carts and wagons. It effectively revived trade, commerce and other activities. The Town Hall became almost like a club where an animated gathering of business people, the bankers, Unani medicine practitioners and eminent teachers assembled. The big hall housed a public library and a Municipal office. Even a European recreation club came up in the vicinity. In course of time, the area saw bustling religious activity with the coming up of the famous Jain temple in 1870. Also, a massive Gurudwara (Sisganj) and a Baptist Chapel among others, came up. The area slowly developed as a religious hub. Christian preachers of different schools made their presence felt in Delhi, felt much before the close of the century. Arya Samaj Missions established their organisations at the start of the century.

Subsequently, because of enhancement of religious and social activities, other areas like Pipal Park (People's park), King Edward's park, which had come up on the ruins of Akbarabadi Masjid, gained prominence.

It is interesting to note the functions and responsibility of the Municipality which was operating from the Town Hall. Initially, the Municipality was spending mainly on maintenance of law and order, that is, on the police force, which was about one fourth of its total income. Conservancy and road maintenance accounted for 15–20 percent. The income of the Municipality depended largely on the Octroi (duty levied on goods) imposed on various goods.

The importance of Fatehpuri Masjid grew, and it established itself as a rival to the much-vaunted Jama Masjid. Lala Chunna Mal, a man of considerable wealth, had purchased it for Rupees 39650 in 1860. It was after 17 years that Lord Lytton brokered a deal which enabled it to be returned to the Muslims for religious purpose. It became a place for animated religious discourses and discussion like the Jama Masjid, which of course had the support of the officialdom. Fatehpuri Masjid became a link between the walled city and the suburbs. It was also enriched through the munificence of Punjab businessmen of the city.

The Victorian civic ethos was to have a Town Hall which would double up as an office of the Municipality and would also house the Chamber of Commerce, a literary society, a museum and an association sort of society where there would be easy exchange of ideas between the local people (called Natives) and the Europeans. The intention was to coalesce the views of the two groups, paving the way for the formation of a coherent policy.

The effort was largely successful. The Municipality managed to buy the building for Rs. 135457. Separate rooms were set aside for a European club; rooms were also set apart for a library. However, no provision was made for Delhi College & Madrasa. In 1869, the Municipality constructed an imposing Clock Tower in front of the Town Hall.

The same year, the Municipality constructed an imposing Serai (a sort of tavern) at a cost of Rs. 100000 which came to be known as Mor Serai, because of a gilded peacock at the top. Two of the richest Hindu residents, namely Seth Chunna Mal and Seth Mahesh Das, were the main donors for this beautiful edifice, the later was particularly credited with having donated almost the entire amount for the Town Hall while the former, Chunna Mal, generously donated for the Mor Serai.

Lord Northbrook, on his visit to Delhi, presented the city with a fountain in Chandni Chowk. Further, the construction of the railway line from the newly constructed railway bridge over the river Yamuna (also known as Lothian Bridge) completely changed the skyline of Old Delhi. The Old Magazine was replaced with a Dak Bungalow and the Post & Telegraph office, in the area between Railway Bridge and Kashmiri Gate, rendering a new utilitarian look to Old Delhi.

Thus, the old world aesthetic architectural purity of Shahjahanabad was changed by the succeeding generation's need based designs and tastes overlaying earlier generation's ethos. In this respect, Delhi paled into insignificance before Calcutta, the then capital of India. This however does not deny Delhi Municipality's steadfast longing for the improvement of the lot of general inhabitants, so far as sanitation and hygiene was concerned.

Various schemes were mooted, including the supply of underground pipe water. It was felt that such a scheme would not be acceptable to devout Hindus and possibly they would refuse to finance the scheme, which however proved to be a misplaced scepticism. By 1867, the available canal water had by and large become brackish and not potable. Sweet water was available in the springs of the Ridge and in the then outskirts of the city like Jhandewalan. Even the construction of water works for tapping the Yamuna water was mooted. Eventually in 1892, Delhi saw the inauguration of the water works.

In 1872, there were two issues which demanded immediate attention. One related to the existence of a high protective wall which appeared as an anachronism as it hindered the modernity of the newly built city. It was the source of congestion in the unhygienic locality with small ill-lit roads with illegal encroachments on both sides and open drains. This atmosphere was a clear invitation to disease, ill health and epidemic, as in the case of the outbreak of Cholera. Military authorities constantly resisted demolition of the wall, even reducing its height for security reasons.

The second was the improper use of Nazul (government) land and property which could be put to a lot of financial and aesthetic advantage. The Punjab government, which was the authority to bring in such changes through their Municipal Act, cold shouldered the proposal, citing their reluctance to go against the Defence Authority who were obsessed with security concerns for the city of Delhi in the face of any anticipated attack and their decision to make Delhi into a secure fortified city.

Regarding the proper utilisation of Nazul property, however, much was done. A recreational and amusement park came up in the place of the demolished Akbarbadi mosque. It may be recalled that the Delhi Municipal Committee was given the status of a first-class Municipality in 1867. Subsequently in 1874, the Municipal Committee was entrusted with the contract of Nazul land upto three miles radius of the city walls. This subsequently increased their functions. The Town Duties Committee which was the precursor of the Municipality, had been established way back in 1824. It performed an important function of conducting classes.

According to the first census conducted in 1833, Delhi's population was 1,19,800. In 1843, it rose to 1,31,000 and in 1853, it rose to 1,51,000. In the aftermath of the revolt of 1857, the population of Delhi registered a dramatic fall. Practically the entire population of the walled city was ejected. One third of the city was destroyed. Muslims fled to suburbs like Mehrauli, Shahdara, Nizam-ud-din and Motia Khan. There were large scale migrations of well to do people and artisans to places as far away as Hyderabad, Lucknow and Jaipur.

It was not before 1862 that the atmosphere started normalising. Hindus were allowed entry to the city first as the British felt that the rebellion had been essentially a Muslim one, not involving Hindus. Initially, after the revolt was put down, nobody was spared. Young and old, city dwellers and villagers, rebels or citizens, all were put to the sword. They were used as gun-fodder and promptly hanged on capture after summary trials. One thing which needs to be lauded about the marauding British troops was that there were no reports of atrocities against women. There was large scale desecration of Islamic holy shrines, already described before.

Even some Hindu temples were not spared from arson and looting, following the pattern of Islamic invaders to India. The idols were broken and pillaged; the underground wealth of the temples was looted.

Allowing a departure from the text, it will be worthwhile to mention the extreme secularism that had been exhibited by the Emperor, Bahadur Shah Zaffar II, who steadfastly maintained his high and noble stance by living true to his dictum that if Muslims were his one eye, the Hindus were his other. Emperor Bahadur Shah even scrupulously practised some essential tenets of the Hindu religion, like veneration for cows as demonstrated by abstinence from sacrifice of cows during the Id festival and practising the use of the sacred Gangajal (water of the river Ganga) for religious purposes. It is indeed a strange coincidence that Timur, the founder of Timur Dynasty and the last incumbent of the dynasty, that is, Bahadur Shah II Zafar who was dethroned by the British in the aftermath of 1847 revolt, were so distinctly opposite in nature and religious tolerance levels.

1865 onwards Delhi witnessed spate of Municipal activity. The Municipality planned to build a general hospital, a women's hospital and a dispensary. The general hospital was built at a cost of Rs. 70,000. However, due to the absence of a proper police force, the Municipality was powerless to enforce laws to contain the spread of Cholera and other epidemics.

From 1870 onwards, through the enforcement of the Punjab Government Municipal Act, some systematic improvement about conservancy, especially about drainage and sanitation, was introduced by dividing the city into sectors. At this time an improvised dispensary and a midwifery school was set up through donations. The Cambridge mission set up a Women Medical School. Delhi Municipality along with the Society for Propagation of the Gospel in Foreign Parts (S.P.G) started a nurses' training school. The Municipal Secretary Smith's untiring efforts in eradicating Cholera from the city earned him rich accolades from citizens.

The Municipality came into picture after it was entrusted with the onerous task of overseeing primary education. It also brought into fore the perpetual animosity between the two warring sects of Islam, that is, the Shias and the Sunnis. Both however opposed the idea of the Municipality as the arbitrator and controller in respect to primary education. The reason for this stance was the composition of the Municipality which was a mixed body of Europeans, Hindus and Muslims, the first two groups outnumbering the Muslims. The matter reached its height of discontentment and as a compromise, W.H. Mill was requested to be the head. In 1885, W.H. Mill had mediated in a debate between the followers of Arya Samaj and the Varnashrama Dharma Sabha. This led to W.H. Mill being offered the Principalship of Anglo Arabic School in 1890. W.H. Mill belonged to the S.P.G (Society for Propagation of the Gospel in Foreign Parts, formed in 1852).

There is no doubt that since its inception, the Municipality in Delhi provided yeomen service to ameliorate the living conditions of the citizens, relating to the conservancy, street lighting, road repairs as the primary objectives and education and health as secondary objectives.

The Municipality had to impose various taxes, among them the house tax was the most important and controversial one. When the Municipality faced the daunting task to extend the facilities of drainage and conservancy to the suburbs, beyond the walled city, there was a fierce debate, as imposition of additional taxes became imperative. Prudently, instead of taxing the food and essential goods, the Municipality opted for the imposition of a moderate house tax. Such a tax had been imposed in Lucknow since 1868.

This tax was expected to be on the same lines as was being levied in Calcutta, Bombay, Karachi and Pune. Delhi (an administrative part of Punjab) was the first city in North India to levy such tax. As expected, there was strong opposition against the imposition of this tax. The protest was simultaneous and it witnessed the participation of all citizens irrespective of communal and class distinctions. In a way, this opposition can be considered a precursor of Hindu Muslim amity which became the cult ritual for the future. Furthermore, it was observed that more than half of the tax would be realised from houses having rental value between Rs. 12 and Rs. 60. Concessions were made in the form of exemptions for three specific categories 1) Persons owning large houses but requiring renovations and improvement, 2) Poor widows who paid Rs. 5 or less as rent and 3) The squatters operating from huts in Sadar Bazar and Teliwara on Municipal land. Also, under strong all-round opposition, the tax rate was lowered from 5 to 3.5 percent. (Information: Dr. Narayani Gupta – ibid).

In this context it is worthwhile to admit the perpetual animosity between the elite members admitted to the Municipality who formed the cream of the Hindu, Muslim and European society, not only by virtue of their abundance of wealth but also their educational qualifications and overall standing in society. These were the qualifying criteria for their selection and appointment in the Municipality as Municipal Commissioners.

During this period, Delhi College had been the cradle, sanctuary and religious edifice for those liberal and secular in spirit, ideals which were also the hallmark of scientific Western enlightened education. The camaraderie between the enlightened and educated Hindu and Muslim youth became an eyesore for the British administration who had the nefarious design of keeping the Indians (imposingly called Natives) perpetually under their thumb and in perpetual suspicion and animosity towards each other. It is to be noted that Delhi, under the administrative jurisdiction of Punjab was denied full measure of self-government even in 1854, on the pretext of Delhi's alleged tendency towards communal violence. However, the Punjab towns like Lahore in 1891, Amritsar in 1895, Multan in 1899 and Ambala in 1906 were given separate representation on the basis of religious grouping. The Commissioner of Delhi, Mr. Clarke, who had ten years of experience in Delhi, categorically informed the Viceroy that 'religion has never been an issue in Municipal politics in Delhi'.

The outbreak of Cholera in Delhi further witnessed the emergence of amity between the Hindus and Muslims. The members of the Municipality, hitherto called the loyalists, subscribed to the views of the British government and supported the official view of the rules and regulations that would come into operation in the event of a cholera outbreak. This prematurely created an atmosphere of panic as the announcement gave officials the exclusive right to frame rules for segregation and treatment during the outbreak of the epidemic. These rules were made in undue haste and were not well thought out. This announcement was in contrast to that of Patna, another major provincial capital where the treatment by medical practitioners like the Vaidya and Hakims were allowed to function, as also a private system of segregation of patients. The panic that ensued after the official warning about a possible outbreak, totally disrupted the trade and commerce of Delhi, particularly the poor section of the society as well as the merchants who apprehended total lockdown of wholesale trade. Marwari businessmen were the most afraid and they shifted their families and stock of goods out of Delhi.

A meeting convened in the Town Hall attracted over 2000 people, including representatives of all European and Indian mercantile firms. A resolution condemning the unnecessary alert notice and consequential panic among the business community was squarely condemned much to the chagrin of the officials and loyalist members of the Municipality.

This was the first show of a general Hindu Muslim amity. A committee was formed with one European as the President, thirteen Hindus, six Europeans and three Muslims as members. A civil surgeon with wide authority was appointed, with an idea to assuage the feelings of antagonism of the general public. However, another vexed issue cropped up, that was the issue of the treatment of women by a male doctor / surgeon, during the possible epidemic. This apart, the news of riots in Bombay, percolating through individuals, dealt a moral blow particularly for the Marwari businessmen class who did not belong to Delhi. They panicked about possible physical harm and loss of property. A consensus that emerged was that the possible epidemic should be handled by working through the affected people, abhorring the strong arm action of the police. The citizens' committee embarked upon a policy of not antagonising the officialdom, rather keeping them in good humour.

Robert Clarke who had a long association with the Municipality but not yet a commissioner, mooted various welfare agendas. The services rendered by the Imam of the Jama Masjid and great physician Hakim Abdul Majid evoked unstinted praise from the officialdom. The fraternisation developed between the Hindus and the Muslims became a source of elation to one group and bellyache to the other. Prompt admission came from press as well as the officials that such a union between the Hindus and Muslims was never seen after the reign of Akbar (1560–1605AD).

Hindus were forthright to seek friendship of the Muslims; Hindus greeted the Muslims at Jama Masjid as they emerged from the Id Prayer. Shri Kishen Das' garden was opened for Jar Mela. Muslims in large numbers participated in Hari Milan. At the height of this Hindu-Muslim amity, a strong vocal section of enlightened Muslims argued that the slaughter of cow at the Id-festival in not sanctioned by scriptures and hence need not be practiced. Even the Emperor was not sacrificing cows at Id, but instead was to sacrifice the camel and told his subjects to sacrifice goats.

All this bonhomie was serious enough for the Europeans during the ghastly days of the 1857 revolt and merciless massacre of British soldiers along with their womenfolk and children, not only in Delhi but distant Bibigarh fort near Allahabad. Even a notorious prank of a handwritten scribble in Clock Tower stating that 1857 had again arrived, triggered the vision of a horrific mob, attacking European enclaves and European families scrambling to reach the fort for safety. A note by H.C.Taushawe is reproduced as follows: - "As Delhi is still the centre of India so is the old Mughal Palace, the centre of Delhi, and it is very important that the people of Delhi should see the garrison in the fort and know that the city was at the mercy of the guns in front of Lahore Gate".

It was felt that Delhi had become even more vulnerable than it was during 1857, because of its rioting. Delhi's importance had increased multifold as it became a bustling commercial centre, a junction of five railway systems and seat of a large number of emerging industries.

A display of fire works during the Moharram Procession, which were enacted by Hindus also, was yet another instance of Hindu Muslim amity, and the authorities banned the procession in 1898. Repercussions of the Grecco Turkish war with frenzied support for Turkey saw the Muslims abandoning English education institution in large numbers and also hospitals but nothing was a bigger proof of Hindu Muslim amity than their sustained and unified agitation against the imposition of house tax as referred to earlier. The agitation started off on the issue of house tax, but snowballed into the larger issue of challenging entrenched supremacy of the prosperous, and literate members of a small but very influential community of the loyalists. It was a challenge against the monopoly of the loyalists. Unable to ward off the charges of perpetual dominance and hegemony against them, the loyalists tried to raise the bar for minimum qualification for voters and candidates. One of these was raising the income tax rating and the other was introducing a higher level of educational qualification. Also, to deal with the grievances, a rate-payers association was formed.

The agitation is notable in the sense that it was jointly organised by Hindus and Muslims. Syed Haider Raza, who had studied in the St. Stephen's College and also a lecturer there for a short period, urged the Hindus and Muslims to unite against the arbitrary levy of house tax. Though in resolving various grievances against the high handedness of the Municipality or local self-government, a Hindu-Muslim amity was noticed, but in the long run it did not sustain the same spirit when pitted against the current and cross current of Muslims politics in the national level. There is indeed no undermining the fact that the Municipality played a vital role in the all-round development of Delhi.

The Delhi society came into existence in 1885, with inauguration by Municipal Commissioner Hamilton. During the revolt 1857, some rich Hindu Khatri families and Jains were traditional bankers to the British and some of them were treasurers of the government. They had supported the British during the revolt by their banking. They had also refused to lend money to the Emperor Bahadur Shah and other nobles of the court. They were suitably rewarded with gifts of large lands after the revolt. Apart from gifts of land, they were inducted to the Municipality which was the local self-government.

Lala Chunna Mal, the Gurwala family (founder of Hindu college), the Naharwala family and all Khatri Hindu families, the Jain families of Saligram and Girdhari Lal - all were government treasurers, who had previously rendered tremendous financial held to the British, and the same time, refused the Mughals as already stated. Lala Chunna Mal owned a palatial building in Nil Katra in the city. He was a philanthropist and donated one lakh rupees for charity, for activities like famine relief during 1860, 1862 and 1869, and also for the propagation of education. All the rich people were inducted as members of Delhi Society when the same was formed. Most of them were alumni of Delhi College and were part of Delhi's integrated cross communal Urdu culture.

These people were rich, cultured and educated, and they sought professional employment with the British government who was more than willing to oblige. They were not interested in occupying the nominated membership of the Municipality. The Hindus, Khatris and Jains were also eager to flaunt their wealth. This found expression in Jain and Hindu festivals where pomp and show emulated the procession of Mughal cavalcades with the exception that it included idols of worship. The processions originated in the walled city and went up to the Jain shrines in Chandni Chowk or Talkatora. Incidentally, the famous Jain temple at the entrance of Chandni Chowk came up in 1870.

The construction of the Jain Mandir at Chandni Chowk made the presence of the Jain community felt in Delhi. There were other communities which emulated the Jain way. The Sikhs made their representation of community felt on Delhi's social fabric through the enlargement of Sisganj Gurudwara. The Fatehpuri Masjid, which was the cradle of Punjabi Sikh businessmen, came up in 1890. The Municipal Commissioner Hamilton was impressed by the success of the Municipal committee in reducing pompish extravaganza during marriage processions. While inaugurating the Delhi Society, he laid down the road map which included the advancement of knowledge and general welfare, especially the knowledge of science and the art of writing. The Society was to refrain from dabbling in trade, arts and manufacturing.

The Delhi Society had a mixed composition, where there were seventy Englishmen and seventy-six Indians. Hamilton was the President, with Moghul Prince Ilahi Bux as Co-President. Lala Sahib Singh was the Vice President and Pyare Lal Ashoob as Secretary. Other active members included mainly Municipal Commissioners who were active English supporters dubbed as 'Loyalists', who were not interested in preserving their identity from members who were the recent products of Delhi College. Right from the beginning of formation of the Society, Pyare Lal, the Secretary, was instrumental in inducting the great Mirza Ghalib as a guest participant.

The members of the Society were held in high esteem with a tag of respectability, primarily because of their social status. Society was interested in assimilating western knowledge, while retaining their conservatism and orthodoxy. It became a meeting point of modern western education and traditional education and culture of the East.

The period also saw a struggle between established commercial interest and the intellectuals. While the intellectuals who were the new entrants in Delhi Social fabric, made their presence felt by forcing the acceptance of their view that education was superior to accumulation of wealth but things didn't go as planned. Commissioner Hamilton banned public debate in 1868 on the public forum between Christian Missionaries and the enlightened youth of Delhi, which was a desired secular move in the public domain.

Secretary of the Society, Pyare Lal Ashoob, left the society for Lahore in 1868. The next Secretary was Lala Chandan Lal, a Christian who was a teacher in Christian Mission School. The Missionaries were elated that this would enable the Society to allow discussions of religious matters which were otherwise banned during the mentorship of Pyare Lal Ashoob, the departing secretary. The new change witnessed a slight difference of opinion between the older generation which belonged to the Urdu language and cultural milieu and the new generation, which was an English speaking one. The latter was led by the nephew of Pyare Lal Ashoob, Sri Ram who was a product of Mission School. He was a brilliant Urdu scholar himself but also a reformist.

One thing which undermined the cohesiveness between the members whether of the Municipality or the Delhi Society was the class differences between the loyalists, the traditional ally of the British for whom acquisition of wealth was the be all and end all, and the new and emerging younger class, for whom education and knowledge was of primary importance.

The Delhi Society which was developing as a forum to concentrate public opinion, suffered a rude jolt with its promising and enterprising members shifting to Lahore, which offered a wide range of opportunities, casting a pall of gloom on the activities of the Delhi Society. This was coupled with diminishing interest in local self-government, along with the mushrooming of various other religious reformist associations relegated the Delhi Society's community activity to the background. This also led to the scepticism about the efficacy of imposition of British innovations and superimposition of new institutions like the Western medical system, displacing Unani medicine and treatment by Hakims.

In respect of education, there was the revival of the Madrassas with their concomitant flaunting of the Urdu language and culture. Nostalgic memories of Shahjahanabad days, with supply of clean Yamuna water through canals along with the Persian wheel were recalled. The much-vaunted resolution of Lord Ripon on local self-government in 1882, was not of much practical help as the Municipality was saddled with much provincial government work. Delhi Society had practically lost its utility. Working on local issues, which was the forte of the Society, slowly lost its importance, as discord between the Hindus and the Muslims came up to the surface. The emergence of Punjabi Muslim immigrant community of businessmen with pan-Islamic issues, were often at odds with the traditionally established rich old Muslim business families. A similar discordant note emerged within the rich industrious Jain families seeking a foothold in Delhi. Similarly, the emergence of the Arya Samaj and the Sanatan Dharma with ideological rivalry, unsettled the tranquil atmosphere that was prevailing before.

With passage of time, these issues were relegated to the background and gave way to the bigger national issue which saw the birth of Muslim nationalism, finally leading to Muslim communal extremism. This led to the unfolding of a different kind of turbulence within the subcontinent.

***

Chapter 18

Contribution of Railways in Bolstering Delhi's Claim as the Mercantile Capital of North India

The Railways has been inexorably linked with the emergence of Delhi as the Mercantile Capital of North India, ahead of the more developed cities of Punjab like Lahore or Amritsar. After the Sepoy Mutiny, for a couple of years, there was chaos and confusion, with revenge and retribution of post 1857 activity ruling the roost. However slowly and surely, with Clemency Canning's deft handling of the situation, peace and sanity were restored. With clamour for all round development of the existing land in and out of city limits and in the suburbs, Delhi Municipality came in face to face for adequate funds to carry out massive projects for the future.

The role of the Railways was a significant one in the industrialization and overall modernisation of the walled city of Delhi. East India Railways was built through Delhi in the 1860s. One notable fact needs to be highlighted in this context: when the Railways first came up in Delhi around 1863, it did not attract due attention. While the railway bridge over the river Yamuna to connect Delhi with the east (i.e. Calcutta or Howrah) was still underway in 1864, the New Delhi Railway Station came up in 1867. At midnight on New Years Eve of 1867, the railway whistle sounded for the first time and the first train steamed into Delhi. Initially, it practically went unnoticed without any foreface or puller gaze.

In the same year Delhi was connected with Punjab and Sind through the Ghaziabad junction. The running power was drawn from Ghaziabad Railway junction. In 1873, the Rajputana State Railway connected Delhi with Bombay and in 1881, came up the Delhi-Ambala-Kalka railways line which afforded a shorter route to the north. In 1900, Ghaziabad-Moradabad line was inaugurated and in 1905 came up the Agra-Delhi Chord ultimately going up to Bombay.

In the early years of the twentieth century, because of the Great Indian Peninsular Railways, the railway staff were provided accommodation in the Paharganj area. This preference is one of the reasons for locating the New Delhi Railway Station in Paharganj area. Subsequently during the Durbar of 1911, the State Entry Railway Platforms came up in New Delhi Station.

There was hectic activity in the Paharganj area following the establishment of the Railway Colony with the coming up of the Great Indian Peninsular Railways. Subsequently, in the early twentieth century, New Delhi Railway Station came to be located in the same area. A major wide road was built from Sabji Mandi through Sadar Bazar to Panchkuian Road which passed close to New Delhi Railway Station and became a hub of industrial activity, mainly furniture and other wood works.

It was in 1900, that the Delhi Municipality became very vocal about the location of the railway lines, the railway yard and the allotment of land to various railway companies. The Punjab Railway Department, which had authority over the Delhi Railway system, asked the latter not to alienate land within a radius of five miles of the Delhi Station to any railway company without its sanction.

Demolition of the wall between Lahori Gate and Ajmeri Gate was a vexed issue which attracted vicious debate. In 1881, it was deemed fit to acquire land, which was in great demand following rapid urbanisation. The Delhi Municipality was very vocal about the location and alignment of the railway lines, land and area for railway yard construction, of level crossings and also allotment of land for new railway companies.

A railway line linking Delhi and Karachi was on the anvil. So was the Great India Peninsular Railway (G.I.P), which would be a massive project. Coming back to the Delhi-Agra Chord, there was a peculiar problem which was about substantial curvature. A major chunk of land south of Sadar Bazar was already allotted to the Delhi-Agra chord. The Municipality insisted on a barrier between the wall and the plot so that the circular road would not be broken. There was also another issue which was very much relevant for the future extension of the city. That was the vexed issue of the demolition of the stretch of wall between Ajmeri Gate and Kabul Gate which was hindering the extension of the city. On top of this, the Agra chord, because of its curvature, would hamper the use of the circular road.

However, the Municipality sought to resolve the difficulty by asking the railways to construct three overbridges at railway cost. One bridge was to be over the Ajmeri Gate for the general public. The second was to be at Farashkhana for the convenience of Muslim funeral processions, proceeding to Mehndion-ka-Mazhar. Third was to be between the main railway station and the suburban railway station outside Lahori Gate. Apart from this, there was an issue of railway crossings for approaches from the north-west and the west to cater to the heavy traffic. The issue of the first and third of the overbridges were mutually resolved. But the second overbridge involved a huge cost and had to be stalled.

Between 1900–05, Delhi became a major railway junction. However, it remained under the jurisdiction of Punjab Railways. Delhi's growing influence could be gauged from the fact that Punjab Chamber of Commerce established its headquarters at Delhi, with branches at Lahore and Amritsar.

As already indicated, the coming up of Delhi Karachi Railway line or the North Western Railway gave an impetus to the Delhi industrialists and merchants as this railway became the supply line for cotton, growing in areas adjacent to Delhi. This helped Delhi to attain the distinction of being a major railway junction of North India.

From 1908, there had been major activity to economically transform the city. With an eye for the future railway companies, other than the existing one, the Government started scouting for land for rail related activities. This was also done in view of the growing clout of Delhi as a major economic hub of North India. A major economic activity was noticed in the form of transfer of a plot of land south of Sadar Bazar to Delhi-Agra chord Railway. Then came the big decision to develop the western suburban area from Mithai ka Pul to Jhandewalan and the more important decision to shift the cantonment to the Ridge. The Army was reluctant to remove the wall. Their concern was indirectly met. Away from the residential locality, they were now supposed to guard the Western Ridges. The demand for more land on the eastern side of the existing track was rejected.

A few months later, the Commissioner urged the Municipality to draw up a comprehensive plan to work on a general scheme for making provision for roads, streets and space for overall development for the next thirty years, based on the rate of increase in land value in the past five years as an index. He further suggested the shifting of troops from Daryaganj to the northern side of the Ridge. Also, a wall was to be constructed on the dry bed of the canal, in the south-west direction; an ornamental garden and a bazaar was also to be created. The new outer road would be made available for Marwari businessmen clamouring for more space for the katras or small markets.

Though not always directly, Railways came to be the fountainhead for all development taking place in the city. Even the Roshanara Garden had to part with land for the laying of the railway lines of the Great Indian Peninsular (G.I.P) Railways, of the Delhi-Kalka line, running up to Rajasthan. The G.I.P Railways quarters had already come up in Paharganj which were at a distance of more than five miles from the new cantonment in Rajpura. Around 1900, more houses started coming up in the civil lines to cater to the needs of railway personnel and also rich factory owners. This was indicative of the influence of the Railways in the overall development of the city. It is also interesting to note the role of Railways in the great showpiece event of the Durbar held in 1911, during the transfer of the capital from Calcutta to Delhi. Railways put up a spectacular show, having twelve railway lines with decorated platforms to receive the Indian princes from the state entry platform of the New Delhi Station specially inaugurated for this purpose. Such was the significance of the Railways. The railways were in the forefront to usher in the overall economic development of Delhi. As already stated, the urbanisation and industrialisation of Delhi were inexorably linked up with the development of the Railways. The impact was such that even the villages were relegated twelve miles away from the Railway tracks; Railways had gobbled up all rural activities. It had replaced all forms of transport other than cart traffic in and around Delhi. Railways hegemony ruled the roost within a precinct of twelve miles between the Railway tracks and the area east of the tracks towards the city. The Railways, along with newly constructed factories totally changed the pattern of urbanisation of Delhi. The location of factories was determined by their accessibility to the wholesale markets and their proximity to the Railway stations.

Barring a few stray factories which came up here and there, in and around the wall of Kashmiri Gate, all important factories were coming up in Sadar Bazar area or the Subzi Mandi, where both Nazul (Government) or private land were in plenty and could be acquired cheaply. Especially in the Sabzi Mandi area, many acres of gardens belonging to the government enclosed in the Roshanara Bagh, were earmarked for development of the Railways. It even included the 'Sardarakhti' estates, which were the estates gifted to private individuals before 1857. Similar lucrative estates were also purchased from wealthy landowners.

From around the year 1890, this area became a hub of industrial activity. Large tracts of land or gardens were earmarked for factories. Railways also acquired a substantial chunk of land, gardens and orchards for future development. There was such a scramble for land that this ward became the most prosperous, accounting for the highest number of taxpayers. Within Delhi, Sadar Bazar, Subzi Mandi and Civil Lines became favourite destinations. These were no longer abodes of workers only. Subsequent development and holding of Durbars in the early part of 20th century, including transfer of capital from Calcutta to Delhi in 1911, all led to an unexpected boom in commercial activities and phenomenal rise in the price of land. This was an unexpected but welcome stroke of good fortune for the land and buildings owners of these areas. However, such an unhindered growth of factories and godowns had its toll on city planning, sanitation and hygiene and over led to crowding. Also, the potential threat of the spread of contagious diseases like Cholera was looming large. This in turn, led to the shifting of some people more towards the suburbs, away from the din of urbanisation.

Chapter 19

Delhi, the New Capital of British India: Its Changing Face, Industrialisation and Modernisation

It was around this time that the face of Delhi began to change. Looking back a few decades, we come to 1714, when the British had succeeded in establishing an embassy of the East India Company in Delhi. Since then the British influence in and over Delhi became more and more overpowering and domineering. Taking advantage of the weak Mughal rulers, new European style structures in the form of bungalows, churches, townhouses and even cemeteries started dotting the skyline of Delhi. It started spreading so far as to encroach upon narrow lanes of the walled city. It is interesting to note that in 1824, a Town Duties Committee was formed. In 1828, the British troops shifted their abode to the Ridge, Rajpura Cantonment and Khyber Pass Cantonment.

Until 1880, there was no industry or factory worth the name where the Factory Act could be applicable. In 1885, only two big factories were there. One was at Bara Hindu Rao, which was Mr. Wilson's Cotton machine, employing 200 workers and the other was an ice factory, at Kauria Pul. In 1888, flour industries and cotton spinning and ginning factories came into existence. D.C.M or Delhi Cloth and Cotton Mills came up in 1889. These were major factories owned by Indians mainly Khatris and Baniyas. This was the time when flour industries became mechanized. In 1892, Delhi Water Works was inaugurated. In 1895, the sewer line in the Chandni Chowk area was completed.

The turn of the century brought many new changes to the walled city, truly epoch-making from the point of view of rapid industrialization of Delhi. In 1902, electricity was introduced in the city of Delhi, paving the way for rapid urbanisation. The electrification of Delhi proved to be a major boost for industrial activity. In 1901, Old Delhi first enjoyed the benefit of electric street lighting. In 1902, House Tax was introduced.

Another important transformation was extension and consolidation of Karol Bagh (known earlier as Bagh Karoli). Karol Bagh came into prominence because of the influx of refugees from West Punjab. Originally the abode of the tanners, it went through a metamorphosis to become a planned settlement of factory workers, workers engaged in the construction of the new city and also the tanners who had been relocated from Paharganj.

In 1908, the army was moved from Daryaganj to a new location on the north of the Ridge. Also, the offices of the Deputy Commissioner and the Commissioner shifted from Kashmiri Gate to the Civil Lines. The rich Indian owners viz Lala Sri Ram, Lala Ram Chand, Lala Basheshwar Nath Goela, Shiekh Hafizullah and some others shifted their activities to this place. In 1912, this area was included in the notified area, with Ridge on the East, Azadpur in the North West, Rajpur Road in the Middle Mall Road and Alipur Road. The cantonment had continued to be in the same location of Rajpur from 1828–57, before it was shifted to the city. In 1915, Delhi acquired land from across Meerut and Bulandshahr, and across Yamuna to the tune of 193 square miles.

The fact of Delhi taking over from Calcutta as the new capital of British India was in the anvil for quite some time. Shifting of the capital to Delhi also opened the floodgates to commercial banking and insurance activities in the form of Joint Stock banks of both British and Indian interest. Delhi quietly saw the opening up of indigenous Mercantile Banks, breaking the hegemony of the Banias and Khatris in the banking business. In 1898, a native commercial money lending bank was established mainly dealing with the activities of buying, selling and lending of money through the age-old method of the Hundis.

Ultimately the declaration of the transfer of the capital took place in 1911. King George V and the Queen Empress arrived at Bombay on 2

December 1911, (at the spot later to be commemorated as the 'Gateway of India') and reached Delhi on the morning of 7 December 1911. His Imperial Majesty declared the shifting of the capital from Calcutta to Delhi, in the Durbar of 11 December, 1911. On the 15th of December, his Imperial Majesty laid the foundation stone of the new capital of India, culminating the decade long debate on the subject. Following the announcement of the shifting of the capital by King George V, and with the addition of hundreds acres of land to the notified area, a new temporary capital came up north of the civil lines, during the period between 1912–1922. The centre of activity later shifted to the Raisina Hill complex, the proposed location of the Rashtrapati Bhavan and the North Block and South Block.

The event of the state entry of Lord Hardinge, the Viceroy of India and his Lady, on 23 December 1912 was extremely ominous. The huge procession of fifty elephants earmarked for a five mile journey from Old Delhi Railway Station to the Coronation ground saw the throwing of a bomb near the Punjab National Bank building which exploded behind the howdah of the Viceroy, killing the servant holding the state umbrella. The Viceroy fortunately sustained only minor injuries, with no injury to the lady. The procession went over to the Diwan-i-Aam in the Red Fort, where the city of Delhi was handed over to Sir Louis Dane, the Lt. Governor of Punjab and Delhi became a province of Punjab for the next 55 years.

Sir Guy Fleetwood Wilson read out the formal reply of the Viceroy. Delhi, then became a separate province under a Chief Commissioner, similar to the District of Columbia, surrounding Washington D.C. Delhi remained important as it also became the Imperial Enclave and official residence of the Imperial Majesty in Delhi, as against the official residence of Lt. Governor in Lahore.

A new and wide road was created linking the civil lines and the city through Sadar Bazar and Jhandewalan. Arrangements were made for the establishment of shops. Sadar Bazar was created to cater to the needs of soldiers stationed at Pahari Dhiraj, Idgah and Rajpur cantonment. Two important roads were constructed. The most important and biggest was the new Jhandewalan Road, connecting east-west and the Idgah Road connecting north-west. The prime motive had been to connect the Subzi

Mandi and Sadar Bazar, the nerve centre of business activity. Also the intention was to accommodate the crowded Khari-Baoli complex.

The Pipal Park (same as people park) was handed over to an Imperial Institution and all public gatherings were stopped. The State Bank of India (earlier the Imperial Bank) came up south of the Red Fort where Sunheri Masjid existed; prayers and religious activity at Sunehri Masjid was also stopped. Viceregal Lodge came up north of the Ridge where Delhi University is now situated. The Commander-in-Chief's residence cum office came up at Alipur Road where Indraprastha College stands since 1932. A number of new hotels came up in the Civil Lines. Some of these are Maiden's hotel (1900- originally single storey), Cecil Hotel in 1920 and Hotel Suisse at Curzon House (subsequently converted into Swiss Apartments).

The Improvement Trust of Delhi did not come up till 1937. The most notable transformation came up with the demolition of the legendary Chandni Chowk following bomb attack on Lord Hardinge. Earlier, Chandni Chowk used to bask in the full moon light with the serene waters of the canal reflecting the full moon and creating a celestial atmosphere, all of this drastically changed. Long rows of big old trees along the road were wiped out. The canal was completely closed and bricked out.

Subsequently, the Town Planning Committee consisting of G.S.Swanton, Edwin Lutyens and J.A.Bordie, after long and arduous deliberation, confirmed Raisina Hills as the seat of the new capital. Lutyens became the Edwardian architect of modern Delhi or New Delhi. His vision was to plan the city in such a way that it would serve as an imperial and majestic capital on the lines of Washington or Paris. Both Sir Edwin Lutyens and architect Sir Herbert Baker are associated with the construction of the Viceroy's House, now the Rashtrapati Bhavan and the two Secretariat buildings, now known as the North and the Southlocks.

It took 17 long years to complete the new capital of British India, arguably one of the best in the world. The total expenditure for the construction of the new capital was around 115 million rupees. It was completed in 1931. The name New Delhi was given in 1927 and the new capital was inaugurated on 13th February, 1931. The city covered a total area of about 3200 acres and was flanked between the Aravalli Range on one side and river Yamuna on the other.

However, the fanfare accompanying the event of shifting of the capital lasted only a few years. It is an irony of fate that the British could rule India for only sixteen more years from the time the majestic capital city was created, as India became free of the British Empire on 15 August, 1947.

Chapter 20

Post Independence Development of Delhi; Jagmohan's Delhi

Jagmohan Malhotra is credited with laying the foundation of 'modern Delhi', the ninth city of Delhi. It was he who first envisioned and initiated the transformation of the national capital in his attempt at making Delhi slum free in the 1970s.

Jagmohan, one of the topmost civil servants cum statesman that India has ever produced in the post-independence period, held the coveted post of Lieutenant Governor of Delhi (1982–84), Governor of Jammu and Kashmir twice, in 1990 and again in 1984–89 and Lieutenant Governor of Goa, Daman and Diu (1981–82). Having served the union government in different portfolios, such as Urban Development, Poverty Alleviation, Culture and Tourism and Communication for the Government of India for a distinctive period of 30 years, he was awarded the Padma Shri in 1971 and the Padma Bhushan in 1977.

The post-independence period of Delhi's reconstruction has been uniquely portrayed by Jagmohan. This was the time of Indira Gandhi's government, and her younger son, Sanjay Gandhi wielded a lot of influence within the working of her government. During the Emergency (1915 to 1977), he entrusted Jagmohan with the task of 'beautification' of Delhi. Jagmohan fulfilled Sanjay Gandhi's vision of modernizing Delhi by a large-scale and targeted demolition of Muslim slum areas, specifically in the Turkman Gate area of old Delhi. The most important chapter that is credited to Jagmohan was the disputed clearance of the Turkman Gate slums.

Turkman Gate derives its name from Shah Turkman, a famous Sufi saint who died in 1240 C.E. His real name was Shams-ul-Arifeen Shah Turkman Bayabani. He was also called Hazrat Bayabani, meaning, a saint of the forest and wilderness, a recluse. His tomb is located within the Turkman Gate. It is also surrounded by a number of smaller graves, which apparently belong to his disciples. In The 13th century, Turkman Gate stood on the banks of the river Yamuna. This is also borne out by the fact that Razia Sultana (1236–1239), the only woman ruler of the Mughal dynasty, was buried near the Turkman Gate. Mubarak Shah in 1944 thought of constructing a new city between the present Ajmeri Gate and the Turkman Gate, but because of his early death, this mission was not fulfilled.

In 1638, the Mughal emperor Shah Jahan decided to shift his capital from Agra and build a new capital, 'Shahjanabad', on the banks of the river Yamuna. He built a massive fort with mighty walls, gates, towers and battlements. This construction was shaped over 8 years. Initially, the fort, which was an imperial township, was designed to accommodate 5,000 persons. A protective wall was constructed around the fort by Aurangzeb. He also constructed a number of gates as an outlet from the imperial township, and Turkman Gate happened to be one of them.

As this area constituted the worst slums of Delhi - Ajmeri Gate area, an improvement scheme was formulated by Delhi Improvement Trust on February 18, 1938. However official apathy stood in the way of alleviation of this area for 12 years and this area gradually became the hotbed of tuberculosis, infantile mortality and enteric fever. Even in 1956, a notification emanating from the office of the Chief Commissioner dated April 24, 1957, described the area as unfit for human habitation and detrimental to the health and safety of the people and the seat of various other illegal activities.

This land was previously occupied by unscrupulous traders and influential persons in the years 1948–52. Some portions of the 'nazul' or government land was taken over by the Ministry of Rehabilitation in the1960s. After paying due compensation, the establishment of DIT / DMC and DDA were carried out by the Delhi Municipal Corporation. Unfortunately, a group of rioters acquired the land which belonged to the Municipal Corporation. The entire land was transferred to Delhi Development Authority in 1974, but not before the unscrupulous mobs, who had no stake on the land, organised riots which had to be quelled by police firing.

The clearing of the slums and the demolition of the illegal structures around the Turkman Gate area was highly controversial. Bulldozers were brought in and the homes of many poor hapless people, however illegally constructed, were razed to the ground. More than 7,00,000 people were displaced from the slums and forced to relocate. The common people living there started rioting.

This period also witnessed the ugly drive of Sanjay Gandhi to sterilize the Muslim population. This sterilisation drive was conducted for a short period of April 1976. People would be rounded off from the streets randomly and forced to be sterilised. The Imam of Turkman Gate had a very objectionable and clandestine role in organising the rioters mobs, in spite of repeated requests from the then Additional District Magistrate, Ashok Pradhan. The activities of the Muslim establishments housed at Daujana House were actually from the Imam of the area, who viciously led the campaign against the sterilization of the Muslims.

Naturally, the local residents started panicking. They were losing their land and homes and also their right to reproduce. More and more people came out of their homes to protest, both against demolition and against sterilisation. As these protesters, including women and children, filled up the streets, it is said that bulldozers ran them over. Violence erupted pretty soon. The police retaliated, first with sticks and tear gas and then were forced to open fire. There are horrific stories of police brutalities, abuse of women and attacks on muslim places of worship. This was the Turkman Gate incident or the Turkman Gate Massacre of 1976.

From the government side, there was only a small consignment of inspectors and sub inspectors who faced the flare-up of the Muslim rioters. They were not strong enough to quell the riots emanating through the vicious machinations of the Muslim clergy. The riots culminated in the closure of the Daujana House by the administration. The rule of the Janata government was also not above board; they were too biased and supercilious to realise the subtle sentiments of the public. Another major block of culprits were the journalists, who resorted to yellow journalism to boost the sale of the newspapers, instead of showing unbiased and socially responsible behaviour.

After the riots, smooth and peaceful clearance work commenced from April 13, 1976. Bulldozers were freely used for clearing the remnants of hutments around the Turkman Gate. The beautification and slum clearance project, which had been originally scheduled around February of 1938 by Delhi Municipal Corporation, finally saw the light of day through the DDA in 1974 after a hibernation period of 38 long years. Thus, after the inexcusable inefficiency and callousness of organisations like Delhi Improvement Trust and the Delhi Municipal Corporation, the proposal of 1938 finally materialised in 1974. Subsequently however, a new block of tenements were built by the DDA in Ranjit Nagar near Patel Nagar. This time also saw the emergence of residential cum industrial and trading complexes in Narayana, Mayapuri and even in Kabadi Market.

Jagmohan sought to achieve the renovation and modernization of Delhi through the demolition of unauthorised colonies and illegal constructions on land that had been acquired by land mafia. For this, predictably, he had to face a lot of criticism and opposition. A report was published in the Indian Express on 14th of September 2000, where the Supreme Court observed, 'Jagmohan is the only sane voice regarding the beautification of Delhi'. That morning, Jagmohan's wife, Uma, thrust the daily newspaper before him and remarked, 'Look what has appeared about you. Unnecessarily you remain disturbed and dejected'. Obviously, her anguish was that Jagmohan's service for the beautification and modernization was not being recognised. Hearing this from his wife, Jagmohan said, 'This could spur forces inimical to my stand against unauthorised colonies and construction in Delhi to exert a greater pressure for my removal and I might suffer another change'. In course of time, this is what exactly happened and in no time Jagmohan was moved from the Ministry of Urban Development.

The very existence of the unplanned and unauthorised colonies in this area also manifested the ugly face of Indian polity and administration. According to Jagmohan, it also demonstrated the insubstantial clay of which a large number of Indians were made. At that time, the Supreme Court was hearing a number of Public Interest Litigations pertaining to the unauthorised colonies, constructions and conversions within Delhi. The news report of the Indian Express of 14 September 2008 fuelled the fire. Jagmohan's insistence on removing the unauthorised constructions from the face of Delhi, spurned illegal colonisers to greater muscle power and the courage to manifest their wrongdoings and they threw to the wind the hoary and cultures tradition of Indian society by unabashedly spreading lies to the nation.

The illegalities and impurities that surfaced, became massive over time, aberrations which became part of the colonisers' thinking and actions. Though there were warning shrieks of a coming storm, it was not encountered with ameliorative measures. Ultimately it caused colossal damage to the civic and the moral fabric of the nation. To say the least, the capital city is the spiritual workshop of the nation. The values embedded in and which emanated from the workshop are expected to be the model for other towns, metropolis and even rural habitats. Thus, we see the grim betrayal of ancient India by the unscrupulous colonisers post 1947. It would not be an aversion of truth to say that this phenomena began to debilitate and destroy the civilisation which boasted of a chequered past.

Certain important facts need to be brought out before the public. A coloniser who intends to develop land in his legal position for setting up of a new colony, has to prepare a proper layout plan first. This plan has to show the standards prescribed under the bylaws for the positioning of the various plots, roads, open spaces, parks and similar other civic infrastructure. It should also earmark the water and sewer lines. Furthermore it is necessary to set out specified lands for the establishment of educational institutions and health centres. The colony developers must certainly specify the lands and other infrastructure and seek out the approval of the Municipality. However, it was observed that the developers never bothered to embark upon the plans for the aforesaid infrastructure. The buyers of the land too pretended that the developers had duped them and that they were not aware of the wrongdoings of the colonisers. Even they were not bothered to look into the titled deeds of the developers which smack of apathy and ignorance on their part

All political parties, without exception, were blind to the unprincipled game of regularisation and closed their eyes to the pace of growth of the unauthorised colonies over the years. Jagmohan states that in the general election of 2009, the number of the colonies stood at 1639. The political parties, due to their own vested interests, overlooked the essential requirements of law for the proper regularisation of the new colonies.

There had already existed a master plan which had to be adhered to, for the proper utilisation of land, development of landscape and other construction requirements. In his analysis, Jagmohan differentiated between two categories of people: one was the middle class, with some knowledge and learning, who legally or illegally wanted a plot of land to fulfil their desire of constructing a house to live in. The other category were the squatters, who just want to squeeze themselves in, to save themselves from the fury of nature.

Both groups were least bothered about the municipal rules and regulations and openly flouted them. They never asked colonisers to show their titled deeds of the land or copies of plans sanctioned by the municipal authorities. There had been no complaints with the police over the colonisers who literally trapped them for misdemeanour. These people became pawns in the hands of the authorities simply because elections to the Assembly and the Parliament were due.

Regeneration of civilization and the so-called second Renaissance of Delhi was Jagmohan's basic intent. Jagmohan conceived the idea of Pragati Vihar, Ahuja Memorial Park - this was the pattern he wanted to follow for the 39 large slums and squatter clusters. Incidentally, Jagmohan wanted to commemorate the great national heroes of India in naming the redeveloped settlement areas. This included Vivekananda Memorial Park, Andrews Ganj, Aurobindo Memorial Park, Sadiq Nagar, Lodhi Colony, Sankata Memorial Park, Maharshi Valmiki Memorial Park, Mandir Marg, Indraprastha Park, Dara Shikoh Park, Humayun's Tomb complex, etc. He even insisted on placing plaques, like the one in Vivekananda Park, where the message is, 'lift up your head. For each one of you carries God within.

Be worthy of him....There are no weak; you are weak because you wish to be. First have faith in yourselves.' In many areas, large clusters in the neighbourhood were cleared on a similar pattern and big parks, reflecting soul-lifting values of ancient Indian philosophy, were built. Some of them were Aastha Kunj of 81 hectares near Nehru Place, Bahai Temple, Iskon temple and Indraprastha Park of 34 hectares.

Another category of area was developed, which were the city forests, district and community forests, woodlands and sports complexes. In this category falls the Hauz Khas (250 ha), Tughlakabad (300 ha), Janpath (50 ha), Rohini Swarn Jayanti Park (101 ha), Ashoka Vihar (32 ha), etc. The standard was that for every 1 million population, a district park of 25 ha was to be earmarked, a 5 ha community park for every one lakh people and a neighbourhood park of one hectare for every 10,000 residential group. An extension of this urban development found expression in Rohini, Dwarka, Narela and the Aravali mountain range ridge of 7777 hectares.

On the 25th day of July 2003, Fali S Nariman, the eminent jurist and member of the Rajya Sabha commented, 'Jagmohan is not only a minister but also a cultural gem and pride to our heritage and our government. He is the source of spirit we need today.... Janardhan Pujari of Karnataka, a Congress member of the Rajya Sabha, had commented on July 30, 2002: "We must appreciate the approach of the minister. His knowledge is superb. The house should be grateful to him. It would do a great deal of good to the nation if the response of all the ministers was like that of Jagmohan."

Jagmohan is ever remembered for the work he had done for Mata Vaishno Devi temple, for which people all over India are grateful to him. In addition, he is the only minister whose name is associated with the Taj Mahal for the immense work he did in the conservation of this great monument. Jagmohan also did immense work to radically improve the cultural heritage of Rajasthan. Congress member of the Lok Sabha, Shri Vijendra Pal Singh eulogised Jagmohan for the work done regarding Chittorgarh, Ranthambore and Maharana Pratap's Foundation. Mulayam Singh Yadav, leader of the Samajwadi party in Lok Sabha, congratulated Jagmohan for the historic act of saving the Taj Mahal and for his reformative upgradation work around Vaishno Devi Shrine. Chandrashekhar, the former Prime Minister of India, said in the Lok Sabha on July 25, 2010: "Minister Jagmohan is doing laudable work and he would be acclaimed by our future generations"

In the aforesaid context, it is pertinent to bring out the mental and physical agony that Jagmohan faced in the course of his drive for the modernization of Delhi. Jagmohan quoted the words of Sardar Vallabhbhai Patel about the physical and mental imbalance of the politicians and the general public. "To cleanse the dirt of the city is quite different from cleaning the dirt of politics. From the former, you get a good night's rest, while the latter keeps us worried and you lose sleep." Interestingly, Pandit Jawaharlal Nehru observed, "I believe in no argument, economic or other, which is based upon the creation of slums. I have a horror of slums. I do not mind a person living in the open like a vagabond or gypsy, But I do mind slums in cities. I have often said, if you cannot provide buildings for those living in slums, give them open space to live in and provide them social services like water and sanitation. The rest follows."

In this context, Jagmohan stated "To me, who has been a long distance walker in the slums and whose tired and aching limbs and smoke and dust filled eyes have refused to surrender before the forces unleashed by the mental slums in the society and the state (power) structure, the agonising reality is far more menacing and messy than perceived so far by the national leadership.

Jagmohan delved little into history when he wrote that once, Edwin Montague had written to Lord Lyde, the then the governor of Bombay, to take measures to improve the housing and sanitation in the city. This he wrote in 1909, when he was the Secretary of State for India. Unfortunately, Lord Lyde, the governor of Bombay, had in return, expressed a deep sense of anguish, bewailing the sanitation and housing conditions of Bombay, calling it 'really a nightmare'. It was only during 1917–22, when Sardar Patel was the chairman of the Sanitary Committee of Ahmedabad, and then the president of the Municipal Board (1924–28), that he showed how an inner impulse to save the city and its people could make up for various other constraints.

Incidentally, the bubonic plague, first noticed around 1900, engulfed the city in epidemic form in 1917. Schools and courts were completely closed because of the scare and people started fleeing to villages. Sardar Patel with his characteristic courage and composure said, "I know what it is to be attacked by the bubonic plague. I was a victim when I lived in Godhra in 1900. In any case, I prefer to die serving the people than live in safety."

At that time, G.V. Mavlankar and his associate civic officers, along with Sardar Patel, went through the narrow streets of Ahmedabad and started ascertaining problems directly from the common people and also started taking immediate remedial measures. The acute problems of sanitation, health, water supply, waste disposal and traffic management were directly solved. Later in 1948, in a civic reception organised by the Bombay Municipal Corporation in his honour, he said, "I had an alloyed happiness in the tasks which I performed. After all, to all of us, to serve our own city, must give unmitigated pleasure and satisfaction which I cannot get in any other sphere."

Jagmohan was also distressed that both Jawaharlal Nehru, President of the Allahabad Municipal Board and Dr. Rajendra Prasad, that of Patna, found themselves helpless against the tactics of the bureaucracy. Dr. Rajendra Prasad tendered his resignation after a year of bitter experience. Sardar Patel however simply bulldozed at the negativity of the bureaucrats and did not hesitate to flex muscles against the mighty ICS (Indian civil services) commissioners, such as John Shilidy, Alfred Master and G.F. Partt. Alfred Master later eulogised Sardar Patel, "I remember Patel as the most efficient chairman of the Sanitary Committee, who stood aloof from the domestic and political intrigues in which some of his fellow counsellors indulged."

Jagmohan effectively emulated what Sardar Patel did for the Ahmedabad Municipal Board. Jagmohan imbibed the spirit of 'iron man with a melting heart'. Sardar Patel showed to all the Indian cities that their leadership needed a sense of discipline, dedication and dynamism, a strong disposition to be in touch with the ground-level conditions and an urge to develop a frame of mind which seeks inner peace and pride through selfless service to the poor and needy. Our conscience is troubled with doubts and despair about the possibility of improvement. We do not seem to be profiting either from history or experience. We appear helplessly to be watching the sickle of time taking away the rich corn, leaving behind the bare and withered stalks."

Jawaharlal Nehru, however, did not show pragmatism in his approach during his visit to the walled city of Delhi. He was so anguished by the spectacle of the dilapidated, dangerous, congested and insanitary buildings of the Turkman Gate slums that shouted at the local leaders and officers who were with him, "burn them". Such a reaction was unbecoming of the Prime Minister of India. On this, Marshall Clinnard, the American scholar and sociologist, after visiting the same locality in the late 1950s, observed, "Houses are one and two storey, so close together that no sun comes through; everything is so damp and this makes the odours of filth and urine all the more noticeable. There is an awful stench everywhere. The area was covered with hordes of flies. Children use the gutter. Saw a man eating his lunch in front of his house a yard away from flies and offal in the gutter. I almost threw up and the educated Indians with me put their handkerchief over their faces. The children have only one small place to play and it is in bad condition. As we drove away, I kept the windows up so that the hordes of flies would not get inside. I couldn't eat my lunch that day... had a feeling as though I had seen enough and wanted to forget the misery.

In all earnestness, the Prime Minister wanted to see a slum free city and he opted for socialistic planning, duly centralised, and set up the Planning Commission. The Planning Commission having taken to heart, the impulsive outburst of the Prime Minister, made a provision in India's first five-year plan (1951–56), to take care of the problems being faced by the slums. No city can be considered healthy which tolerates within itself, the existence of a highly congested area. Slums are a national problem. From the national point of view, it is better to pay for the cost of clearing slums than to continue to pay the mounting cost of slums and suffer destructive effects upon human lives and property indefinitely.

Much later, when the Prime Minister visited Bangalore (now Bengaluru), where now a prolific software industry has developed, he witnessed to his chagrin, a plethora of slums unattended. On one side there was modernization and beautification of the premier city of the south, on the other, there remained the ugly slums. There were more than 1000 slums in Bangalore, where 2 million people squatted. The metropolitan cities of India have proliferated, but the living conditions of the poor have continued to deteriorate. One of Asia's largest slums is at Dharavi in Mumbai, which has a population of about 10,00,000. The Census Commission, in March 2014 stated that 64 million urban Indians live in unsanitary slums that are distinctly unfit for human habitation. In Delhi itself, there are about 35% people who live in settlements full of dirt, decay, disease, danger and despair.

Jagmohan has also recorded the history of different slums across the globe. The earliest slums recorded were the Jewish Ghettos, which were labelled as 'nauseous and deadly'. Again, the Irish and Chinese slums earn the notoriety of being the most 'fearful'. English slums of the nineteenth century were called 'frowzy dens' by Charles Dickens.

Indian slums and the living conditions as exist, approximate the 'fearful', 'frowzy' and 'deadly' slums of the ages gone by. Jagmohan observed that no site is too slushy, too filthy and too dangerous for the precarious huddle of huts to be put up and for human beings to dwell in them. In many places, people live inside the huge asbestos water or waste pipes, lying abandoned. Most obnoxiously, these asbestos pipes are the places where the have-nots live with their spouses, copulate, give birth to children and finally breathe their last. This is the most agonising story of slum dwellers, a condition that sadly exists even today.

In this context, Jagmohan draws attention to a lengthy report of The Hindu Daily of 28 March, 2014, about the Indira Camp slums of New Delhi, which had 1600 'jhuggis' and 6000 inhabitants. Jagmohan quotes the report: "In order to reach the stinking slum, one has to wade through a bumpy uneven passage, with massive heaps of garbage on both sides. It was not only garbage- it is a marshland filled with human and animal excreta, coming from the two overflowing government toilets close to the water pipe." These were the only toilets for the hapless inhabitants residing there. Dilshad Muhammad, a resident, lamented that a lot of children had died by slipping into the filth. He added that when it rained, they pick their kids on their shoulders to take them to their schools and also bring them back the very same way. The most pathetic and inhumane observation came from a resident, Sushila, who had lost her aunt when rain water had flooded her jhuggi in 2008. "She was trying to pull her trunk to save medical documents of her hospitalised husband. She fell into the water that had reached her waist line. We found her body only when we saw her clothes floating a few days later, said Sushila.

Jagmohan questioned, why do such in human conditions exist? Why do the spectacles of 'disease and horror' that the slums in the 1953s evoked, still remain? Jagmohan laments that this long apathy remained because of not only the 'physical' slum but also the 'mental' slums of the Indian polity. The resolute practicality of Sardar Patel, the poetic and humanitarian passion of Jawaharlal Nehru or even the allotment of adequate funds for this purpose in the Five Year Plans were insufficient to solve this problem.

In June-July 1960, the 'Jhuggi-Jhopri Removal Scheme' was approved by the Union Cabinet, which sanctioned 80 square yards of plot to each eligible squatter family on a lease of 99 years. The plot was to be provided with the latrine, a water tap and a plinth on which the lessee could construct a house or hut, according to means or requirement. However, there was heavy corruption among the allottees to make quick bucks by selling the land to the land sharks and to continue squatting somewhere else. Modifications were made on the scheme from time to time to maintain the ownership of the gullible squatters.

Later on, a high level study group, under the leadership of the Minister of House and Housing, Jagannath Rao was appointed, with some other members being the Lieutenant-Governor of Delhi and other senior leaders of political parties represented in the Metropolitan Council. This committee castigated the municipalities for the bureaucratic negligence and corrupt practices. Two recommendations came out of these deliberations on the slums and the problem of squatting. It was decided that no members of any political party should interfere with any ground level implementation. Also, most importantly, the unauthorised occupation of public land would be made a cognizable offence, punishable with imprisonment upto three years. However, the huge allocation of central funds too, could not mitigate the squatter problem.

It is worthwhile to note that under the stewardship of Dr. A.N.Jha, the eminent scholar of Sanskrit and ancient Indian tradition, many repairs were carried on in various burning ghats in the city, including the famous Nigambodh Ghat. However, despite their best efforts, there is hardly any recognisable improvement of the ghats and sewer treatments. The effluents from industries continue to flow into the Yamuna without proper check.

In terms of vision, the comradeship between A.N.Jha and Jagmohan started moving in slightly different tracks and they fell apart in their zest to beautify and sanctify the age-old burning ghats on the banks of the river Yamuna. As Jagmohan was appointed Commissioner of the DDA (Delhi Development Authority), he found a proper forum to pursue his cherished dream of beautifying the ghats of the Yamuna as well as ameliorating the miserable conditions as prevalent in the 'jhuggis' and 'jhopris'. At that time, the other prominent government functionaries, apart from Dr. A.N.Jha were Dharmaveera, Bhagwan Sahay and Viswanathan. Jagmohan also faced hostility from muscle men known as 'dadas', who opposed the resettlement plan and did not allow the work to continue in an orderly fashion.

The Congress Party that was in opposition at that time, singularly opposed any plan of the Delhi Government to beautify Delhi. The use of the bulldozers to remove unauthorised constructions was vehemently opposed by them. It was a miserable situation with three parties, namely Dr. A.N.Jha, the senior most administrator, Jagmohan, the executor of the formalised plans to remove debris and the Congress in opposition, were at loggerheads, putting obstacles in the path of the beautification and formalised development of Delhi. At one point, Jagmohan lamented that he was perhaps the centre of the crossfire between the administration (party in power) and the Congress party (opposition). Things came to such an ugly pass that on 27th July, 1967 the Congress Party organised a very offensive procession where an effigy of Dr. A.N.Jha was burnt with other shocking indecencies. Obviously, the Congress party had a vested interest in retaining the slum dwellers and squatters whom they thought of as their vote bank. In the years to come, the impunity with which the squatters tried to destroy the fabric of the cultured heritage of Delhi, was undoubtedly the most agonising for both the administrator and the executor.

Once, when Mir Mushtaq Ahmed, senior leader of the Congress, rang up to ask for an appointment with A.N.Jha, he replied, "Mir Sahib, you have to come to hell because your friends have already sent me there". This demonstrated the magnanimity of Dr. Jha in spite of the constant provocation by the Congress to malign him in the public eye. In this context, it may be mentioned that when Y.B.Chavan was the Home Minister, Dr. Jha, though otherwise a cheerful and gracious personality, didn't mince words when he expressed the deceit and hypocrisy of the Congress leaders. He stated, "To me, the attitude of ambivalence on the part of the political parties has been, to say the least, most disappointing... I must in the end, confess to a feeling of being let down by everyone and shown up as one who has been acting arbitrarily and tyrannically- the only person lacking in sympathy, while everyone else has been falling over each other to be humane and helpful and generous.

The immense pain that Dr. Jha suffered never rendered him spiritless and at the end, the stupendous amount of development work done on the beautification of the age-old traditional Hindu burning ghats revived the cultural heritage of India. Jagmohan quoted a beautiful hymn for the departed souls whose last rites were conducted at Nigambodh Ghat: 'Be upward and divine. There is no power that can undo your existence. You are an inextricable part of the all-pervasive Divinity who is invisible, undying and formless and whom no sword could pierce, no fire could burn and no water could drown. You have not come out of zero and you will not go back to zero.'

Lamentably, a litigation was brought against Jagmohan before the Delhi High Court. The complainant advocate started a harangue against Jagmohan. The presiding judge of the court however interrupted him gently and remarked off the record: "He has done an amazing service in transforming the area. Now I would not be very unhappy when death comes; at least my soul would pass through a clean, open and elevating park and not a smoke-laden and filthy slum." This shows the level of thankfulness and gratitude that the citizens of Delhi felt towards Jagmohan. Thereafter, redevelopment and resettlement work, on the lines of Nigambodh Ghat, was done in the clusters of Paharganj, in the Prasad Nagar 'quarry pits',

Nizamuddin Basti, Motia Khan's Idgah, Firozshah Kotla, Daryaganj, Jama Masjid, Tilak Bridge, Patel Nagar hillock and Humayun Temple of Connaught Place.

Bhavani Sengupta in the Hindustan Times wrote about Jagmohan: "One has only to read Jagmohan's awesomely documented book to realise the truth. He has minced no words about the indifference and incompetence and worse of Indian leaders of all hues…". Truly, Jagmohan is remembered as the architect of post-independence Delhi after Lutyens; the sanctification, beautification and practical designing of important buildings speak of Jagmohan's contribution. According to Professor B. Bhattacharya, ('Management and Change'), "Jagmohan… developed an agenda for action which attempts to blend practical hard-nosed reforms with fundamental ethical behaviour". Perhaps the most flattering praise came from India Today "He takes no foes, he knows no friends. For him, nothing or nobody is above Delhi, its beauty, its heritage, its historical places and public spaces. He is citizen one."

PART 2

SELECT ESSAYS ON DELHI AND BEYOND

Essay 1

Benevolent Despots

Britain's colonial past has been a source of unquestioning pride to them within their own nation and, even to this day, two thirds of Britons genuinely believe that the Empire was 'something to be proud of'. Indians, however, have always been acutely aware of the dark colonial past: the horrors of British rule, the savage exploitation and the resulting collapse of our age-old social institutions, our agriculture and industry. Thus, it stands to reason that many have questioned and many have grudgingly acknowledged some of the good that the British did in India.

If we had to count some of the good that the British did in India, we should start with their abolition of the infamous and inhuman practice of sati. By 1829, the practice was officially banned and by the 1870s, it was practically wiped out from the country. The British were also responsible for the removal of other cruel and inhuman social practices like infanticide, child marriage and untouchability and for promoting widows remarriage.

Concepts of western liberal education and western sciences were also introduced by the British in India. They promoted the English language and made English the official and literary language of the country. Though at the time, this was done to serve their own purposes, it had far reaching results. The Bengalis, especially of Calcutta, the 'Bhadrolok' class, highly appreciated the introduction of English language and wholeheartedly supported the move to make English the official language.

The British were responsible for laying the foundation stone of one of the largest railway networks in the world and introducing the post and telegraph system, leading to a faster and more efficient means of transport and communication. This was done mainly to oversee their expansion over the native states and the native princes and also to introduce a system of quick deployment of British forces to any troubled areas where they were facing opposition from the native princes.

They set up the department of Geographical Survey of India in 1851 which had the responsibility of surveying villages and cities and making maps for India during British rule. The British started the census in 1871 that is taken once in 10 years to collect statistical data of age, gender, religion, caste, occupation and education of the population. The pride and honour of our nation, the Indian Army, was also formed during the British Era, around 1895. The culture and discipline and many of the army's practices that still persist belong to the pre-independence era. The British also developed an irrigation system which increased the amount of land available for farming by eight times. They set up a large network of irrigation canals in the areas which did not get the benefit of the monsoons, and which were not fed by major rivers They set up a coal industry which had not existed before. Public health and life expectancy increased under British rule mainly because of improved water supply and introduction of quinine treatment against malaria. Interestingly, the Indian middle class and Indian landowners and princes gained in terms of education, job opportunities, business opportunities and careers in areas like the law and medicine.

This period can be called a period of benevolent administrators. In this category we can put Lord William Bentinck (Governor General from 1828 to 1835), Lord Dalhousie (Governor General from 1848 to 1856), Lord Canning (Governor General of India, from 1856 to 1858, and also the first Viceroy from 1 November, 1858 to 1862) and Lord Mayo (Viceroy of India from 1869 to 1872)

Lord William Bentinck

William Bentinck was the Governor General of the British East India company from 1828 to 1835. The most famous reform associated with his name is the prohibition of Suttee or sati enacted in 1829. Bentinck's regulation of December 4, 1829 declared ' the practice of Sati or burning or burying alive the widows of Hindus, illegal and punishable by the criminal courts', and rightly pronounced it to be ' revolting to the feelings of human nature and nowhere enjoined by the religion of the people as an imperative duty'. By this regulation, the people who abetted sati were declared guilty of 'culpable homicide'.

The practice of Sati had become extremely prevalent in Bengal where in some years more than 800 women were being sacrificed at the funeral pyres of their dead husbands. The most strenuous opposition to Lord Bentinck's measure, however, also came from Bengal. The ban was challenged in the courts, but the Privy Council of London upheld the ban in 1832. Another Reform associated with Bentinck was his suppression female infanticide and making it a punishable offence. Further, Lord William Bentinck along with William Henry Sleeman are credited with the suppression of organised bands of thugs. These were bands of criminals travelling in disguise and murdering helpless travellers. Bentinck passed a series of special acts to regulate their proceedings and more than 3000 thugs were caught during 1831 - 1837 and India was eventually rid of this great scourge.

Bentinck is also known for his judicial and financial reforms and his arrangements for the employment of Indians in appointments hitherto reserved exclusively for Europeans.

The administration of Bentinck was a landmark in Indian history also for the momentous decision to make English language the official and literary language of the country. The Charter Act of 1813 was the first step where education was made an objective of the government. The act sanctioned a sum of Rs. 11 lakhs towards education of Indians in British ruled India. In 1835 it was decided by Lord Bentinck's government that western sciences and literature would be taught to Indians through the medium of English language. The English Education Act of 1835 was a legislative act of the Council of India which reallocated funds for the education and literacy of India. English became the official language of India, the language of law courts, of administration and instruction and this had far reaching consequences. In February of 1835, Bentinck laid the foundation of the Calcutta Medical College and Hospital.

Thomas Babington Macaulay

In 1834, Thomas Babington Macaulay, appointed as the first Law Member of the Governor General's Council and served on the Supreme Council during 1834–1838. He eloquently pleaded in favour of Western education and denounced classical Indian learning. According to him '...a single shelf of a good European library was worth the whole native literature of India and Arabia'. In his famous Minutes on Indian Education, in February of 1835, he decided that henceforth all available public funds should be spent on English education, 'on imparting to the native population a knowledge of English literature and science through the medium of English language'. He wanted to reform Secondary Education on utilitarian lines, to deliver 'useful learning'. Macaulay's Minute on Indian Education was primarily responsible for the introduction of Western instructional education in India. His view was also accepted by Bentinck's government, that 'it is possible to make natives of this country thoroughly good English scholars, and that to this our efforts are to be directed'. He propounded that

1. Education in India should be imparted in English in place of traditional Indian languages because the Oriental culture was 'defective and unholy'.
2. Macaulay believed in educating a few upper and middle class students. In due course of time, this education would trickle down to the common people. This system was known as the infiltration theory.
3. There was a huge demand for clerks and officials in other administrative roles in the company's functioning and it was cheaper to get Indians with a working knowledge of English, rather than Englishmen from England for these jobs.
4. All public services were to be filled through an open competitive examination held by the Council of Education; preference being given to those with the knowledge of English.

According to Macaulay, 'we must at present do our best to form a class who may be interpreters between us and the millions whom we govern, - a class of persons Indians in blood and colour, but English in tastes, in opinions, in morals and in intellect.' Virtually, English language became the only passport to higher appointments available to Indians and this in turn assured its popularity and rapid progress.

Though English was basically introduced so that Indian people could be used as cheap workforce in the company's administration and therefore open to too much criticism at the time, not many can dispute the propriety of the decision to make English the vehicle for higher instruction and administration. The existing system of education in India is based on the lines laid down by Macaulay.

It is true that the English language was taught to the Indians by the British, not so much as an act of benevolence, but mainly to facilitate the work of administration. English was an 'instrument of colonialism', to be taught to only a select few, for their own purposes. It is indeed a remarkable irony that the Indians mastered the language and used it as their own instrument, to express and spread nationalist sentiments across the country and beyond.

Lord Dalhousie

Lord Dalhousie, known primarily for his policy of annexation of Indian states through his infamous Doctrine of Lapse which became one of the major reasons for the revolt of 1857, was also known for his framing of a system of government on modern lines.

As the Governor-General of India from 1848 to 1856, he introduced many reforms. He decided that India should have a Railways of her own; amidst a lot of predictions of failure, he persisted and was able to open a short railway line in 1854. Dalhousie also founded the Postal department and introduced the electric telegraph. Roads, irrigation works, navigable canals and many other such improvements relating to public works were designed and executed under his personal guidance and supervision.

Dalhousie is also known for some social reforms like abolishing child marriage, advocating for widow remarriage and encouraging women's education. Lord Dalhousie, along with John Elliot Drinkwater Bethune were pioneers in the field of women's education. Bethune Collegiate School, also known as the Calcutta Female School, was established in the year 1849 by Bethune, which is the oldest women's college in Asia. Dalhousie also introduced the Hindu Widows' Remarriage Act in 1856, which allowed Hindu widows to get married again. This became an act after it was approved by the next Governor General, Lord Canning.

It was Lord Dalhousie as Governor-General who received the Wood's Dispatch from the President of the Board of Control of the East India Company, Sir Charles Wood in 1854, containing a scheme of education for all of India and which formed the foundation on which the education system of British India was subsequently developed. This document provided for the establishment of aided schools in all districts, colleges and universities throughout India. Dalhousie was prompt in giving effect to the policy outlined in the Dispatch and organised the Departments of Public Instruction in all provinces.

The Wood's Despatch of 1854 is considered as the 'Magna Carta of English Education in India'. This played a very important role In the spread of English education and female education in India. Charles Wood recommended that primary schools adopt vernacular languages and that English be the medium of instruction in colleges and for higher education. A lot of emphasis was also given to vocational training and women's education in India.

1. Woods dispatch provided for a more systematic method of education starting from the primary level up to the university level.
2. The medium of instruction at the primary level was to be the one occurring in Indian languages while at the higher levels it would be English
3. All private schools should be given grants-in-aid for proper functioning and there should be at least one government school in every district. Also, Universities modelled on the University of London would be established in big cities such as Bombay, Calcutta and Madras.
4. An education department would be set up in every province.
5. There was a lot of focus on Teachers training, women's education and mass education.

6. The goal was to enhance the moral character of Indians through education in English and to supply the East India company with civil servants who could be trusted upon.

Lord Canning

Lord Canning was the last Governor General of India from 1856 to 1862 and the first Viceroy from 1858 to 1862. At the time of the revolt of 1857 Lord Canning was the supreme British commander holding the fort for both the military and civil administration. The vengeance wrecked by the Indian sepoys of Meerut and Bareilly upon the hapless British residents, irrespective of their age, sex and gender was most abominable. Whereas the British desperately sought revenge for the atrocities committed by the sepoys, Governor General Lord Canning at that turbulent moment, brought in some degree of sensibility. He stopped the mindless massacre of the Indians, both Hindus and Muslims, who were being mercilessly used as cannon fodder by the British forces. Lord Canning with his vigorous administrative activity was able to establish some semblance of order and stability for which he was derided by the revengeful British as 'Clemency Canning'. He deserves the highest credit for the manner in which he fulfilled his official responsibilities and attempted to heal rather than to inflame the wounds inflicted by the mutiny.

As the revolt ended, Lord Canning proclaimed peace throughout India. Many British, both in India and England, demanded the pursuit of a ruthless and indiscriminate policy of vengeance. Even Brigadier General John Nicholson, who played a major role in bringing down the revolt spoke of legalizing the 'the flaying alive, impalement or burning of the murderers of the women and children at Delhi'. But Canning, uninfluenced by this clamour, handled the matter with a statesman like prudence and arranged for the proper trial and punishment of only those who are really guilty. At the time, he was derided for his decision by his peers, but his policy was wise and expedient and mindless revenge would only have added bitterness between the rulers and the ruled.

In the Darbar of November 1, 1858, the Queen's Proclamation promised to respect the rights, dignity and honour of the native princes and to pay due regard to the ancient rights, usages and customs of India. It granted general amnesty to 'all offenders, save and except those who have been, and shall be convicted of having directly taken part in the murder of British subjects' and proclaimed a 'policy of justice, benevolence and religious tolerance'.

Lord Canning bravely set himself to the work of reconstruction. Even at the height of the mutiny, it was the greatness of Lord Canning to establish three universities at the metropolitan centres of Kolkata, Bombay and Madras. Initially these universities were only centres of examinations for colleges and under their territorial jurisdiction. However, within a short time Lord Canning converted these universities into full-fledged teaching universities. The impulse given by the universities to the study of English and other subjects taught through the medium of that language had a profound effect on India.

Lord Canning was instrumental in introducing the codification of the Indian rules. He spearheaded the stupendous task of conversion of the Muslim jurisprudence to modern jurisprudence based on British hierarchy. He wanted to remodel the justice system based on the jurisprudence prevalent in England. The Penal Code on which Macaulay and other experts had been long at work, saw the light of day in 1860 and was followed the next year by the Code of Criminal Procedure. The Penal Code has stood the test of experience wonderfully well and has needed only a slight amendment.

It was he who first introduced the idea of budgeting of finance. Prior to that, the mutiny and the British military expenditures had completely reduced the treasury into naught and it was observed that in 1858, the total debt to the exchequer was approximately 98 million pounds sterling.

By the act of 1858, the rule of the East India Company in India was terminated, and the governance of India was transferred to the Crown of England. Certain drastic steps were taken by Lord Canning. As the Act of 1858 had transferred the Governance of India from the East India Company to the Crown of England, Canning took advantage of this and proclaimed that henceforth, the expenditure of revenue should be exclusively vested with the Secretary of State in Council in England, and that no part of the grant or appropriation of any revenue from this fund should be made available without the concurrence of majority vote in the meeting of Secretary of State in Council. Within the overall authority of the council, a limited expenditure of certain nature was allowed to be transacted by the government of India as a special delegated power.

As the situation regarding the government finance was totally chaotic, a proper financial management was sought to ameliorate the situation by adapting the traditional English pattern. The major crux of unbridled expenditure was the demand of the British military forces which were regularly engaged in the annexation of the Indian states. However, Canning brought a semblance of discipline in financial management and properly delegated the power to the executive provincial authority, which had been reduced to the status of executing agencies without any authority to transact even the minimum financial requirements of the state. Skilled financial experts were brought in from England to set the finances in order. They introduced the income tax, enforced a strict economy and soon converted the deficit into a surplus.

Lord Canning is credited also with the introduction of the system of budget as was prevalent in England in 1860–61, with the end of the financial year fixed on 31st of March. Another important landmark act which is credited to the ingenuity of Lord Canning was the introduction of the Rent Act of 1859 which was thought to be applied to the Bengal, Bihar and Agra province then known as the Northwestern province and Central provinces (known as CP and Berar). This act did much to secure the rights of the cultivating tenants, which the regulations of the permanent settlement had failed to protect. This regulation conferred 'tenancy right for the cultivator cultivating the land having continuous cultivating possession of land for 12 years and will be entitled to a right of occupancy'. For the first time the right of occupancy was made legal. In several provinces however, the Tenancy Act of 1859 could not be properly implemented as it suffered from lack of definite legal force.

Lord Canning retired in March 1862. His incessant work, mostly of complicated legal nature, took its fatal toll and he expired within 3 months of his retirement. Lord Canning's successor, Lord Elgin, died at Dharamshala in November 1863. The two stalwarts having expired in quick succession within a very short span of time, the mantle of the successor fell on the Chief Commissioner of Punjab, Sir John Lawrence, in early 1864, because of stupendous work in suppressing the mutiny in Punjab and also recovering Delhi from the mutineers. He was appointed as Viceroy and Governor General in a dual role. As he was a member of the civil service, any restriction to his appointment to the highest office under the Crown was specially waived. He was raised to the status of peerage to be designated as Lord Lawrence. With his appointment, the period of reconstruction after the mutiny, came to an end.

Lord Mayo

Richard Bourke, 6th Earl of Mayo was the Viceroy of India from 1869–72. Lord Mayo is credited with the founding of the Mayo College of Ajmer, to cater to the special education of Rajput princes. This college of the Chiefs was inaugurated after the death of Lord Mayo. Similar institutions were subsequently established in Lahore (then in undivided India) and Rajkot in Saurashtra (Kathiawar).

Lord Mayo who is known for his measure of decentralisation - the government of each province was responsible for its own finances within certain limits. To his government belongs the credit for taking the first important step towards financial decentralisation in India by giving to each Provincial Government a fixed grant for the maintenance of certain definite services such as police, jails, education and medical services with certain powers assigned to them to allocate revenues at their discretion and to provide for extra expenditure if needed, by raising local taxes.

During his tenure, a regular census of Bengal was taken for the first time, in 1871, which revealed the astounding fact that the population of the province far exceeded the official estimate by 26 million. He was instrumental in establishing the Statistical Survey of India and the

Department of Agriculture and Commerce. Lord Mayo also paid a lot of attention to public works, especially roads, railways, forests, irrigation works and canals. The most important legal reform during his time was the passing of the Indian Evidence Act in 1872. Earlier, the law system was differentiated and was applied as per caste community and social group in question. This act introduced the standard set of laws applicable to all Indians, thus removing distinction and differentiation.

It was his diplomacy that helped to bring back the Amir of Afghanistan, Sher Ali, who was disgusted by the cold and selfish policy of Lord Lawrence. It was a major tactical diplomatic victory for Lord Mayo, as the Amir of Afghanistan was veering towards Russia. Lord Mayo was permitted to promise the Amir general support against Russia, on the express condition that the government of India should be the ultimate arbitrator on the manner of help to be given to the Amir. This way, he was successful in stabilising the northwestern frontier of India and establishing close relationship with the Amir.

However while inspecting the convict settlement at Port Blair in the Andaman Islands in 1872 he was assassinated by an Afghan convict, who stabbed him with a knife. One effect of his assassination was that there were demand for the creation of an Intelligence Bureau in India which would assist in tracking down suspects and subversive elements by the British colonial administration. Lord Mayo is primarily remembered for the educational institutions set up in his name in India.

Essay 2

Emergence of Delhi as the New Capital of British India

On December 12, 1911, at the Coronation Durbar in Delhi, King George V announced the momentous decision on the closely guarded secret of transfer of the Capital of India from Calcutta to Delhi. The new seat of the Government was to rule the empire from Kashmir to Colombo and from the North West frontier to Rangoon. This change was expected, having been on the cards for the about fifty years.

The association of Delhi for the vast majority of Indians, was historical. For the Hindus, Delhi was a name to conjure with, being associated with sacred legend going back to the days of the Pandavas which was before the dawn of history. Purana Quila marks the site of the city the Pandavas called Indraprastha. This was at the fringe of the city of Delhi, barely five km from the southern border of modern Delhi. For the Muslims, Delhi retained a nostalgic association of pride and gratification being the capital of their conquered part of India from the days of the Sultanate. As against this Calcutta was a distant place in the east of India where the authority of Mughal rulers of Delhi was marginal.

This was further demonstrated as the mutinous sepoys at the height of revolt of 1857, rushed towards Delhi to make the ageing Mughal Emperor, Bahadur Shah Zafar as their leader. The storming of Delhi by the sepoys sparked off uprisings all over the Gangetic plain. Thus re-annexation of Delhi by the British and deposition of Bahadur Shah Zafar were the most urgent objectives of the British.

It was a deft move on part of Lord Lytton who in close collaboration with Disraeli, the Prime Minister of Great Britain and Lord Salisbury, the then Secretary of State for India, decided to hold an Imperial Assemblage in 1877 to proclaim Queen Victoria as the Empress of India at Delhi, even though Calcutta was the capital of British India. The move was obviously intended to stamp the authority of the Queen on the seat of the Mughals for centuries, Delhi being held with reverence and awe as the seat of supreme power. On this count alone, the status of Calcutta could hardly match that of Delhi.

Delhi had scored over Calcutta. It is worth recalling the historical and political situation in Calcutta during the first decade of the twentieth century before the decision of shifting of the capital in 1911.

The Battle of Plassey in June 1757 and defeat of Siraj-Ud-Daulah, at the hands of the British force led by Robert Clive, saw the emergence of Calcutta as the centre of operation and conquest of North India. The British possessions and conquered territory of North India up to the Khyber Pass in the Northwest Frontier, were for all practical purposes, administered from Calcutta. The Bengal Presidency, as originally constituted, extended up to the northwestern border of the British conquest.

With the conquest of Bengal and establishment of Calcutta as the administrative capital began the association of the British with upper class Indians, leading to the establishment of Western (English) educated Bengali elite groups. They were steadfastly pro-British, so much so that they remained totally aloof from the mutiny of 1857, with Calcutta being the citadel of British India. The exposure of Bengali elites to Western education and ideas, in its wake, brought advocacy of social reform and learning the value of freedom and consciousness of their subordinate status and sense of economic exploitation at the hands of the British. The feeling of this discontent saw the emergence of a feeling of nationalism which found expression in the formation of Indian National Congress in 1885 to articulate grievances through discussions once a year. Hardly, any substantial objective was achieved in the annual deliberation. However, there was a dramatic transformation in 1905. In October 1905, Lord Curzon brought about the partition of the province of Bengal, which was actually a conglomerate of the provinces of Bengal, Bihar, Orissa and Assam. The area covered 189000 square miles with a population of nearly 1 crore.

Though the arguments advanced for the partition were administrative, that the Bengal province was of unwieldy dimensions for efficient governance, the serious consequence this announcement generated was purely political in nature. Curzon's idea was to nip the rising sentiments of nationalism in the bud as it was held that 'Bengal united is a power, while Bengal divided will pull the separated provinces in different directions'.

However, Curzon's idea of dividing the Bengal province to facilitate ruling of smaller provinces, had just the opposite impact. It united Bengal against British Rule. There were big meetings in the Town Hall of Calcutta in March 1904, and January 1905, apart from submissions of petitions, press conferences and smaller protests. However, these were on moderate lines as were the deliberations of the Indian National Congress those days.

Then followed more aggressive form of protests. In July 1905, emerged the boycott of British goods and use of 'Swadeshi' or indigenously produced goods like textiles, soaps, detergents and other manufactured goods of British origin. There was some amount of coercion adopted by the volunteers. Boycott, then extended to educational institutions. There was picketing before government run educational institutions. The date of partition was 16 October 1905. On that day, Bengal witnessed a unique solidarity of brotherhood and unity by exchange of Rakhi (a traditional coloured wrist band tied by siblings) among the society without colour, creed or religious distinction. Massive support came from the great poet Rabindra Nath Tagore also. The movement saw the emergence of the great scholar and revolutionary, Sri Aurobindo Ghosh, (later on, the famous spiritual leader and saint of the Pondicherry Ashram).

Aurobindo held the partition as the 'pettiest and narrowest' of all political objectives. He along with brother Barin Ghosh, a diehard revolutionary, propagated that Swadeshi or switching over to indigenous goods and boycott of all British goods represented the first step to 'Swaraj' or freedom from British rule.

However, the protests did not cut any ice with Lord Curzon. The alternative proposal of reducing the size of the provinces without dividing Bengal down the middle was also summarily rejected. The final plan to divide Bengal was sent to London in February 1905 and accepted in March

1905. A new province of Eastern Bengal and Assam with the capital at Dacca, came into existence on 16 October, 1905. With his job accomplished Lord Curzon demitted the office of Viceroy in November 1905.

The spate of protests that the partition generated did not subside even after the departure of Curzon, rather it culminated in the initiation of a regular protest movement known as Swadeshi movement. As peaceful protests turned militant, repression to curb the protests was equally swift. The British government resorted to harsh measures of mass arrest, deportation, preventive detention, sending of the militant youths to the gallows, apart from general censorship of the press.

Around 1909, the intensity of the 'Swadeshi' movement started dying down and its place was taken over by a general sense of despair among Bengalis, particularly the youth of Bengal. With the charisma associated with the grandeur of state of undivided Bengal gone, the injury to Bengal's pride having received a thorough and sound beating in the form of the partition of Bengal and the Swadeshi movement slowly taking a backseat in the political scenario, the rudderless yet the vibrant youth of Bengal drifted into the vortex of abysmal despair and indignation.

There was, however, a general recognition, including at the level of King George V, that the partition of Bengal was not a wise and tactical decision. The king wanted to revoke the partition and wanted to do so at a Coronation Durbar which he was determined to hold in India.

Then there came a stunning event which terribly shook the ruling authority and ruled subjects out of their lulled mental frame. The event came not from the field of politics but from the least expected field of sport, that is, the game of football.

In an epoch-making afternoon of July 9, 1911, at the Maidan of Calcutta, a local football club, Mohun Bagan Athletic Club inflicted an unbelievable defeat on a crack outfit of the British Regiment, East Yorkshire Regiment football team in the final of I.F.A. (Indian Football Association) Shield, the blue riband tournament of football in India.

Mohun Bagan Athletic Club was founded in the Shyambazar area of North Calcutta in 1889, with the support of a couple of elite Bengali families of the area. The team, consisting of local youth, caught the eye of football administrators of those days of Calcutta, having done well in the local open tournaments like the Trades Cup. It won an invitation to match the giants of football at I.F.A. Shield.

In a stunning and frenzied display of determination, the skill and efficiency of the group of barefooted footballers, except for one booted player, Sudhir Chatterjee, (later on Reverend Sudhir Chatterjee) battled the might of the British military players to eke out an incredible victory which created a feeling of national pride and resurrected sagging morale and patriotism of the Bengalis. This sense of joy and feeling of oneness with the heroes of the day percolated beyond the boundaries of Bengal to engulf the whole of Eastern India, the erstwhile province of undivided Bengal.

Even after a hundred years of the event, the names of the heroes who made possible the utterly impossible act, are remembered with reverence, awe and love. The heroes to remember were: Hiralal Mukherjee (played as Goalkeeper), Bhuti Sukul (a native of U.P. who migrated to the state of Cooch Behar) played at Back. Sudhir Chatterjee (the only booted player playing at Back), Monomohan Mukherjee (Back), Rajen Sengupta (Back), Nil Madhav Bhattacharia (Half Back), Kanu Roy (Forward), Habul Sarkar (Forward), Abhilas Ghosh (forwards) Bijoy Das Bhaduri (forward), Shil Das Bhaduri (Captain and forward). Truly, a game of football was elevated to the level of a 'battle between British Rulers and ruled Indians', in the context of India's freedom struggle.A question remains unanswered, whether there was a coincidental connection between the event of July 9, 1911 and the proclamation of the date of revocation of partition of Bengal at the Delhi Durbar coronation of King-Emperor, King George V on December 12, 1911. The King announced the transfer of the seat of Government of India from Calcutta to the ancient imperial capital, Delhi. A simultaneous announcement was made for appointment of a new Governorship for the Presidency of Bengal, administering the areas of Behar, Chota Nagpur and Orissa and of a Chief Commissionership of Assam, with such administrative changes and redistribution of boundaries as the Governor General in Council with the approval of the Secretary of State for India in Council may be in due course determine. The King expressed an earnest desire that these changes may be conducive to the better administration of India and the greater prosperity and happiness of his beloved people.

Talking about the football match, it remained more of a nostalgic romantic feeling among the Bengalis rather than a path breaking event in the history of the freedom struggle, unlike the armed struggle of the Chittagong Armoury Raid carried out in the cantonment town of Chittagong, a port town on the eastern hilly tract of East Bengal (now Bangladesh) bordering Burma, under the leadership of Surya Sen (Master-da) by a band of local Bengali youth in the year 1930, with two girl leaders Preetilata and Kalpana, among others.

Now, reverting to the issue of transfer of the capital, it's worthwhile to look at the factors that played a decisive role in shifting of the capital from Calcutta, which remained so for over one hundred fifty years, including the days of governance by East India Company, and the factors that were considered for choice of Delhi. Regarding the first factor, Calcutta became the capital during consolidation of British power in India following their victory over the Nawab of Bengal, Siraj-Ud-Daulah of Murshidabad, at the Battle of Plassey, in 1757. As the East India Company incorporated in London, originally venturing into south India as a trading company moved to Bengal, it transformed itself into a force of invaders eyeing for annexation of territories with political motives. Calcutta was the natural site for the British as the capital of annexed Indian territory.

The origin of Calcutta draws reference to the exploits of a servant of the English East India Company, with headquarters at Leadenhall Street, London. Job Charnock of the company arrived in Sutanuti in August 1690 after being driven out of the town of Hugli, a few miles up river Hooghly (Ganga) by the Mughal administrator of Bengal. Charnock, rowing down the river, landed at Sutanuti, which had a port facility and was already a thriving market. There were two other adjoining villages, Govindapur and Kalikata. Successors of Charnock, selected Kalikata, as their headquarters and built a fort on river Hooghly, named Fort William. By 1781, Kalikata with completion of Fort William as apex, had become the administrative centre. This was the forerunner of Calcutta, the capital and the second city of the British Empire after London. The political presence of the British in India was monitored from Calcutta, as also the trading of the company across the ocean. With the defeat of the Nawab of Bengal by a force led by Robert Clive in June 1757 and the establishment of the East India Company as rulers of Bengal, Calcutta became the centre of operations for the British in the east and north of India. This included both trading and administrative operations. The main objective of the British was trade and administration; However, their social and cultural life too flourished. They left a very distinct mark on the city of Calcutta, and demarcated areas with their exclusive Churches, educational institutions, hospital, and clubs and many invaluable properties including libraries (National Library), museums, literary academies, amusement centres, including the Botanical Garden and 200 other gardens, printing and security forces and a judicial system. Calcutta became a city worthy to be the capital of the British Empire in India.

This position remained unchanged till 1868, when the issue of the change of capital cropped up, on the grounds that there should be separate capital for provincial and federal governments. However, not till the Morley-Minto Reforms and the partition of Bengal did the need for an independent capital start engaging attention. King George V announced his decision to visit India, which would be a first by a ruling monarch of Great Britain, in the British Parliament on February 6, 1911, when Lord Asquith was heading the cabinet.

He wanted the occasion to be memorable by making a handsome political gift to his subjects. King George V himself wrote to the Viceroy of India Lord Harding on this subject. "Why not make the two Bengals into a Presidency like Bombay or Madras? That would flatter the Bengalis very much, allay discontent and stop sedition, and well be worth the extra cost to the country. Think it over." The proposal did not find favour with the Viceroy and Secretary of state. But the King was adamant even after the sanction of money for King's visit to India by the House of commons.

King's desire for a royal gift to his Indian subjects was finally solved by John Jenkin who was Home Member. He suggested in June 1911 that the partition of Bengal be revoked, the boundaries of Bengal be redrawn, and the imperial capital be shifted from Calcutta to Delhi. The Jenkin's scheme won approval from all. Lord Hardinge, the Viceroy of India wrote on 25 August 1911 to Lord Crewe from Shimla, which reasoned out the moving of the capital from Calcutta. The main portion of the letter was as follows:

> *'That the Government of India should have its seat in the same city as one of the chief Provincial Governments and moreover in a city geographically so ill adapted as Calcutta to be the capital of the Indian Empire, has long been recognized to be a serious anomaly. The considerations which explain its original selection as the principal seat of power long since passed away with the consolidation of British rule throughout the peninsula and the developments of a great inland system of railway communication. But it is only in the light of recent development, constitutional and political, that the drawbacks of the existing state and urgency of a change have been fully realised. On the one hand the almost incalculable importance of the part which can already safely be predicted for the Imperial Legislative council in the shape it has assumed under the Indian Councils Act of 1909 renders removal of the capital to a more central and easily accessible position practically imperative. On the other hand, the peculiar political situation which has arisen in Bengal since the Partition makes it eminently desirable to withdraw the Government of India from its present provincial environment. While its removal from Bengal is an essential feature of the scheme we have in view for allaying the ill feeling aroused by the partition amongst the Bengali population. Once the necessity of removing the seat of the Supreme Government from Bengal (is) established... there can be, in our opinion, no manner of doubt as to the choice of the new capital or as to the occasion on which that choice should be announced. On geographical, historical and political grounds, the capital of the Indian Empire should be at Delhi and the announcement that the transfer of the seat of Government to Delhi has been sanctioned should be made by His Majesty the King Emperor at the forthcoming Imperial Durbar in Delhi."*

The political reason for shifting of the capital was that such a transfer would materially facilitate the growth of local self-government on sound and safe lines. It was argued that the central government should be at an independent place and at the same site as that of a provincial government. Delhi's claim for the seat of Central Government was supported by the fact it had by that time a splendid communication being connected on all sides by railway network.

With regards to the climatic suitability, Delhi could boast of at least seven months of tolerable climate and also salubrity could be ensured at a reasonable cost. The Government of India could be able to stay in Delhi from the 1st of October to the 1st of May. Also, the sunset in Delhi, one hour after Calcutta, will allow one extra working hour in the evening, with the prospect of finalising issues calling for urgency.

As to the factors of industrial and commercial interest, though Delhi would become away from Calcutta, the industrial and commercial hub, none the less it would be closer to Bombay and Karachi, important centres of industry and commerce of western India. On the historical association of Delhi to be the capital of India much has been said earlier. However, even at the cost of repetition, it would be worth it to quote the letter of Lord Harding dated 25 August 1911. "Delhi is still a name to conjure with. It is intimately associated in the mind of Hindus with sacred legends which go back even beyond the dawn of history... The Purana Q̲ila still marks the site of the city they founded and called Indraprastha, barely three miles from the south gate of modern city of Delhi. To the Mahomedans it would be a source of unbounded gratification to see the ancient capital of the Mughals restored to the proud position as the seat of the Empire. Throughout India, as far as Mahomedan conquest had extended, every walled town has its 'Delhi Gate'. The change would strike the imagination of the people of India as nothing else could do and would send a wave of enthusiasm throughout the country, and would be accepted by all as the assertion of an unfaltering determination to maintain British rule in India. It would be hailed with joy by the ruling chiefs and the races of North India and would be welcomed warmly by the vast majority of Indians throughout the continent." Incidentally, a conclusion could be drawn that the Viceroy had admitted that Delhi had to be revered as the seat of former Empire, which would automatically imply that the British acknowledged that Bahadur Shah Zafar, whom they removed and sent in exile to Rangoon, had legitimate claim as a ruler.

To stamp their authority over the annexed territory of India, the first move that the British took was to reannex Delhi, deport Bahadur Shah Zafar and kill his descendants. It is not for nothing that Lord Lytton in association with Prime Minister Disraeli and Secretary of State for India Lord Salisbury chose the old, semi-dead city of tombs, dilapidated havelis, that was Delhi for the Imperial Assemblage in 1877 to proclaim Queen Victoria, as Empress of India and not the modern Europeanised capital city of Calcutta. They felt that Delhi, the age-old throne of the Mughals, would carry the halo that Indian subjects associated with the splendour of supreme power. Calcutta had nothing in comparison to offer. The geographical location of Delhi as capital had envisioned an immediate contact and direct control of varied types of Indian society. It was close to Punjab which was the meeting point of different creeds and races: Sikhs, Hindus and Mahomedans, each contributing to a virile and vibrant race. The United Province of Oudh and Agra was in close proximity as also the principalities of Rajputana, Central India and North West frontiers. Calcutta and Bombay were also equally accessible distance wise.

Another point was that there were very few Native states like Cooch Behar in and around Calcutta. Except for the border states of eastern India, other native states hardly had any political significance. On the other hand, the contacts with Rajput principalities, states of Maratha chief of Central India and Sikh chief of Punjab would be easier.

There were mixed reactions from different states and linguistic societies. The Beharis were enthusiastic at the coming formation of the new province. People of the United Province and Punjab warmly welcomed the scheme. The Rajputs were elated at the proximity of the would be seat of power.

So far Bengal was concerned, it was distinctly a bane and not a boon. The Bengalis, while welcoming the reunion of Bengal, felt badly let down with the new seat of capital with its accompanying power and glory gone.

They felt that they had lost more to Delhi than they could ever recover from Dacca. Muslims of eastern Bengal were also not amused as they felt deserted. It will be interesting to know the reaction from Calcutta including its large European residents, connected mainly with commerce and social activities of education, health, legal professions, scholars, researchers and others.

The announcement of December 12, 1911 was received in Calcutta with an incredulity which soon turned into indignation. The European community regarded this as unfair to Calcutta and mischievous to say the least, especially the secrecy which shrouded such a momentous change. They felt that it was an outright insult to the great city. Neither the Government of Bengal nor the Chamber of Commerce was consulted. The commercial class apprehended the shifting of the capital and associated it with the removal of all contacts with the Government leading to weakening of their clout. The government, henceforth, would be out of touch with public opinion, leading to a hegemony of a small coterie of officials. They felt that in the future, correspondence would only be the means of settling grievances and disputes between the Government and commercial interest, and questions which could be promptly disposed of in a personal interview will be protracted for months. Regarding public opinion, a letter to the English press from Welbore Grantham is worth mentioning. In verbatim the letter was as follows:

> *"There is one serious drawback to the alleged advantages secured by the change of the capital of India from Calcutta to Delhi which has not, I believe, received notice in any of the comments, which appeared in the press. That drawback is the withdrawal of the Supreme Government from the wholesome influence of a weighty European public opinion. The Government of India is a bureaucracy whose unceasing tendency is, like the tendency of all bureaucracies, to become more bureaucratic. In Calcutta, outside official circles but in constant association with officials, there is a large, instructed, intelligent European Community."*

Opinions on this issue were sharply divided among the key pillars of the Government. The most serious debate on this, took place in the House of Lords on 21 February, Wednesday 1912. Lord Curzon of Kedleston, who was the stormy Governor (Viceroy) General of India of the Partition of Bengal fame, took up the gauntlet on behalf of the critics against the change. In a scathing criticism against Lord Crewe, Lord Curzon stated in the House of Lords:

> *"It was on December 12 last that Lord Morley told us in this house of the new and far reaching step, which has been announced that morning at Delhi by the King and commended them to the consideration of this House. We were all taken by surprise. Lord Landsdowne and myself had only been similarly responsible for another ten years, I believe not one of us had been consulted or had the slightest inkling of what was going to be done.*

But I think it should be known that this step was taken on the initiative of a Viceroy — I speak of him with respect because he is a personal friend of mine — who had only been in India a few months, while a Secretary of State who had not long enjoyed his great position." (Reference here is to Lord Hardinge and Lord Crewe)

Lord Curzon, in the same castigated the Ministers in no uncertain terms….."All these steps had been decided in secret without consultation with those whom you ordinarily consult, without any intimation to representative bodies or persons, without any consultation of public opinion, behind the back of Parliament. Then there is the extreme secrecy and almost indecent haste of your procedure. Your policy was not referred to a single Local Government; not a single Lieutenant Governor was consulted. Even the Lieutenant Governor of the province concerned only learnt of it the night before it was announced at Delhi.

Finally Lord Curzon spelt out his opinion as to the real reasons for the change in these words… "They desire to escape the somewhat heated atmosphere of Bengal and to say goodbye to the Bengali friends for whom they have done so much. As to the future of Calcutta, I am not one of those who think that the removal from Calcutta will seriously and detrimentally affect it. The importance of Calcutta results from its position on the sea, from its proximity to the great source of supply of jute and coal and tea, from the enterprise of its merchants. I have little doubt that the mercantile community in Calcutta will bend their backs to win for their city as great and famous a place as it had in the past. Personally, I think the removal of the Government is much more injurious to the Government than it will be to Calcutta."

It is worthy to note here, the reaction of the Indian National Congress, which was under the dominance of Surendra Nath Banerjee, its President. He declared that the influence of Bengal in the Government of the country did not depend upon whether Calcutta was or was not the capital for three months, but upon the moral and intellectual character of the people of Bengal, which remained unaffected by the change.

For Lord Curzon, Delhi was the deserted city of dreary and disconsolate tombs. Continuing the criticism of the Government on its decision to shift the capital, there were further sarcastic remarks in the House of Lords. About Lord Hardinge's despatch in favour of the change, strongly supported by Lord Crewe, the Secretary of State, Lord Curzon in his sarcastic criticism on the eloquent passages about the historical association of Delhi derided the reason given by the Secretary about the older times of Hindu history and satisfying the historical sense of the million. Without denying the mythological glamour of Delhi, Curzon clearly stated that the modern Delhi was only 250 years old and the capital of Mughals in the expiring years of their regime. Obviously, he was stating that Delhi had come to be the capital after the shift from Agra and thus effectively, it was the capital for a period of little more than 100 years, i.e. from the reign of Shah Jahan. He however observed that earlier also, Delhi had been the capital but then all had perished one after another. Delhi was the capital of Prithviraj Chauhan, Qutubuddin Aibak, Razia Sultan, Alauddin Khilji, Mohammad bin-Tughlak, Feroz Shah Tughlak, the Sayyids and the Lodhis. He accordingly advised his Majesty's Government not to dwell too much on the dead capitals of the past and to look forward to creating a living capital for the future. On the point of the centralised location of Delhi compared to that of Calcutta, the opponents of the shift argued that while Delhi was more central to Bombay, it was at a greater distance from Burma, Madras and even from Mysore and Hyderabad, the two great royal Principalities. This apart, they questioned the healthiness of Delhi, its strategic position, and thirdly the access of the Government and the capital to public opinion.

It was indispensable that the capital should be in a place where naval superiority of Britain should be brought to play. Calcutta was ideally suited for such a situation. Another argument expressed against shifting at the House, was that Delhi as capital of the Government would become more isolated, more bureaucratic and less in touch with public opinion.

On the issue of business interest, Delhi stood nowhere in comparison to Calcutta. Delhi could not either be an industrial or manufacturing city, nor a distributing centre, since the trade of India must exist and be linked with the sea. On the point of isolation, a member said in the House,... "Your new city is to be placed outside the walls of a quite small nature town of 200,000 people and there the Government will live shut off, as I think, from the rest of India.

In the first place, it will diminish its prestige, in the second place, it will react upon the efficiency of the administration and in the third place it will shorten your rule in India". The cost of the change also dominated the discussion. The Government of India said: "The cost of transfer will be considerable, but we can not conceive that a larger sum than £ 4,000,000 will be necessary, including the three years interest on capital, while the works and buildings are being completed."

As against this must be set the rise in the value of Government land in Delhi, the sale of government land and building at Calcutta, and utilisation of Durban works at Delhi. I ask, is it conceivable that these can be completed in three years? I tell you they will not be done in ten years."

This was a prophecy which came to be more than true, as the future course of the economic situation demonstrated, with the onset of World War I being the biggest villain. The great war nearly put the completion of the new Indian capital at Delhi into jeopardy apart from enormously increasing the overall cost.

In August 1918, the press had highlighted the news of the shift of the capital which received serious opposition as the war was closing. Even as late as 1920, Delhi was by no means the unanimous choice for the site of British India's new capital, even though the construction work had already started in earnest. During the War, the buildings of the new capital, which were under various stages of construction, were taken over by the Delhi War conference, as decided earlier. Care was however taken to ensure that the material used in the construction of buildings still at temporary stage, will not be wasted, while buildings which were already under construction to meet permanent requirements could be utilised. Thus, there was constant effort to keep the expenditure in building the new capital under control.

Before dealing with the cost of construction of the new capital in detail, it would be worthwhile to examine, when and how, the opposition to Delhi as capital was resolved. It was only in February of 1920, the opposition to Delhi as the capital of India was brought to a head by a resolution moved in the Imperial Legislative Council, proposing that the Government of India should be situated in one place throughout the year. The resolution was rejected after protracted debate, so also, the recommendation to appoint a committee to select a suitable place for the capital. The argument advanced by the Government for a change was equally forceful. In the course of the debate, Mr. Curzon, representing the Bengal Chamber of commerce, castigated the Government on their estimates about the cost of the change of capital which was originally pegged at £ 4,000,000, whereas he claimed that more than £ 3,600,000 had already been spent, including improvement of Delhi city and the outlay on the temporary capital. The actual expenditure of New Delhi was over £ 2,300,000 or about 3 1/2 crore rupees. He held that the total cost would not be less than £ 6,600,000 or around 10 crores and above. He however, admitted that Calcutta had become too congested for the new capital. Places as diverse as Bombay, Karachi, Nasik, Ranchi, DehraDun, Poona, Allahabad, Panchmari and Jubbulpore were recommended by different speakers.

The stand of the Government was clear and categorical. Sir William Vincent, speaking on behalf of the Government, declared that the Government of India was a subordinate Government and unable to accept any resolution which would go against a matter already decided by the King Emperor. He further reminded that for eight years the council had not objected to the expenditure being carried out. He held that the advantages of Delhi had been underestimated. He also held that the summer capital at Shimla was in the interest of officials who are required to work at high pressure throughout the year. The aforesaid declaration of Sir William Vincent, drew its authority from the reply of Lord Crewe in the House of Lords in the year 1912.

Lord Crewe defended the secrecy shrouding the announcement about the transfer of capital stating that had the issue been placed in the parliament for necessary sanction, there would have been public discussion and it would not have been possible to announce the same at the Durbar held on 12 December 1911.

Furthermore, the partition of Bengal was treated by the Government of India and Secretary of State as an administrative action not requiring sanction of the Parliament. Lord Morley, dwelling upon the Final Constitutional Doctrine, held that the Indian system of government is a written constitution resting on statutes and instruments, warrants and the like which were as good as statutes. The ultimate responsibility for the Indian government rests, beyond all questions, with the Imperial Government represented by a Secretary of State, and in the last resort, therefore, through the Secretary of State by Parliament. The cabinet of the day, through a Secretary of State, has an indefeasible right, within limits laid down by law, to dictate policy, to initiate instructions, to reject proposals, to have the last word in every question that arises and the first word in every question they think they ought to arise.

In the ultimate analysis it had bypassed the Parliament, since the declaration of transfer, which was a package that the King had in mind, could not have been announced in the Durbar. The king's wish had ultimately prevailed.

Once again reverting to the criticism and controversy about the mounting cost for construction of the capital over the initial projection of estimate, it may be borne in mind that the escalating cost was the result of the great war and dwindling value of money. But then the opposition to the shifting of capital continued even as late as 1920. It would have carried on, unless Sir Edwin Lutyen, the main architect of modern Delhi, had not issued a clarification on certain vital financial aspects in a letter to Morning Post, London in December 1923. He observed that many statements were made which revealed a sad ignorance of fact and seemed inspired from a lively if somewhat malignant imagination. He stated that the statement, that up to now 20,000,000 pounds were spent on New Delhi, was not true. The expenditure up to March 31, 1923 was 841 lakhs (£ 5,600,000) and the total expenditure is estimated at 1300 lakhs (£ 8,600,000). This expenditure would establish the Government in the new capital. Rising expenditure due to the great war and falling exchange rates were the two factors contributing to the rising cost of building capital from the original sanctioned amount of Rs. 900 lakh to 1321 lakh, in September 1922.The central showpiece of the new capital is the Rashtrapati Bhavan known earlier as Viceroy's House. It stands in the midst of 330 acres. Its construction had absorbed 4 1/2 million bricks, nearly 1 1/2 million cubic feet of stone, 7500 tons of cement and 1350 tons of Iron and steel. It consists of 340 rooms, 1 1/2 miles of corridors, 227 columns, 37 fountains, 14 lifts and 300 telephones.

Before proceeding further, it is worthwhile to have a look at the time and the people who transformed the eastern ridges spanning out to river Jamuna into a spiralling city of New Delhi. It was the village of Malcha outside the city of Shahjahanabad, in the midst of Raisina Hills, where the new city was conceived. Shahjahanabad was the last of 'seven cities' that preceded Delhi. The earlier cities were — Lalkot, Siri, Tughlakabad, Jahanpanah, Firozshah Kotla and Purana Qila that stood on the same ground as the ancient legendary city of Indraprastha. Shahjahanabad was indeed a city of unparalleled beauty with skilled craftsmanship and majestic buildings.

Its central showpiece was the magnificent 'Red Fort' perched on the banks of river 'Yamuna', a sister of the mighty Ganga. The 'Red Fort', with Divan-e-Khas, the hall of private audience, boasted of its association with world famous ornate 'Peacock Throne'. This was a city with secular landscapes and cultural excellences; its social fabric was a blended mixture of diverse culture where its poetry and music, its myriad trade and profession, its respect for diverse faiths and above all its respect for deep rooted human values made it a resilient, dynamic, vibrant cultural city, till the uprising of 1857 took away much of the shine of the city.

In this background, the search for the creation of a new location to make it the seat of the British empire, was really a mind-boggling exercise. The consensus was that the new city should be such that it could stand up to the monumental city that the Mughal Emperor Shah Jahan had built on the banks of the Yamuna.

The Government had an extremely tough job to locate a place for the new capital. The first choice, obviously, was around the place where Durbar was held in 1911. But then the search for the location upon which the foundation stone was to be laid, was to be conducted with diligence, uninterrupted by energetic discussions and debates. Before the final plan for Delhi was approved, Henry Vaughan Lancaster, an important architect of his time, presented five schemes to the then Viceroy Lord Hardinge. The main theme of Lancaster's scheme was that there should be a link with Shahjahanabad which in turn would allow integration of the inhabitants of Delhi with the new city, which will be political and administrative in nature, being the new capital. He wanted to maintain the intrinsic character and soul of the old city. He did not want to impose a cold, sterile seat of a foreign administrative power superimposed alongside a virile tactile living Delhi.

To create a tract of land from the Yamuna at the foot of the coronation site to Jama Masjid, was beset with logistic problems. This would have covered a largely populous area which had to be uprooted at an enormous cost of human relocation, and was in itself an ill-conceived proposal and hence not accepted.

The proposal for having the city on the reclaimed marshy land along the banks of the river Yamuna, after converting a part of the Yamuna into a big lake along with embankment, was also rejected as impractical. The suggestion to locate the site on the ridge which was a forested undulating tract that lay between Lodhi and Safdarjung tomb on one side and Shahjahanabad and river on the other, was rejected by Lord Hardinge who found it hostile and inhospitable. King Emperor George V and Queen

Mary held that the site for the coronation, which was in close proximity to the Civil Lines and other British establishments, could well be the site for a new capital.

The King and the Queen, themselves freed the architects and the planner from their preference for the Durbar site, and instead opted for the Ridge where British troops had enforced their authority over the last Mughals during the 1857 uprising. The final choice was Raisina Hill and the direction of the main avenue faced the Purana Qila and Delhi Darwaza. Thus, the location was disconnected from the existing capital of the Mughal empire. Raisina Hill was considered as the control point of the capital.

Sir John Jenkins, home member of the Viceroy Council was entrusted with the job of searching out a suitable architect. Of the various names which came into consideration, the front runners were Henry Vanghan Lanchester and Edwin Landseer Lutyens, the decision of final selection being left to Lord Crewe, the Secretary of State, London. The choice fell on Edwin Lutyens, who was brought in as the primary architect for building of the imperial capital. Herbert Baker, a friend and colleague of Lutyens, came to be associated with Lutyens. Lutyens was the architect of elite residences of Lords and County manors and Sir Herbert Baker, designed government buildings in South Africa, before they joined hands for building the new capital of India.

Sir Herbert Baker, the chief architect dwelling upon the selection of site for the new capital wrote: "The largest mass of rock on Raisina Hill was chosen as the focus of the city and its central buildings. In the winter of 1913, the writer (Baker) was sitting with the present Prime Minister on this rock and wondering how a beautiful city could arise from what Lord Curzon described as the 'deserted cities of dreary and disconsolate tombs', when the sun, setting beneath the rain clouds, formed a full rainbow, arching the destined central vista. The good omen then acclaimed has been triumphantly fulfilled.... The last of Sikh Gurus who lay buried here, when condemned to death by the emperor Aurangzeb went to it with a prophecy on his lips that a great white race would come from the west to destroy the Empire of his executioner.

Delhi came to be so deeply associated with Lutyens that it had come to be known as `Lutyens Delhi' in common parlance. Apart from chief architect Lutyens,.and Baker, there were Walter George, Robert Russel and Sir John Marshall, who also belonged to the larger team of architects. This team also had Delhi Town Planning Committee members namely John A Brodie and George S.C. Swinton, and also Sir Alexander Rouse, who was the Chief Engineer of the Public Works Department.

The plan of the new imperial capital was finalised by the Delhi Town Planning Committee in March 1913. It also made blueprints for the layout of the city showing arterial road networks and avenues over a terrain map of the ancient city. The most prominent among them was the Imperial Avenue, Kingsway (now Rajpath) which faces the Purana Qila. In the whole scheme of things, Purana Qila or Indraprastha the legendary first capital of Delhi occupied a prominent place.

While the architects were entrusted with the job of designing the new capital, the final execution of the architects' design into reality fell on Indian contractors. As the actual execution reached its starting point, as Lutyens communicated to his wife Emily (daughter of Lord Lytton, the first Viceroy of India), people of all sorts flocked to where architects were staying with a hope to view or catch any one of them. While architects and marble merchants sought to meet him, engineers and plumbers headed for Brodie, member of the Town Planning Committee.

Among the people seeking their attention were hordes of rich and industrious Sikh contractors, who had flourishing business in west Punjab (now Pakistan). Among them was the father-son duo Sujan Singh and Sobha Singh, who were to become household names as contractors of modern Delhi. They managed to get a contract for levelling of the Delhi Durbar land in 1911, and from there, they never looked back. Sobha Singh (knighted as Sir Sobha Singh) went on to construct some of the most prestigious and prominent buildings. The most important were South Block and the War Memorial at Kingsway or Rajpath). He also built the front court of the Government House, a major portion of Connaught Place, Regal Buildings, Baroda House, Scindia House to name the major ones.

The other Indian to be knighted for competence and professionalism was an engineer with the Public Works Department, Jeja Singh Malik, who worked with Sir Alexander Rouse. Among others, the prominent one was Baisakha Singh, contractor for North Block. Narain Singh was the main contractor for laying most of the roads for Coronation Durbar. Dharam Singh won the contract for the supply of marble and Dholpur, Agra stones for building the Government House and Secretariats.

Seth Haroun-al-Rashid of Karachi was the main contractor for the Government House (Rashtrapati Bhawan). Another prominent contractor was Seth Lachhman Das, known for his impeccable honesty and principles; he was entrusted with the work of the Council House i.e. the Parliament House. Akbar Ali, a Punjabi Muslim, built the National Archives. The famous Mughal Garden at Government House, was the creation of Nawab Ali (not related to Akbar Ali). It is worth appreciating the untiring efforts put up by these people for hiring labour from neighbouring states and supervising their work tirelessly at the building sites. Sir Sobha Singh, also built the huge complex, 'Sujan Singh Park', named after his father, which was designed by an Englishman, Walter George. It is a unique conglomeration of seven apartment blocks on a sprawling garden quadrangle with high ceilings, spacious rooms and verandahs, unique in itself. Much of the Prithviraj Road constructions were created by Baishakha Singh. The Imperial Hotel was built by Narain Singh. This hotel had a chequered history, during the time of independence and the transfer of power.One of the fascinating structures that dotted New Delhi's skyline was the All India War Memorial and the statue of King George V. The Memorial arch was built by Sir Sobha Singh and completed in 1931. This was dedicated to the thousands of Indian and British soldiers who showed unflinching loyalty to the crown during the First World War and third Afghan War 1919 and North West Frontier Province, as described by the Duke of Connaught and later Lord Irwin who formally inaugurated it. 500 feet away from the memorial, Lutyens designed a memorial for King George V who died in 1936, after holding the reins of emerging New India with the new capital for twenty five eventful years.

The mention of New Delhi will be incomplete without a reference to Connaught Place. With Nicholls, the Delhi Committee's architect envisioned the need for a circular arcade as part of the aristocratic business district for the British rulers and their families, the Indian nobility and administrators and wealthy Indians. After Nicholls, it was only in 1928, that the chief architect to the Government of India R.T. Russel arranged for the beautiful, colonnaded circular arcade, the 'Connaught Circus', the shopping centre.

The Eastern and Western Courts which were to serve as hostel for Legislators was designed and built by R.T. Russel in 1932. It was much against the wishes of Lutyens as it blocked the view of Purana Qila from Rajpath, the stadium originally known as Irwin Amphitheatre, that was designed by Anthony S Demello and built in 1933. The unique feature of the courts was that they were built on a platform one floor tall, with two colonnaded floors with arches at different points.

Russel also built the National Stadium where the first Asian Games were held in 1952. It is at the extreme end of Rajpath, earlier known as Kingsway. Incidentally, it blocked the direct view of Purana Qila from Vijay Chowk where 'Beating Retreat' parade is held now. Gole Market, the octagonal market was architectured by Lutyens in 1921, mainly to cater the needs of government servants. The architect and visionary of modem Delhi after the transfer of capital had envisaged and hoped that the Maharajas of states around Delhi would queue up for acquiring places and palaces of their own in the proximity of supreme power. The hope was not belied as by 1913, many Maharajas had applied for substantial plots to build their palaces. Among these palaces, those of Maharaja of Jaipur, the Nizam of Hyderabad (said to be the richest in the world), rulers of Bikaner, Baroda and Patiala were granted large tracts of freehold land to build their palaces.

Lutyens himself was commissioned by the seventh Nizam to build the Hyderabad House. It was the most gorgeous, yet beautiful building which bore the stamp of Lutyens' genius. With its archways, obelisks, jaali work, grand stairways, fountains and chandeliers, patterned floor and marble fireplaces, it was next only to the Government House in design and decoration. It is now the official banquet hall of the Government of India for visiting dignitaries.

The Gole Dak Khana, amidst busy traffic, was designed by R.T. Russel of PWD and built in 1931. Lady Hardinge college had the distinction of being the first women's medical college. Built at the initiative of Lady Hardinge, the college was started in 1916, with 16 students enrolled for a seven year course. Dr. Kate Plate, was the first Principal. The college was affiliated to Delhi University in 1950 and its post graduate course started in 1954.

Lok Nayak Jai Prakash Narayan Hospital, known earlier as Irwin Hospital, started in 1936, with 350 beds. Its foundation stone was laid by Lord Irwin in 1930, and it became operational in 1936, under Lt Col Cruickshank. It was the largest hospital in north India in 1950 and also the venue of Maulana Azad Medical College in 1957. In November 1977, it became Lok Nayak Jai Prakash Narayan Hospital. The oldest club of Delhi is Delhi Gymkhana club, which was started in July 1913 at the coronation ground. It came to its new abode after Lutyens designed it. It was built in 1928, on 27 acres of land. Its first President was Sir Harcourt Butler, the then Governor of the United Province of Oudh. Agra 'Imperial' was dropped in 1947.

The oldest hotel in New Delhi was 'The Imperial Hotel', built in 1934, the architect being F.B. Blomfield. Inaugurated by Lord Willingdon in 1936, it started running under Ranjit Singh, son of Narain Singh, a leading contractor of Delhi. It had the flavour of a 19th century English manor, and was known for its collection of art. The other most important hotel was Hotel Ambassador, which was built in 1945. Its designer was British architect Walter Syker George, a close associate of both Lutyens and Baker. Incidentally Hotel Marina, in Connaught Place was a contemporary hotel.

Two of the best known Churches, the Cathedral Church of Redemption was built in 1931, the architect being H.A.N. Medd. He had been selected for the job after a close competition of design under the presidentship of Edward Lutyens. The second most well known Church was Sacred Heart Cathedral, which also houses Jesus Mary School and Saint Columbus

School of Irish Christian Brothers. It took five years to complete; from 1930 to 1935. Its architect was again H.A.N. Medd.

The New Delhi Railway Station was started in 1926, with a single platform near Ajmeri Gate. It was in 1927–28, the New Delhi Railway Station came into being, with the State Entry Road for the viceroy and royals, which still retains its old world glory.

Viceregal Lodge, the Circuit House, was yet another landmark building, which was the residence of Lord Hardinge, when he shifted from Calcutta. Subsequently, five viceroys made it their abode and it was the seat of authority from 1912 to 1929. Now it is part of Delhi University. Delhi University was established in 1922 with three colleges, St. Stephens College, Hindu College and Ramjas College. The first English daily, The Hindustan Times, was launched in 1924.

The next palace, the `Baroda House' was truly like a British royal house with American plumbing, Anglo-Saxon furnishing and when started, it had a conglomerate of the best French cooks, English valets and maids and table linen woven in Belfast. The palace now houses Northern Railway Head Office with all its grandeur destroyed.

Similar is the case with the palace of the Maharaja of Patiala, now reduced to a judicial court. The palace of the Maharaja of Jaipur retains its pristine glory as the Museum of Modern Art. Bikaner House has become the official establishment of the Rajasthan Government.

During the annual events of meeting of the Chamber of Princes, occasioned by garden parties, polo competitions, and balls where the most opulent Indians flaunted their wealth to attract their attention, two hotels namely Maidens and Cecil Hotel were most prominent as they used to house princes without permanent palaces in Delhi.

R.T. Russels designed the bungalows of the top executives of the Government, as well as other gazetted officers. The most prominent religious place for Christians, namely the Roman Catholic Cathedral of the Sacred Heart was built by H.A.N. Medd in 1934.

The Central Secretariats, the seat of Administration was inaugurated on 10th February 1931 by the Viceroy amidst great fanfare and gaiety. The project cost was Rs. 1,53,91,000 raised and revised from an earlier estimate of Rs. 1,24,00,000 as a result of the First Great War and falling value of rupees.

The designing of the Legislative Building i.e. the Council House (Parliament buildings) witnessed a fierce exchange between Lutyens and Baker. For both of them, winning the architectural consent was a matter of immense prestige. While Baker rooted for a triangular building plan with the three angles being replaced by semi circular design, Lutyens opted for a complete circular design. Finally, Lutyens' view prevailed. The Duke of Connaught laid the foundation stone of the Council House (Parliament House) on 13th February 1921. The Council House (Parliament House) was inaugurated on 18 January 1927 by the Viceroy Lord Irwin.

New Delhi as the capital of India was formally inaugurated on 10 February 1931. Lord Irwin was the Viceroy.

Indian House of Parliament was the most important building as it represented the rapidity and extent of constitutional progress of British India. The Duke of Connaught delivered a stirring speech at the laying of the foundation stone of the Legislative House —

"These buildings will not only be the home of the next representative institutions which mark the vast stride forward in the political development of India and the British empire, but will, I trust, stand for future generations as a symbol of India's rebirth to yet higher destinies".

All great rulers, every great people and every great civilization have left their own record in stone, bronze, or marble, as well as in the pages of history and I need only recall the Acropolis of Athens, the capital of Rome and the great cities of the East which were famous in their past ages for their splendour and culture. India herself is rich in such precious legacies, from the granite pillars on which Emperor Asoka engraved his imperishable edicts to the chequered centuries down to the splendid palaces and forts of the Mughal Emperors. Every age has left behind it some monument commensurate with its own achievements. Is it not a worthy ideal that equally noble buildings shall consecrate India's great achievements in the 20th century and her solemn entry upon the path of responsible government which Great Britain and the self governing dominions of the Empire have trod before her.

My earnest hope (the Duke concluded) is that New Delhi may not only become a capital worthy of the future greatness of India, but also one of the great national capitals which will link the peoples of the Empire together in enduring peace and prosperity under the aegis of the British Crown".

While the tone of the speech of the Duke was a call for a subservient India, or even as a dominion, it was observed that the tenure and mood had undergone a complete transformation. The importance of the occasion was emphasised in the message from the king and the speech of the Viceroy, both characterised by a sympathy for India's constitutional aspirations, as also the acceptance of the new building as a symbol of sincerity of the British Empire towards them.

In the actual ceremony, two Guards of Honour were presented to the Viceroy and Lady Irwin. One Guard of Honour was presented by the 2nd Battalion of the Royal Warwickshire Regiment and the second was the 2nd Battalion of the 2nd Punjab Regiment.

The attendants for this spectacle was about 2000 guests, meticulously attired English men and ladies, who merged with the gorgeously bejewelled Indian ruling princes and their spouses. Noticeably among the large body of Indian Legislatives who thronged on the left of the throne was a white clad Pandit Motilal Nehru along with other swarajists. The Viceroy and Lady Irwin, as they entered the Royal Pavilion, were received by an Indian member of the Viceregal council, Sir Bhupendra Nath Mitra connected with the Building department, who paid handsome tribute to the geniuses of the architecture: Sir Edward Lutyens, the principal architect of the city, Sir Herbert Baker, the architect of the Council House and Mr. Rouse, chief engineer of the Public Works Department. The Maharaja of Patiala, as the Chancellor of the Princes, received the Viceroys.

There were murmurs of appreciation for the excellence of the buildings and its architect Sir Baker, which included the frank appreciation of Indian nationalists and swarajists. The greatest showpiece of the monarchy's sympathy for India's aspirations and their express desire for political understanding, itself was instrumental in mounting the battle for India's constitutional aspirations, which finally sealed the fate of the

British Empire in just sixteen years, when the sun of the mighty Empire sank into oblivion.

It is worthwhile to dwell a little on the architecture of the capital city of Delhi which stands proudly in the comity of capitals of this and mighty countries of the world.

Lord Curzon, the last viceroy with Calcutta as capital, whose preference for Calcutta knew no heights, agreed with his successor Lord Hardinge, the first Viceroy in Delhi, the new capital, for turning Delhi into an architectural marvel, so as to make it a real jewel on the crown of the British Monarch, not only surpassing Calcutta, the erstwhile capital of British Raj for a long hundred fifty years, but also to take on the capitals of the important countries in the world including USA and Canada, in architectural beauty.

Most of the modern capital cities (obvious exceptions are Paris, Rome, Cairo, etc.) came up in places which were not a continuation of the old city/ capital. Contrary to this, Delhi as a capital had to reckon with its chequered past, starting from the prehistoric capital of the Pandavas, an ancient Aryan race, who fought the battle with Kauravas, their close relatives, at the battle of Kurukshetra, a battle immortalised in the epic 'Mahabharata' from where the most holy scripture of the Hindus, the 'Bhagavad Gita' emanated. The present day Qutub Minar Complex which dots Delhi's skyline, dates back to the era of Gupta Dynasty (350 BCE to 315 BCE), a dynasty of Hindu emperors.

Anang Pal of the Tomar Dynasty built the Lal Kot or Red Fort (not to be confused with the present Red Fort) in the Mehrauli area of Dhillika sometime in the 11th Century. The great Chauhan King, Prithvi Raj Chauhan (1178–1192) while constructing the Qila Rai Pithora in the 12th Century incorporated the area of Lal Kot. Though his capital city was Ajaymeru (present day Ajmer), Prithvi Raj Chauhan ruled from the Qila Rai Pithora till he was defeated by Mahmud Ghori. This part of Delhi then saw a successive rule of Turks and Pathans till the arrival of Timur Lang (1370–1405), a marauding chieftain of wild Persia (Central Asia) who continued plundering and destroying Delhi and its inhabitants at the point of sword. Then came the crucial day of April 21, 1526 when a descendant of Timur, Babar swooped down with an army of horsemen and defeated Ibrahim Lodhi at the battlefield of Panipat, a sleepy hamlet north of Delhi about 50 miles away.

Coming back to the Qutub Minar Complex, Qutub Minar was built by Qutub-ud-din Aibak, the slave general of Mahmud Ghori, in 1193 as a Victory tower celebrating the victory of Mahmud Ghori over Prithvi Raj Chauhan in 1192. Qutub-ud-din's son-in-law Shamsuddin Iltutmish continued the construction which was finally completed 1230. The 73 meter tower was named after Qutbuddin Bakhtiar Kaki (1173–1235) a Muslim Sufi mystic. The Minar was damaged by lightning in 1368. It was again repaired in 1503 by Feroze Shah Tughlaq (1351–1388) when it was damaged by lightning a second time. In the centre of the complex stands an iron pillar 7.2 metres in height, defying all principles of corrosion and thus a subject matter of great interest even to the present day metallurgists. From the inscription on the pillar it seems that this one was built by one King Chandra, a name that generally refers to Chandragupta II of Gupta dynasty. It is not certain when the pillar was moved to Delhi from its original location, Udayagiri in present Madhya Pradesh.

Till this time there was no edifice of the rulers worth the name in Delhi except the tombs with sprawling gardens built by the Lodi Kings. The first monument to attract attention is the Humayun's tomb with its marbled dome raised on a high pedestal

Neither Babar, nor his great grandson Akbar had built any building worth noting in Delhi. Babar's son Humayan was defeated by the Afghans after the premature death of Babar. It was a young Akbar who faced the challenge of the Afghans just 30 years after Babar had defeated the Afghans at the first battle of Panipat. Akbar, still young, won the second battle of Panipat to enter Delhi as king. However, neither Babar nor Akbar, made Delhi, their capital and preferred Agra as the seat of their capital. So far as Delhi was concerned makers of modern capital had nothing particular to fall back.

The Hindu architectural monuments were a combination of exquisitely ornamental works including carvings but were dimensionally small to be used as a model for the modern Indian capital. The Afghan or Mughal edifices, which were mostly tombs with high domes on raised platforms, in the midst of sprawling gardens, could hardly be conceived as a model for a modern capital. After Jehangir, his son Shah Jahan built Delhi with its massive fort of Red Sandstone with a huge raised line of walls guarding the fort which housed the seat of administration and also served as a residence. The fort city was completed by Aurangzeb, who confined his father, Shah Jahan, within the walls of the Agra Fort, overlooking the Taj Mahal, the acquisitively wonderful mausoleum, a poetry on marble, built by him to commemorate his wife Mumtaz Mahal.

Aurangzeb had a turbulent period of reign. His huge Mughal Empire had started to show signs of disintegration, misery and gloom even by the end of his reign. Nadir Shah, the marauding Persian ruler taking advantage of the chaotic and turbulent conditions in Delhi, swooped down on the capital and the fort and decamped with the legendary Peacock Throne among others. The looted booty was said to be 32 million rupees. After Nadir Shah, another scourge over Delhi descended in the form of the invader, Ahmed Shah Abdali who invaded Delhi six times in the course of fourteen years.

The great confederacy of the Marathas thrived around this time with its base in Poona. The Marathas after repeated forays into Delhi and adjoining areas, challenged the Afghan invader from the North, at the third battle of Panipat, where the Marathas faced a crushing defeat, ending thereby their elusive dream of conquering Delhi. It also ensured a quick subjugation of the Maratha chieftains by the British, including that of the legendary state of Jhansi, with its brave queen Lakshmibai, who fought the might of British tooth and nail.

Shah Alam II who was the ruler of Delhi at the time of the third battle of Panipat, fled to Allahabad, which was already under the dominance of the East India company. After staying there for some years, Shah Alam returned to Delhi, only to be captured by the Rohilla Chieftain, Ghulam Kadir who blinded him at the Durbar Hall of Delhi's Red Fort.

While all the upheavals were going on around the capital city of Delhi, the white race from the West started making slow inroads into India. It started with Portuguese trade inroads into the west coast of India.

The Portuguese were the first to open up the sea route to India in the sixteenth century, Dutch, Danes, Spanish, French and finally the British followed suit. The British trade forays, well organised, under the stewardship of London based East India Company started making firm strides. During the reign of Farrukhsiyar, a Farman was granted in 1717 to East India Company allowing duty free trading rights in Bengal, confirming their foothold in Bengal. During the period 1717–1757 the Company grew in such military strength that under the command of Robert Clive, they defeated the Nawab of Bengal, Siraj-ud-Daullah, at the battle of Plassey near Murshidabad in June 1757, thereby bringing Bengal under company's military and administrative jurisdiction. Around this time Shah Alam II was in reign in Delhi, but the sun was slowly setting over the Mughal Empire. Shah Alam II, whose reign from 1759 to 1806 saw the invasion of Ahmad Shah Abdali, also defeated the mighty Marathas in 1761, in the third Battle of Panipat, as stated earlier.

Akbar Shah II remained a titular figurehead under British protection during 1806–1837. The last Mughal Emperor Bahadur Shah Zafar ruled from 1837 to 1857, when he lost to the British at the height of Sepoy Mutiny, only to be exiled to Rangoon, Burma, where he breathed his last. The calculative journey of the British which started during the reign of Jahangir (1605 to 1627) when Sir Thomas Roe came to the darbar of Emperor Jahangir, and slowly and steadily, captured a prominent position there, culminated in complete control over North India. Incidentally, the British had already annexed the kingdom of Mysore in the South in 1801, with victory over Tipu Sultan. Though there was comparative calm in Delhi after 1761 till 1857, there was hardly any architectural activity of creation of edifices with structural excellence during this period. When the British annexed Delhi in 1857, it was a desolate city of dreary and decaying ruins, with the exception of the massive Red Fort of Shah Jahan. There were stray edifices, mostly mausoleums and gardens. Thus, Delhi did not have much to offer as an architectural model for the proposed capital whose shifting from Calcutta was on the anvil.

The King's decree to build a new capital of India at Delhi brought into reckoning the question of style and architectural design to be followed.

Ideally, the architecture would be a blend of the east and the west and ought to have a stamp of Imperialism showcasing the might of the British Empire. However, the Western architectural style that had emerged in England as a synthesis of Roman arts and Gothic style, could hardly be planted in India, considering that India had a wide divergence of climate, race and culture compared to England and Europe in general.

Herbert Baker, the architect of South African fame and a lifetime friend of Lutyens, who along with Lutyens was commissioned to undertake the building of New Delhi architecturally, believed that the architecture of the new Indian capital should essentially incorporate the best of the Indian style and designs. However, being the centre of administration of British India, it should also categorically reflect the spirit of British sovereignty which must be reflected in the stones.

Baker had also held in his brilliant article on aesthetic and architectural paradigms, the historical significance of style in building the new capital. The article appeared in The Times, London, dated 3rd October 1912.

Baker had observed: "The new capital must be the sculptural monument of the good government and unity which India, for the first time in its history, has enjoyed under British rule. British rule in India is not a mere veneer of government and culture. It is a new civilization in growth, a blend of the best elements of East and West. The effect of this will remain should British sovereignty ever depart from the shores of India. In the words of Lord Curzon, "Our work is righteous and it shall endure. The architecture of Delhi should bear that testimony. Everybody who was associated in conceptualising an architectural paradigm for the new capital agreed that there should be a blending of Indian architectural design with that of modem day requirement along with a stamp of Imperial sovereign authority. But the difficulty that the architect for the new capital faced was to find a truly Indian style, the constructive and geometrical qualities necessary to buildings that had to be raised to accommodate the spirit of synthesis. It was obvious that the Indian style can neither be predominantly Hindu or Mughal nor predominantly English.

The difficulty was furthermore aggravated because true models of Hindu building style with all its paraphernalia was not available, since with the advent of Muslim power and repeated invasions of India from the early period of the eleventh century, there had been ruthless demolition of notable Hindu structures, be it temples or palaces, as part of the Holy war of the Muslims against whom they considered as infidels. What was available at hand was Mughal or Indo-Saracenic architecture which abounded in Delhi and its neighbourhood. This architecture consisted of Arabian art with Persian, Indian and even Chinese influences. Then it was imperative that the impression of the art and style of the imperial conquerors had to be put on the Indo-Saracenic style.

The Indian architecture could be found expressed in rural palaces, temples and tombs. None of these were kindred enough to the architectural problems that the new capital faced. Artistic and architectural design of the Hindus found its manifestation in these intricate ornamental works. However, large constructive works were not available for the reason stated earlier.

The Turks and Pathans who followed them built giant edifices namely fortresses, mosques and tombs whose architectural designs could hardly be emulated in designing a modern seat of government. Moghuls who followed them were more artistic in designs. They built tombs with beautiful gardens enclosing them with lofty portals, beautiful fountains and pathways. In respect of their seat of government and residential quarters, they made massive and magnificent gateways with mighty protective walls inside which would be dwelling units with courts, pavilions and towers with carefully manicured garden and garden paths. In spite of all their beauty, as an architectural piece, it could not be found suitable for modern capital.

The British were very clear that the new city should bear an imperial stamp and authority signifying the conquest of India, and not merely a city for administrative manoeuvre. They wanted to showcase the legacy of the Roman Empire that brought western civilisation to its pinnacle.

While the architect Baker rooted only for an imperial scheme of architecture, Lutyens held a rather different view. Lutyens had a soft corner for Indian architecture and visualised the grand new palace set in an ancient and multi-layered city, though he was still not familiar with the cultural patterns and landscapes of the Indian subcontinent. Though not appreciating Indian architecture, which according to him veneered jointly in stone concrete and marble on gigantic scale without any architectural finery, Lutyens incorporated various Indian elements and motifs which attracted his attention as he was travelling through different places. He was greatly impressed by various historic relics and ornamental works and motifs like the ones of earlier Hindu age of Asoka, the great, who built stone railings of height 7 to 8 feet to protect the Buddhist shrines. But the most fascinating of all to attract Lutyens attention was the Stupa of Sanchi, the dome structure of which found expression as architectural beauty in various buildings including the Viceroy Palace (Rashtrapati Bhawan). The famous Asoka pillar, 'Chhatris' and 'Chajjas' abounded in buildings of monumental importance. The eternal symbols of Hindu's religious belief found expression in his use of concentric circles representing interpretations of cultural beliefs, the crescent moon, the temple bells, the elephant heads, snake fountains and the like. Intricate 'Jali' works to embellish windows, long arched corridors with painted ceilings forming colourful canopies, the lions guarding the grand stairways and spewing water from their mouth were some of the Indian ornamental designs to embellish architectural beauties. Lutyen was greatly fascinated by Mughal architecture of well conceived formal gardens that beautified and added richness to massive stone buildings. Even he was appreciative of 'vaastu' in buildings, a belief that the frontage should be smaller in width compared to the back like a cow head and not lion-shaped where the frontage is dimensionally larger than the back.

Lutyens evolved the city of Delhi with interspersing of gardens, broad circular avenues with massive trees like neem, jamuns, gulmohar, jacaranda lined along the wide roads. The thick bushes that donned the boundaries of the bungalow were hedged to prevent dust, hot wind and noise pollution. Another interesting feature that Lutyens conceived related to the roads and avenues was that, instead of roads running parallel to each other and cutting one another at right angles the roads were radically designed, joining at a circular avenue. This dispersal of roads was designed to reduce the effect of the hot dusty summer wind, known as 'Loo'.

Another trait of Lutyens' ingenuity relates to his fascination for decorating the city with gardens and trees. In his hand Delhi truly became a city of gardens and trees. His abiding passion for gardens and his instinctive skill regarding the placement of the trees and bushes, hedges and creepers within an open space radiating beauty, colour and shade created the Mughal gardens of the Government House (Rashtrapati Bhavan). Lutyens was full of appreciation for Mustre, the head of the Horticulture Department, who in a span of a year turned the huge mass of debris and desert into a blooming garden of roses. The garden, which complimented and enhanced the grandeur of the structure of the Government House, consisted of water bodies, water channels, low level fountains spraying gentle spring of water, deftly woven colours and shades of flower, fragrance of roses and colourful fountains creating artificial rainbows, which made the garden a real paradise.

The beautiful structure, one of the most picturesque residences in the world as abode of the head of state, was formally completed on 23rd December 1929, when Lord and Lady Irwin entered the house. Lutyens poignantly wrote to his wife: "At a given signal, the doors were opened - no key as there was no lock - and they, Lady Irwin and he went into the house and we left them alone and for the first time in 17 years the house closed on me. The Mountbattens were the last British family to live in this palace before it passed on to C. Rajagopalachari, India's first Indian Governor General.

Lutyens died in 1944 and Baker, his friend and co-author of New Delhi, in 1946. Lutyens was buried in St. Paul's Cathedral, while Baker's tomb is in Westminster Abbey.

* * *

Essay 3

Famines in Bengal and the Role of the British Government in India

The traumatic travails which the state of Bengal had to suffer due to the outbreak of famines over the past century is too pathetic and heart-wrenching to recollect. It is an abject chronology of human failure before the wrath of the almighty.

Bengal had always been the land of milk and honey through the bounty of nature, which had left Bengal with insured and abundant rainfall, the lifeline of agriculture. Occasionally however, rainfall played truant, rendering the good earth dry and desolate. And such occasions have recurred throughout history, with pitiful results. It was during these frequent occurrences of famine, caused by the failure of seasonal rains, that the sufferings of the poor peasants knew no bounds. This was accentuated by the failure of the governments to make any systematic and sustained efforts to provide relief to the affected areas and people. Whatever little they did was not sufficient to alleviate the acute miseries of the people who died of starvation and the disease and pestilence that closely followed it.

Bengal witnessed the worst famines in human history during the 1940's. One and half million people died in the interior districts of Bengal, both in rural and urban habitats and many more in the streets of Calcutta, the Metropolis. This was the time when the World War II was in full swing in the battlefields of Europe in the South Eastern part of Asia which included the vast tracts of the Malay Peninsula including Singapore, the whole of the Indian archipelago of Indo-China with the battlefield of Pearl Harbour where the Japanese and the Axis powers were pitted against the

Allied powers. Dwight D. Eisenhower, the US President, Sir Winston Churchill, the British Prime Minister and Charles de Gaulle, the French Supremo were in the forefront.

As World War II was at its devastating height, the province of Bengal was witnessing the most dreadful famine of 1943, a famine not seen in hundred years of history. The horrible Bengal famine of 1943 brought untold miseries for the people of the province. It was undoubtedly a direct result of the war conditions but it was also heightened by the 'carelessness and complete lack of foresight of those in authority'.

Throughout history, there have been many instances when famine has struck various parts of India. There is a record of a terrible famine that had broken out in 1556–1557 around Agra where the condition turned so bad that men ate their own kind, the whole country was converted into a desert and no man remained alive to till the land. Again, famine and pestilence struck Gujarat in 1573–1574, when the inhabitants both the rich and poor, fled from the land. The country was again affected by another severe famine lasting from 1594–1598, where it was said that the streets and roads were blocked with dead bodies and no one was left to help with their removal. In 1630–1632, another equally horrible famine occurred in the region of the Deccan and Gujarat. There are records of the extreme horrors of this famine where it is said that the shortage of food became so acute men began to attack and devour each other. All efforts made by the then Mughal administration were insufficient in the face of such acute calamity.

Coming back to Bengal, one of the earliest times when famine struck the state of Bengal was in the 1740's, which was the direct outcome of the Borgi invasion of Bengal (Maratha invasion). More than 400,000 people were killed. Local shortages greatly increased food prices. The severe food shortages and consequential price rise contributed to famine conditions. Conditions worsened till 1752 when the monsoons failed, and the famine came. This was the great famine of 1752 which wrought havoc upon the province, with the price of rice soring 6 times its previous level. Multitudes of death and dying and thousands of walking skeletons covered the streets of Calcutta. This famine was mostly restricted to the traditionally poor districts of the western part of Bengal. The recurring losses and the exactions by the invaders completely crippled the landed proprietors and the tillers. This famine specially inflicted heavy damage to the rich and the highly productive areas of Western Bengal.

Again In 1761, just a few years after the fateful Battle of Plassey of 1757, there was a great scarcity of grain around Calcutta leading to very high prices. The next severe attack of famine which Bengal witnessed was in the year 1769–70, when there had been a failure of rains spread over two consecutive years. In 1768 and 1769, rains failed over most parts of Bihar and Bengal, and by 1770, mortality rates in West Bengal skyrocketed to astronomical heights. It was estimated that one-third of the Bengali population perished in this famine. There are other estimates that more than one fifth of the population perished. Be that as it may, the truth was that core areas of Western and Central Bengal were completely devastated; many people died of starvation or disease. The prosperous districts of Bengal namely Murshidabad, Nadia, RajShahi, Hooghly, Birbhum even Bardhaman came into the vortex of almost total destruction. It was recorded that an estimated one third of those engaged in silkworm rearing in Murshidabad had perished in the famine.

Normally, the effect of the famine was less in the low-lying delta areas of East Bengal. Another discernible fact is that those who did not have the provisions of permanent storage of grain suffered the most because of the fury of the famine.

Next came the memory of 1783 when north India had to encounter a ravaging disaster of famine known as the terrible 'Chalisa'. The 1784 and 1787 famines were caused due to excessive flooding in parts of eastern Bengal. 60,000 people were estimated to have died in Dhaka alone. The famines were marked not only by death and desolation but also by suicide and even cannibalism. Often, such conditions were worsened by attacks of ravaging armies. The horrors of such devastations was recorded in 1802, when the Maratha chief Jaswant Rao Holkar, marching from the north to Pune, completely devastated the agricultural fields and decimated the wealth of the farmers in the form of domesticated cattle, who then resorted to cannibalism. The establishment of the famine amelioration policy was left to the conscience of the local government officials. Some measures were taken, like digging of wells, storage of food grain, giving of alms, and remissions of revenue, but it was commonly felt and widely accepted that famine was a calamity that was totally beyond the powers of men to mitigate.

Following the sepoy mutiny of 1857, there was a spectacular rise in prices of day-to-day goods. In the years 1866–67, a severe famine took a heavy toll of human lives in Orissa and along the eastern coast from Calcutta to Madras. The cause of this famine was the failure of the autumn rains in 1865 and subsequently two thirds of the rice crops failed. During the next 10 years there were many local famines which occurred in the United Provinces in Punjab and Rajputana during the year 1868–69. The next famine of 1876–78, which occurred in Madras, Mysore, Bombay and Hyderabad, also resulted from two deficient monsoons. The policy of the central government of the time was to spare no efforts to save the populations of the famine affected areas, but also not to interfere in the local trade and not to give in to charity.

There was a series of severe famines that ravaged Bengal during this time, especially the famines of 1874–76 and 1887 to 1889 and unusual drought and floods of 1883 to 1885. The following is a study of the movement of prices of rice in Bengal in the period of 1861 to 1885:

The average price of rice (number of seers for a rupee), for six 4-year periods is as follows:

1861–64	1865–68	1869–72	1873–76	1877–80	1885
26.29	18.66	22.27	18.9	16.05	15.18

One thing was common in those days: as and when tragedy befell the poorer Western districts of Bengal, the people in large hordes sought to find succour in the Eastern side of the Bhagirathi, notably in the Calcutta district, which had a more stable economy under the British rule.

Having recounted the major visitations of famines in Bengal, we may now pay attention to the aspect of famine management by the British Government in India. The British government's management of the famine situation in India was mostly on the lines of mismanagement. In the face of the recurring famines, the British government lay the blame on providence and the invocation of the Malthusian theory, that the growth in population beyond limits of what the land can sustain, will inevitably lead to death, through which the level of population was to be restored to the correct balance. So, famines and epidemics were nature's own way of dealing with overpopulation. The British administration believed in financial prudence, that they should not spend money that they had not budgeted for. The British government also had strict ideas regarding non-interference in market forces. According to Dinyar Patal, 'It was common economic wisdom that government intervention in famines was unnecessary and even harmful. The market would restore a proper balance'. Thus, keeping with their principles, Lord Lytton, (Viceroy of India from 1876–80), refused to reduce the prices of grain during the famine. This way, the British government in India absolved itself from the allegation of human element, that is, the proper governance to combat the recurring incidences of famine.

In a rough estimate, 30 to 35 million people needlessly died of starvation during British rule all over India. William Digby pointed out that in the entire 107 years from 1793–1900, only an estimated 5 million people died in all the wars fought around the world. Whereas, in just ten years, from 1890 to 1900, 19 million people had died in India in famine alone. During British rule in India, 35 million people died of famines and resulting epidemics. Shashi Tharoor calls this the 'British Colonial Holocaust'. (An Era Of Darkness, The British Empire by Shashi Tharoor)

The British government did set up relief camps, but relief rarely reached the local inhabitants who were barely fed and nearly all died. The frequent famines that occurred in India were not so much a direct result of food shortage but the inability of the people to buy food grains. Even as the famine raged, millions of tonnes of wheat were exported from India to Britain. During the Orissa Famine of 1866, the British exported 200 million pounds of rice to Britain at a time when one and a half million people starved to death in India. Add to this the brutal collection of very high taxes and rents even during the height of the famines, the already impoverished and starving peasants could never pay up their dues. The British government was willing to provide work to the able-bodied, but generally frowned upon any kind of charity or almsgiving, even to those 'living skeletons' who were starving to death.

Attempts to formulate a general system of famine relief or its prevention was hardly discernible before 1858, though a part of the system or its wide extended region came under the grip of severe famine as a consequence of huge floods or continuous drought over a couple of seasons.

It was in the year 1858 when the onslaught of famine had attracted the attention and the need to formulate a permanent commission to go into the depths of the causes of the famine; its origin, duration and final consequences in the form of mortality, desolation of agricultural land and its grim consequence in the form of half-fed moving skeletons roaming the streets of Calcutta begging for a morsel of food to partially alleviate their hunger. In its worst visitation, there are instances when hunger led to the cannibalism of man eating the flesh of other human beings and domesticated animals.

The Governor General at the time, Lord Lytton felt that it was necessary to formulate some general principles of famine relief and accordingly he appointed a Famine Commission under General Sir Richard Strachey. The Famine Commission recommendations formed the basis of the Famine Code which was put into effect in 1883 by the Government of India. The Commission started with the basic principle that it was the duty of the state to offer relief to the needy during the times of famine. This relief was to be provided in the form of providing employment to the able-bodied men, distributing food and money to the aged and infirm, prior planning for relief work, suspension of land revenue and rents and offer of cheaper loans to peasants. Further, to meet the unforeseen expenditures caused by famine, it was decided to set aside 15 million rupees every year to constitute the 'Famine Relief and Insurance Fund'. This Famine Code formed a guide for the various provincial famine codes which were subsequently prepared and put into force as and when situations demanded.

In 1896–97, and in 1899–1900, there were a series of terrible famines which affected the United provinces, Bengal, Central Provinces, Madras,

Punjab and Bombay. It was during this time that relief measures were undertaken on an extensive scale and the principles of the Famine Code put into effective operation. The famine of 1896–97 affected around 225,000 sq miles and a population of sixty two millions. After the famine of 1896–97, another Commission was appointed under Sir James Lyall, which approved of all the principles adopted in 1880. The famine that visited India in 1900 was the greatest in extent and seriousness what the land had experienced in 200 years. More than 400,000 sq miles and a population of about sixty million were directly affected in this famine. The famine brought in its wake fever, dysentery and cholera which further enfeebled the population and claimed many victims. In 1900, another Commission was appointed under Sir Anthony McDonnell, which presented its report in 1901. This report laid emphasis on the need for 'moral strategy' or 'putting heart into the people'. This meant helping the people with loans, like 'takkavi' loans (short term loans which were given to poor farmers to buy seeds, fertilisers and for other agricultural requirements) and being aware of the signs of the approaching calamity. The report laid stress on early and detailed planning in the face of famine. This Commission further emphasised the importance of development of agriculture, irrigation, water storage, industry and other public works to facilitate relief operations and to build up a Famine Relief Fund. Here it may be added that the development of Railways also served as an important means of famine relief because it facilitated transport and distribution of food grains to areas affected by the famine.

Finally coming back to the Great Bengal famine of 1943–44, in which an estimated 4 million people lost their lives, out of a total population of 60 million. This was the most notorious famine to hit Bengal, with people dying from starvation, aggravated by malnutrition and compromised immune systems and diseases like malaria, dysentery, diarrhoea, cholera and smallpox. There was a total breakdown of the social fabric, with mass migrations, exploitation of women and children, poor living conditions, lack of hygiene and sanitation, poor quality of water, no proper disposal of waste or of the bodies of the dead littering the streets and pavements. Millions were impoverished and many in the rural areas lost their homes and lands, travelling to the cities in search of relief or work.

It is widely believed that this famine was largely man-made, created by the harsh and inhuman war-time colonial policies, and not by failure of the monsoons. Wartime inflation had raised the prices of rice and other food grains, making them out of reach of the common man. Winston Churchill willfully diverted food supplies from the starving Indian population to the British soldiers fighting in the World War and to stockpile grain in parts of Europe. According to Churchill, the famine was the fault of the Indians themselves, for 'breeding like rabbits'.

Humanitarian aid, either from the British Government in India or the Bengal Provincial Government was slow to arrive and was not adequate in the face of this calamity. The first official intervention for famine management came in the form of the Famine Enquiry Commission presided over by Sir John Woodhead; their report, published in May 1945, was as follows: "It has been for us a sad task to enquire into the course and causes of the Bengal famine. We have been haunted by a deep sense of tragedy. A million and a half of the poor people of Bengal fell victim to circumstances for which they themselves were not responsible. Society together with its organs failed to protect their weaker members. Indeed, there was a moral and social breakdown as well as an administrative breakdown."The wound inflicted on Bengal by this terrible calamity was extremely slow to heal.

* * *

Essay 4

India's Foreign Trade During British Rule: A Comprehensive Study

India's land mass is encircled by sea on all sides. On the west is the Arabian Sea, at the southern tip, the Indian Ocean and in the east, the Bay of Bengal. The Indian subcontinent holds a strategic position in the Indian ocean with sea routes connecting it to the east and to the west. India is and has always been, a seafaring nation.

Throughout the 19th century, there was cutthroat competition among the European trading companies that had started business in India. After 1813, all the European Nations were placed on equal footing so far as foreign trade was concerned. However, Britain continued to enjoy unrivalled supremacy because of its political dominance over India. The years 1815 to 1914 were the golden period of British trade with India. In India, Britain found a steadfast supplier of raw material and food stuff which were complementary to the meagre agricultural products of England. Britain in turn took advantage of the burgeoning Indian market and made it into a lucrative dumping ground for consumable goods manufactured in Britain. The agriculture based manufactured items like cotton goods along with woollen textile, which had a high demand in India, were staple import items. This apart, the most sought-after products were steel, tin and other metals and hardware which had a ready market in India.

A major chunk of the foreign trade of India was carried out through Bengal. The Bengal Province had been the richest province of the Mughal empire. Not only was the land extremely fertile for agriculture, but it was also an important commercial centre. The overseas trade of the Mughal empire was carried on primarily through the eastern ports like Calcutta. And throughout the British era, Bengal continued to be the major exporter of agricultural raw materials and also the major importer of British manufactured goods. There were mainly two major items of trade: agricultural products like indigo, opium, jute and rice, and finished products from the textile industry, like muslin and silk. The muslin of East Bengal was a prime product which had a very lucrative market in Europe. It was in great demand among the aristocrats and gentry of Europe. Exports from Bengal to Europe were financed by silver bullion from Europe.

The Charter Act of 1833 finally put an end to the commercial activities of the East India Company. The company's trading activities were closed down and it became an administrative body for the British crown. This charter also came to be known as the Government of India Act, 1833. India's foreign trade was naturally influenced by this turn of events.

Indigo was once the most favoured item of export for the East India Company. However, the British traders completely lost their importance following the development of industrial substitutes of Indigo manufactured in European countries, especially like Germany and France. After the 1830's, the cultivation of jute and tea gave the British ample opportunities for trade. The companies dealing in jute were initially British owned and flourished on the banks of the river Ganga; they continued to retain their importance. Equally important was the development of the tea gardens producing high quality tea. The lion's share of these two items was under British ownership and remained the main source of income from foreign trade.

Trade prospects from Bengal developed in leaps and bounds after the opening of the Suez Canal in 1869, which reduced the naval distance between England and India by 4,000 miles. England already had supremacy over her European counterparts as a manufacturing country. Now, sailing ships were replaced by steamboats which were not subject to the vagaries of natural weather. The construction of the Howrah Bridge in Calcutta over the river Hooghly in 1874 vastly facilitated the changing pattern of external and internal trade. Bengal's interior was brought into the ambit of international trade through quick transit over waterways along with the transportation through land, which proved to be a real boon for the ryots of the interiors. Moreover, telegraphic communication between Europe and India was introduced in the year 1865 when India was connected with Europe through cable. A few years earlier, an effective postal service had been introduced in India in the year 1854, that was both efficient and cheap. In 1870, there was a complete overhaul of the Port Administration of Calcutta. The Port Trust of India came into being and opened a floodgate of jobs for Indians and also facilitated cargo handling. England emerged as a supreme naval power over the east. Furthermore, this period witnessed relative political peace and stability, except for the Afghan war and the Burmese war. Consequently, Bengal reaped a strong bonanza in foreign trade. Even during the 1857 mutiny, Bengal was not directly drawn into the vortex of the sepoy revolt. Bengalis were of English educated 'bhadralok' elite class with a majority of them being brahmins. They did not have any social bonding or sympathy with the sepoys and could not easily associate themselves with the mutineers of Meerut, Kanpur and Lucknow.

Professor H.H. Dodwell M.A, in his introduction to Volume 6 of The Indian Empire 1858–1918, eulogised the role of Lord Cornwallis in Bengal and Munro in Madras in the development of the administrative system up to the time of the Sepoy Mutiny of 1857. He stated with conviction how the Company's government was not obscurantist or reactionary; that without exception, the Governor-Generals had been aware of the obligations and responsibilities assigned to them. They are not merely administrators but also benevolent welfare officers for the Indian subjects at large. It was common knowledge that District Magistrates often endeared themselves to the Indian subjects, that even long after their retirement, they continued to be lovingly remembered by the Indians. The Montgomery district, presently in Pakistan, remains a stunning example.

It was this kind of political stability which was the prime factor leading to the successful expansion of trade and commerce both internationally and internally. Except for the Santhal Rebellion of 1865 and the inhuman treatment of the Indigo plantation workers, this period presented an ideal atmosphere in unhampered overall development. The period of the second half of the nineteenth century was a period of sustained commercial life and organisational betterment.

It will be worthwhile to list out the items of import and export related to India's foreign trade. Bengal principal imports were as follows: cheap Manchester cotton goods, woollen goods, silk goods, metals and hardware, cutlery, liquors, salts, spices and provisions, railway and telegraph machinery, kerosene oil and some minor items like matches. These goods practically accounted for 91% of imports. There were some items manufactured in Boston like clocks, watches, umbrellas, instruments and appliances, glassware and some chemicals.

The principal exports from Bengal were raw cotton, dyeing materials like indigo, food grains, oil seeds, opium, saltpetre, some minerals like mica and manganese, raw silk, silk products, jute and jute products, cotton twists, yarns and cotton piece goods.

Later on, by 1905–06, jute and jute manufacturers along with hides and skins entered the exports list. Tea and opium also became major export items. The bulk of exports however was related to agricultural products. Jute, tea and opium continued to be major export products, but there was also a slow introduction of manufactured goods, mainly jute and cotton goods.

The other countries with which British India started importing large quantities of products were China, France, The United States of America, Singapore and Ceylon. The main imports from China were chinaware, camphor, copper, paints, silk, tea and the chief export items to China were opium, raw cotton, gunny bags and saltpetre. From France, the main items of import were silk piece goods, white cotton piece goods, precious stones, wines and spirits, while the exports were indigo, wheat, seeds, silk, sugar, tobacco, hides and skins. From Singapore, Bengal received tin cans and rattan, cutch and gambier, betel nuts, pepper and tea. Export items to Singapore were wax, opium, gunny bags, rice and castor oil. Ceylon, presently Sri Lanka, exported coir, yarn, coconuts, coconut oil, betel nut and shells to India. From India, they took gram and pulses, paddy, rice, wheat, oil cakes, opium and sugar. To Mauritius, India used to export large quantities of paddy and rice for the indentured labour. Also, gram and pulse, castor oil, oil cakes and saltpetre were sent to Mauritius. From the USA, the main items of import was mineral oil while exports consisted of indigo, cutch and gambier, hides and skins, raw jute, gunny bags, shellac and linseed.

Australia also had good business ties with India. Horses and copper were imported from Australia. Tea was sent to Australia. The Calcutta tea Syndicate was established to popularise tea there. China was the main exporter of tea. Since the retail trade was handled by the Chinese residents, even the products manufactured by Italy and Germany were handled by the Chinese retail traders. Thus, Italy and Germany too enjoyed a brisk business with India.

Italy used to export a large number of goods to India. These were coral goods, glass beads, false pearls, claret, brandy, lametta stone, and marble. Italy also imported indigo, raw cotton, raw hide and skins, shellac, oil seeds, raw silk and tobacco. The trade with Trieste represented one of the routes by which Central Europe was brought into communication with Calcutta. The main imports to Calcutta were cotton twist, coloured piece goods, glass beads, lametta, brass leaves and woollen piece goods. These were mostly German manufactured goods dispatched to Calcutta from Italian ports. There were also exports to Austria, mainly Indigo, raw cotton, hides and skins, jute, shellac and tallow.

In 1890–91, a direct steamer service started from Hamburg in Germany to Calcutta. Two regular services of steamers started plying between Hamburg and Calcutta. In 1893–94, Germany became the largest consumer of Bengal cotton valued at Rs. 20,70,079. Russia emerged as a partner in Bengal foreign trade from 1887–88, when import of mineral oil from Batum started competing with oil from the USA and Europe. By the end of 1888, Japan also entered the Bengal market and started competing with Manchester goods. Japan also imported Bengal raw cotton. It will not be out of place to make a mention of the high quality of cotton textile manufactured under the authority of the British East India Company which had established specialised manufacturing units in Dhaka, Shantipur, Tangail and Birbhum.

During 30 years, (1839–40) to (1869–70), the value of imports of Britain cotton goods and plain goods jumped from Rs. 97,60,911 to

Rs. 8,12,54,482, which accounted for 62% of the total Bengal imports in the year 1876–77.

Another notable feature was the awakening of local Bengali trading associations. The non-official Calcutta Chamber of Commerce was founded in 1834. During the Governor-General ship of Lord William Bentinck, Indo-British firms like Carr Tagore and Co, Rustomjee Cowasjee and Co were established. In 1853, the Indo British Chamber was reconstituted as the Bengal Chamber of Commerce. This body however, represented the British interests. So, a need was felt to organise a chamber of commerce catering to the interests of indigenous traders. This led to the foundation of the Bengal National Chamber of Commerce in 1887, which was completely devoid of British participation. This opened the floodgates of establishment of chambers of commerce in East Bengal. This started with the foundation of the Chittagong Chamber of Commerce in 1906 to represent the common trading interests of both British and the Indian traders.

The next to come up, closely on the heels of the Chittagong Chamber of Commerce, was the Narayanganj Chamber of Commerce to promote the commercial interests of the manufacturers of East Bengal with no specific reference to Indian manufacturers in particular. Along with the formation of Chambers of Commerce, this period saw the opening of specific associations like the Calcutta Wheat and Seed Trader Association in 1884 and the Calcutta Jute Fabric Shippers Association in 1893. This was a union of the shipper fraternity of Calcutta embracing both European and Indian shippers' interests. The next to emerge was an association which catered to the needs of exclusive ethnic communities like the Marwari community of Calcutta in 1898.

The Calcutta stock exchange as a commercial exchange was mooted in Calcutta much earlier and established in 1858. With a change in nomenclature, the Royal Exchange of Calcutta was formed in 1893.

A cheaper and safer banking system was the need of the day, so to enhance the business spirit and also to give fillip to the burgeoning trading activities, there was the need to open commercial banks. The ethos of free trade and reforms, as propounded way back by Adam Smith, continued to influence the British government's administrative and trading policies. The growing volume of Bengal's foreign trade required a cheap and efficient banking system. Ultimately, the government granted a charter to the Union Bank, (founded in 1833) in 1835. It signalled the fruitful culmination of the struggles of the free trader. Subsequently the Bank of Bengal was established. However, the government had some very stringent restrictions in regard to exchange operations. In this context, the contribution of Dwarkanath Tagore, the scion of the Tagore family and the grandfather of Rabindranath Tagore, is worth mentioning. The Union Bank 1833 of which Dwarkanath Tagore was a director, however, crashed in 1847–48 due to some private banking and agency concerns.

The steady and rapid growth of India's trade with Britain and the far east called for an immediate introduction of an exchange banking system. The British government gave permission in 1851 to the Oriental Bank to establish agencies in India for the purpose of deposit, exchange and remittances. The Chartered Bank of India, Australia and China started functioning in Calcutta from 1858.

Next came the National Bank of India, the Hongkong and Shanghai Banking Corporation and the Chartered Mercantile Bank of India, London and China. At the beginning of 1866, there were 22 exchange banks in Calcutta. However, as a result of the recession of trade and commerce, there was a huge casualty and only seven exchange banks were left in India.

This phenomenal growth was not permanent as fissures started creeping in. To start with, there was a fall in the price of silver, making it difficult to maintain the level of business. In the period between 1872–94, there was a fall in the value of silver in terms of gold. Indian foreign trade was such that the proceeds from export of Indian goods was more that the import from Europe, Middle East and the Philippines. This balance of trade was adjusted through large scale export of silver bullion by the European nations, Philippines and the Middle East. The European countries were the main exporters of silver. Imports by the English East India Company averaged around 200,000 pounds a year in the time of Alivardi Khan's reign around the year 1750. The Dutch companies, which were incidentally more established and bigger in size, exported silver varying between 30,000 pounds and 475,000 pounds a year. Even the French companies used to send 2 to 4 ship loads of silver per year to adjust the negative balance of payment, even after the disruption of French trade from the middle of the 1740's.

It is estimated that Persia, which had a huge trade with India, was being paid for in spices, so that most of the loot taken by Nadir Shah in 1735 during the sacking of Delhi, found its way back to India

The first half of the century, up to 1750, was dominated by the European traders, of whom, the private British traders of Calcutta were predominant. They also included the servants of the Company and others who were allowed by the Company to carry on their private trading activities with their own ships. P.J. Marshall records that in late Mughal Bengal, more ships were coming to the British port at Calcutta than those going to the Nawab's port on the Hooghly river. In the 1730's, the French chief, Dupleix believed that the Europeans could impose any terms they wished on the Nawab by blockading his ports and depriving him of silver. Shipping and dealing with silver were not the only trading activities by the Europeans. They were the major purchases of high-quality textiles. They were directly or indirectly, stimulators of commercial agriculture by increasing the demand for mulberry for silkworms.

The cost value of the English East India company's investment in Bengal goods for the London Market was about 400,000 pounds a year. This was only the official figure, there was a very flourishing clandestine market operated by the private European traders, the estimate of which is hard to make. But in any case, it was not less than the official figure. In the 1740's, the average purchase of the Dutch companies for the Netherlands was the equivalent of about 200,000 pounds a year, rising to 250,000 pounds in the 1750's. The French company's purchases may have been about half of this value.

A major issue was the division of business into Pound Sterling and Rupees, the former being restricted to the companies operating out of London and the latter operating out of India. The British could only invest in Sterling companies, while the Rupee companies are open for both

British and Indian investors. Incidentally, out of 385 joint stock companies, 376 companies were based in Calcutta, dealing with tea and jute, which were reserved for the British. This was the state of affairs till as late as 1914. Again, up to 1915, the British had 100% ownership of jute mills which eventually came down to 78% by 1929.

The Indian economy went through a series of monetary and exchange rate moderations. These included among others, a transition from gold bullion sterling standard exchange rate to a controversial fixed exchange rate system, which was done to manage the deliberate depreciation of the value of the rupee. Meanwhile the Reserve Bank of India was established and made functional in 1934–35. Initially, it had limited authority. This period witnessed a severely chaotic condition in respect to international trade, with the price volatility of 20% to 30% a year. Britain had continued to maintain fixed exchange rates as it was beneficial to them. It was a shock absorber for the British economy, as it managed to adjust current account deficit and also to meet other domestic exigencies. No consideration was forthcoming for ameliorating the financial woes of India, their most important colony, proving that the British had scant sympathy in dealing with the vicissitudes of India's trade and international obligations.

The Great Depression of 1929–30 exposed the Indian peasantry into utter deprivation as the poor cultivators found that their produce remained unsold due to lack of purchasing capacity of the consumers. Incidentally, the potato producing areas of Ireland and America were also facing similar crises. Farmers in the USA faced the same torment when they found that the grain grown on their soil was in plenty, but there were no buyers who could afford to buy them. Agricultural prices had collapsed. The British, speculating that there would be devaluation of the Indian currency, leading to a corresponding decline in the sterling value of their assets in India, resorted to the restriction of Indian money supply. The British insisted that the Indian rupee should remain static at the fixed rate of one Shilling and sixpence. Also, the British government in England commanded the Indian government to take out of circulation notes and coins to keep the exchange rates high. The total amount of cash in circulation fell from 5 billion rupees in 1929, to 4 billion rupees in 1930, which further reduced to 3 billion in

1938. The British saw to it that their assets in India were secured and their currency remained at a high level, with scant sympathy for their starving Indian subjects, pushing millions of them into the doom of starvation and famine.

The Indian currency had been at one time, the strongest in the world. Prior to the British invasion till about the 17th century, India accounted for 27% of world trade, with the treasury of Aurangzeb flush with 100 million pounds of tax revenue alone in the year 1700; this went down to 3% by the time of the departure of the British in 1947. India was thus reduced to penury through the shameless machinations of the British.

Essay 5

The Loot of India

The systematic plunder of the wealth of India and specifically the state of Bengal formally started with the conquest of Bengal in June of 1757, following the victory of Colonel (later Lord) Robert Clive, in the Battle of Plassey, located about 150 Km north of Kolkata and to the south of Murshidabad, the then capital of the Mughal empire in Bengal. It was the Battle of Plassey that led to the conquest of the whole of India and to the destruction of an old civilization by the British East India Company without an iota of scruple and with the sole aim of satisfying their insatiable greed and avarice.

Right from the beginning of Siraj-ud-daulah's ascension to the throne of Bengal, following the death of Alivardi Khan in April of 1756, there was total change in the power equation in Bengal. As wished by Alivardi Khan, his grandson Siraj-ud-daulah was appointed as the Nawab, but his relationship with the British started worsening, without any possibility of compromise. On one hand, the Nawab resented the interference of the British in his court, while on the other, the British felt that the Nawab was bent upon slashing their trading privileges.

Finally, things came to a head with the Battle of Plassey. The Battle of Plassey was the epoch-making watershed in the history of India since it paved the way for an uninterrupted subjugation of Bengal, and then the whole of India for a period of 190 years, that is from 1757 to 1947, when India got its independence from British rule. In the afternoon of June 26th, 1757, Robert Clive inflicted defeat on the army of the Bengal Nawab Siraj-ud-daulah in the famous Battle of Plassey. This was not even a full-scale battle, but a mere skirmish, where the Nawab's commander-in-chief Mir Zaffar treacherously surrendered to the British without an iota of fight and even restricted another royal commander of the Nawab, Mohanlal from engaging with the British. The victory at Plassey was thus handed over to the British on the platter. Siraj-ud-daulah, completely lost and desolate, was forced to flee the battlefield only to be caught and put to death by the order of Mir Zaffar's son, Miran. Mir Zaffar was installed on the throne of Bengal by Clive himself, under the authority of the East India Company. With the victory at the Battle of Plassey in 1757, the British, camouflaged as a trading company, emerged as the rulers of the country.

It was much before 1757 that the British had planted themselves firmly on Indian soil and exercised their authority over the native territories of India and their rulers. The British explorer, Job Charnock, is credited with planting the authority of the British in Calcutta, the centre of English dominance, a city few miles downstream from the riverine Hugli villages of Sutanuti, Govindpur, as well as the fortification of Fort William on the River Hugli on the outskirts of Calcutta. Calcutta was destined to be the capital of British India from 1765 up to the shifting of the capital to Delhi in 1911. Calcutta, the town, located on the bank of the river Hooghly and stretching lengthwise parallel to the river without much width, became the eastern capital of the British Empire as it had all the ingredients of administrative, cultural, social, political and educational activities, as befitting the capital of British India. It was studded with iconic and monumental structures of Victoria Memorial, the National Library, the huge International Museum, the famous educational institutions like the Asiatic Society, the huge zoo and many prominent social and cultural hubs of the British and the Indians. Most importantly, Calcutta became the pivotal centre of trade and commerce through the sea routes, both towards the east and to the British capital, London, towards the west.

Being a capitalist trading nation, the British embarked upon international and domestic trade through the arms of the East India Company, which owed its establishment to the Charter bestowed by Queen Elizabeth I of England, in the year 1600. The charter of 1600 authorised the East India Company to trade in specific Indian articles namely silk, spices and profitable Indian commodities, which had a market in Europe. It was during the reign of the Mughal Emperor Jahangir that the British trading companies first made their foray into India, exploring the possibilities of trade here. The first British Ambassador, Sir Thomas Roe presented his credentials to the Mughal Emperor Jahangir in 1615 at his court in Agra. At that time, Emperor Jahangir was the richest emperor in the whole world, with his empire stretching from Kabul to Assam and from the Himalayas to Karnataka. During 1615–18, the Mughal Emperor granted the British trading company permission to set up their factories on Indian soil. The first English factory in India was established at Surat in 1613, followed by the second one at Masulipatnam.

Armed with this Charter from the Crown of England, with its principal functioning offices at Calcutta, in due course of time, the East India Company acquired trading rights, and established itself strongly in India. The Company flourished in leaps and bounds and expanded its prolific trading activities, both internal and international, through sea routes. Slowly but steadily, it spread its tentacles to all parts of India and established itself in the metropolitan cities of Calcutta, Bombay and Madras and even acquired the rights to proper self defence of their establishments including the right to recruit soldiers and stationing of military garrisons there. After planting their feet firmly on Indian soil, it extended its military arms to wrest power from local traders and appropriating authority over the local rulers. While the administration of the three prosperous states, those of Bengal, Bihar and to some extent Orissa vested completely with the Mughal emperor of Delhi, with clever manipulation, the East India Company acquired not only exclusive trading rights to India, but also great military and political power.

Coupled with that, the Mughal Empire had gone into a coma following the invasion of the ruler of Iran, Nadir Shah, the scourge of India, who invaded Delhi in 1739. In eight weeks, the total accumulated wealth of the Mughal treasury was completely ransacked. Treasure accumulated over centuries and by generations of Mughal emperors, worth over 500 million rupees was seized and the entire contents of the emperor's fabled treasury and even the peacock throne along with the Kohinoor diamond were taken away by Nadir Shah. Delhi was left desolate and impoverished and was reduced to a city of mass graves. The staggering butchery of the civilians and the military alike, left Delhi at the mercy of any foreign invaders and this was an ideal situation for the British East India Company to make inroads into the already weakened territory.

With the authority of the Mughal emperor completely weakened, the British deepened their hold on the local zamindars and princes. With the Battle of Plassey and subsequently with the Battle of Buxar in 1764–65, the British East India company acquired political, military and administrative rights over the Bengal Province (which included Bihar and Odisha), which was at that time the richest province of the Mughal Empire. The Mughal emperor, Shah Alam II ascended the throne of Delhi in the year 1760. He was a weak, young and inexperienced emperor, ruling over a crumbling Mughal Empire. The Battle of Buxar was an even more decisive battle for the East India Company. In August 1765, following his defeat, Shah Alam II was browbeaten to surrender the Diwani rights (right to collect revenue) of Bengal to the British, which entailed the withdrawal of his own revenue officials from that province in favour of the East India company's officials. The East India Company thus became the imperial tax collectors of the huge Mughal province of Bengal.

Mir Zafar had ascended the throne with a huge financial obligation to the British. An amount of three million sterling had been pledged by Mir Zafar to the company. Jagat Seth, the chief banker of the nawab, had to pay up 50% of the indemnity immediately and the balance was to be paid off over a period of three years. Clive, however, was not content with the aforesaid arrangement and insisted that the Company must be given assignments of revenue of specific parts of Bengal.

An additional loan was imposed on the Nawab Mir Zafar to pay rupees 1,10,000 a month for the use of the company's troops. According to Clive,

Bengal was the inexhaustible fund of riches and apart from its own trade expenses, had to support the expenses of the British troops with divisions in the British settlements of Bombay and Madras. While the trade in Bengal, including overseas trade, was financed by a positive balance of payments with silver bullion, Bengal was being forced to generate extra revenue from the areas over which the British had administrative authority. That apart, Clive intended to seize and capture the territories under French control. It was from this time onwards that the internal trade of Bengal also witnessed a massive invasion from the Europeans, especially the British private traders. Clive was determined to make the British the sole European authority of trade in Bengal.

The loot of Indian wealth by British imperialism can be divided logically into two parts. First, the loot of wealth which was in the form of money, that is, prevalent Indian currencies: gold, silver and such other resources. Secondly there was the drain of India's wealth in the form of restrictions on national and international trade due to the imposition of restrictive laws and statutory rules.

The drain of wealth from India was basically in the form of flow of revenue from India into the London treasury. The British forces, under the command of Colonel Robert Clive, had won the decisive Battle of Plassey to dethrone the Nawab Siraj-ud-daulah. In return for this victory, Robert Clive was able to transfer a princely sum of 2.5 million pounds, the entire contents of the Nawab's treasury, to the Company coffers in Britain. Robert Clive himself too amassed a huge personal wealth. In his first visit to India, he took away 234,000 pounds (Which will make 23 million pounds in today's money) from his exploits in the country, in the form of presents and tribute, making him one of the richest men in England, while publicly extolling his self-restraint in not stealing even more. Clive came back to India in 1765 and returned to England in 1767 having amassed a fortune estimated at 400,000 pounds (40 million pounds in today's terms). Apart from this, he was showered with millions of rupees worth of gifts, he extracted promises of annual tribute and helped himself to any rare jewels that caught his eye which fetched him five times of its value in India when sold in the England markets.

Clive had the temerity to declare, "…an opulent city lay at my mercy, its richest bankers bid against each other for my smiles; I walked through vaults which were thrown open to me alone, piled on either hand with gold and jewels….When I think of the marvellous riches of that country, and the comparatively small part which I took away, I am astonished at my own moderation". Ironically, Clive was lovingly conferred the title 'Clive of India' by his lackeys for his shameless perfidy in ensuring that a good portion of the country belonged to him.

Shashi Tharoor in his book, 'An Era of Darkness' quoted the biographical Essay by the 19th century politician and historian, Lord Thomas Babington Macaulay who went beyond the details of Clive's life to investigate some of the larger forces his success had set in motion. Macaulay had served the East India company in various capacities and called the Company the greatest corporation in the world. His diatribe was aimed at the 'nabobs' (mispronounced for Nawab). The term applied to East India Company employees who returned to England extremely rich after amassing huge fortunes in India.

This was the first instance of major loot of the Indian treasury by the British. This theft or embezzlement which started from this time, continued for long after. It was described by the Earl of Chatham as 'the redemption of a nation…a kind of gift from heaven'. 'Each year, between 1765 and 1815, there was the extraction of approximately 18,000,000 pounds from India. 'There were few kings in Europe', wrote Comte-de-Châtelet, the French Ambassador to London, 'richer than the Directors of the English East India Company'.

The young American historian and philosopher Will Durant, known for his 11 volume 'The Story of Civilization', came to India in 1930, to collect data for his book. He was filled with utter astonishment and indignation by the conscious and deliberate bleeding of India by the British and he wrote a scathing denunciation of this greatest crime in history. His short book, 'The Case for India', is a profoundly emphatic work of compassion and outrage that attacked the self-serving justification of the British for their long and shameless record of rapacity in India.

One of the most vocal critics of the illegal activities of the East India company was the playwright Richard Sheridan who castigated the East India Company board members with these words, "The operation of the company combined the meanness of a peddler with the profligacy of a pirate. Thus, it was that they united the mock majesty of a bloody sceptre with the little traffic of a merchant counting-house, wielding a truncheon with one hand and picking a pocket with the other."

John Shore as Baron of Teignmouth went on to serve as Governor General of India from 1793–97. He pointed in a minute as early as 1789 that the East India company were both merchants and sovereigns in India; in the formal capacity, they engross its trade whilst in the latter, they appropriate its revenue. Teignmouth pointed to the inequity of the policy of extraction, the drain of currency (silver) from the country to Europe, and resultant collapse of India's internal trade, which had flourished before the company depredations.

The company mainly adopted a policy of shameless perfidy and cupidity in extracting wealth from the native princes, thereafter, overthrowing them and gradually grabbing their estates. This was a well-known policy since the late eighteenth century.

The high priest of this high handedness was none other than Warren Hastings, the most rapacious of the company's Governor Generals. He had no qualms in resorting to extreme treachery in taking action and waging war against his bribe-giving Indian princes and zamindars, ostensibly to show the world that he could not be purchased with bribes. It will not be irrelevant to point out that Hastings adopted the same policy of Subsidiary Alliance as was adopted in the kingdom of the Nizam of Hyderabad, where in a huge amount was extracted from the Nizam for the maintenance of the British soldiers in his capital. This was ostensibly to guard the Nizam's territory against the Maratha onslaughts. The expenditure was so staggering that the Nizam had no option but to borrow the amount from the British banks at an astronomical interest rate of 24% of the principal. As an alternative, he had to cede certain portions of his territory to the Company, from where the British were allowed to appropriate or realise tax revenue exclusively. The same policy was adopted towards the Nawab of Arcot.

Hastings' personal avarice knew no bounds; he shamelessly proclaimed that he tortured the widowed begums of Oudh and extracted every bit of their treasure and assets, not less than 10 lakh rupees, a princely sum in those days. Further, he requested the company to allow him to retain the entire assets and spoils for himself. The company immediately gave him permission because the company's coffers would be richer in the future because of Hastings' manoeuvrability.

Warren Hastings, the Governor of the East India Company till 1773, was promoted as the Governor General of India. In 1788, Hastings was impeached by the House of Commons in the British Parliament for rampant corruption and abuse of power. The main attack came from Edmund Burke. Burke in his opening speech accused the British East India Company of cruelties unheard of in human history and devastation almost without name which have their roots in the wicked disposition of men; their pride, cruelty, malignity, haughtiness and insolence knew no limits. He described in painful detail the violation of Bengali women by the British tax collectors: 'They were dragged out naked and exposed to the public view and scourged before all the people... they put the nipples of the hapless women into the sharp edges of split bamboos and tore them from their bodies', leading Sheridan's wife to swoon in horror in parliament, from where she had to be carried out in distress. More indictment followed in the stentorian voices of Sheridan and Charles James Fox. In the end however, Hastings was acquitted, restoring the image of the Empire in the eyes of the British public, which served to justify the continuing rapacity for a century and a half more. It will be interesting to quote another extract from the opening speech of Edmund Burke in the impeachment of Warren Hastings. Alarmed at the wanton embezzlement of Indian resources, William Burke commented 'Today the Commons of Great Britain prosecutes the delinquents of India. Tomorrow, the delinquents of India may be the members of the Commons of Great Britain'.

But the problem went well beyond Hastings. The preacher William Howitt felt that the mode by which the East India Company had possessed itself of Hindustan was the most revolting and unchristian that could possibly be conceived. The system, which for more than a century, was steadily at work to strip the native princes of their dominions, was a system of torture more exquisite than legal or spiritual tyranny ever before discovered. William Howitt speaking in 1839, while the Company was still in power, lamented that 'the scene of extraction, rapacity and plunder which India became in our hands, and that upon the whole body of the population, forms one of the most disgraceful portions of human history.... There was but one object of going thither, and one interest when there. It was a soil made scared or rather doomed, to the exclusive plunder of a privileged number'.

The highest officers in the government had the strongest motive for corruption and therefore there could be no possibility to check the same corruption in the officers below them. Every man, in every department, whether civil, military or mercantile, was placed in a beneficiary position of receiving splendid presents.

That the actions of Hastings brought forth a sharp reaction of disapproval from the Government of the Earl of Chatham was evident as he sought to exert the supremacy of the Parliament over the Company way back in 1766. However, his mission was not successful since many of the MPs were shareholders of the East India Company. It was only in 1773 when Lord North passed the Regulating Act that the Parliament gained some control over the activities of the East India Company. However, the large number of MPs who were shareholders of the company did not accept this without challenge and they passed enabling legislation which were just short of restrictive laws. It was William Pitt who finally passed the Indian Act in 1784 establishing a Board of Control with powers to dictate orders to the Company, to bring to heel, malpractices which were bringing illegal riches to the Company shareholders. In this context, the London Chronicle in 1784 listed the names of 29 MPs who had direct connection or who were East India Company shareholders. It would not be wrong to say that the nawabs (Indian rulers of the territories encroached upon by the British) and their money, eventually changed the course of British politics.

As we discuss the unabashed plunder of the richest province of the Mughal Empire, the Bengal province, we have to remember the open and unapologetic loot of the wealth of Bengal by the British. Even the most prolific Anglophile has to accept the wanton and systematic destruction of India's industry and trade, notably the ship building and shipping industry of Bengal.

Before the forays of the British East India company into Bengal and other parts of India, there was a thriving ship building industry in many parts of India like Bengal, Surat, Masulipatnam and Calicut. Even in the 16th century, during the halcyon days of Shivaji, the great Maratha warlord, there was a substantial fleet of ships to guard the coast of the Arabian Sea against the Portuguese predatory.

Further down south on the Malabar Coast, the Zamorin of Calicut, (the Nair ruler of the kingdom of Calicut or Kozhikode) even in the mid-16th century, had declared that all the fishermen living in his territory must bring up at least one of their sons as a Muslim to join his all Muslim ship crew. Needless to say, the Malabar coast of the Arabian Sea, had a very striking shipping and shipbuilding industry, apart from that of Bengal in the East.

Bengal, in fact, had the most flourishing shipbuilding industry. The Bengal fleet in the early seventeenth century, included 4000 to 5000 ships at 400 to 500 tons each, entirely built in Bengal with men and material of Bengal. Its huge popularity paved the way for the increased production and trading of goods in the mid-18th century, as stated earlier.

The versatility, acumen, craft and architectural beauty of the Bengal built ships begs no commendation from even the British authorities. That the Bengal built ships were far superior to the ones built in the dockyards of England by the English craftsmen, was not even a point of contention. The ships built in Bengal had a lifespan of over 20 years without repairs as against the ships built in the shipyards of Britain which could not last more than 10 years without repairs under identical open sea voyage conditions. The reason that led to the superiority of Indian ships as compared to the

British made ones was that the Indian shipbuilders used the best quality of Burma teak and sal which could withstand and survive the vagaries of the saline water of the seas and the extreme weather conditions. As against this, the ships built in the dockyards of England were made from British oak and fir which was less suitable to withstand the vagaries of high sea weather and the salinity of water. This apart, the Indian workers were far more advanced in the use of hardware components, so essential for shipbuilding including the use of iron and high tensile brass, which was indispensable for the manufacture of wooden ships. High tensile brass was widely used for fittings, service water pumps, shaft liners and nails.

Since the longevity of the Indian ships was much more than that of the British and their cost of construction much lower, the Indian ships were able to charge low freight rates for the hauling of cargo as compared to the British ones. This resulted in mounting pressure of unemployment among the British dockworkers. This unfortunate competition between the Indian-built ships and the ships built in the English dockyards rendered various types of labourers like caulkers, sawyers and shipwrights jobless, since British enterprises dealing with the shipping industry refused to place orders for costlier ship building projects.

Another success story of the Indian shipping industry may be highlighted here. There was always a clamouring by the British shipbuilding industry to put some legislative factors against the Bengal shipbuilders because of the obvious superiority and revenue yielding calibre of these indigenous shipbuilders. In the period after 1757, the East India Company and their ship builders were given a monopoly on oceanic trade routes which had been so long open to Indian traders. Duties were imposed on the Indian trading ships moving to and from Indian ports. This adversely affected the Indian shipbuilding industry to the point of irrelevance, as Indian ships were allowed to apply only on the Indian coastal routes and for supplying goods for the local population.

However, the long-drawn Napoleonic Wars changed the whole spectrum. As the war progressed, there was a systematic depletion of British merchant ships. It is reported that the Napoleonic war of 1803 destroyed 173,000 tons of British shipping, which forced the British Government in London to employ 112,890 tons of foreign vessels to conduct British commerce. To comply with the Navigation Acts, the British government was forced to classify Indian shipping as British shipping and Indian sailors were classified as British sailors, which permitted them access to the trade routes hitherto permitted only to the British.

The meanness of the British Government became immediately apparent with the cessation of the Napoleonic Wars. As soon as the war ended, the Navigation Acts were suitably amended, and Indian ships were again barred from those trade routes just as before the war. A legislation was enacted to that effect. Thus, it is apparent that the British authorities utilised the Indian resources and industries, only when it suited them and suppressed them whenever their need disappeared.

As already stated, the fleet made in the early seventeenth century in the Bengal dockyards had 4,000 to 5000 ships, which could each carry 400 to 500 tons of freight. These numbers obviously increased till the mid-18th century, when the goods and products carried by the Bengal built ships far outnumbered those carried by the English ships. By 1800, the Governor General Wellesley reported that the British Indian port of Calcutta had 10,000 tons of cargo shipping built in India. Between 1801 to 1838, there was a further increase of 327 ships in Bengal, all owned by the British.

British shipwrights highly valued the superior nature of Indian workmanship at shipbuilding; because of this, they started constructing their ships in Calcutta itself, using Indian workers. They adopted the Indian naval architectural designs while constructing their own ships. Indian craftsmen were experts in shipbuilding, building cheaper and durable vessels that stood the test of time. This led to a situation where the British based businesses just could not keep up.

To mitigate their plight, in 1813, the British shipbuilders petitioned the British government to enact a legislation to bar the Indian ships below 350 tonnes from plying between the Indian colonies or from Indian docks to Britain. It was the first death nail for Bengal built ships as it led to the total suspension of 40% of the ships. By a further legislation act of 1814, Indian built ships were denied the name of British registered vessels to avail trade facilities with the United States and the European continent. Only the trade with China was not restricted; the ships could ply to and fro from the Calcutta port to the Chinese port. However, no market of Chinese goods in India was available. So, this sector was unprofitable for India and was not used. Over the years, slowly and steadily, due to nonprofitable trade and oppressive legislation, India's thriving shipbuilding industry collapsed, and by 1850, completely died out.

The British also orchestrated the collapse of Indian Textile industry. At the beginning of the eighteenth century, India's share of the world's trade was 27% but by the time the British departed in 1947, it had come down to up to a meagre 3%. The export of silk from Bengal alone was 6.5 million rupees until 1753. The combined export of textile and silk from Bengal was 33% till the 1760's. With the British acquiring political power around 1765, the textile industry was the hardest hit. First, the British started paying for the textiles and silk from the revenues extracted from the province itself instead of in British pounds. Secondly, extremely cheap, machine-made British textiles began flooding the Indian markets and the Indian weavers could not keep up with these low prices. Almost overnight, the skilled Indian weavers and artisans became unemployed and impoverished and had to migrate to other places in search of work. Now India became a mere supplier of raw cotton to England, while the British started exporting cheaply manufactured textiles into the country. Thus, from a manufacturing country, India became an exporter of raw materials, not only of cotton, silk and jute, but also tea, spices, opium etc.

Another Indian industry which suffered at the hands of the British was the steel industry. India had a long history of highly developed steel industry which went way back to the 6th century. Right from the sixth century when crucible-formed steel variously known as 'Wootz', also 'ukku' in local Kannad dialect mistranslated in English as 'wook' or 'wootz' was being manufactured in India. Indian steel was so superior in quality that it acquired global attention and was regarded as the world's finest. In the 12th century, Arabs got hold of the Indian steel manufacturing technology and started manufacturing the world-famous Damascus Steel. Indian steel swords had a long legendary history: the swords manufactured in India by Rajputana craftsmen dwarfed all other swords in terms of workmanship, weight and battle worthiness. In the days of British colonial expansion, the Indian battle swords were found to be far more superior compared to the swords manufactured in England and Europe. It was common practice of the British engaged in battle, to dismount and swap their own battlefield swords with the superior swords of the vanquished Indian soldiers.

The British were systematically opposed to the development of the Indian steel industry. The British metallurgists adopted the Indian metallurgical formula for sword making and used it to their own benefit. But having acquired this knowledge, they crushed the Indian steel industry by the end of the 18th century. The Indian steel industry was never allowed to raise its head again.

Not to industrialise India, was a deliberate policy of the British. To say that India stagnated when the European countries surged ahead, would be an oversimplification. This happened only because stringent barriers of regulatory high tariff and other oppressive measures, restricted India on the path to industrialisation.

Excessive Taxation was rampant during the British rule. Bishop Heber acknowledged that taxation on the crops produced on the land had always been an important source of revenue to the Muslim rulers. In times of extreme emergency, like war with neighbouring states, the Muslim rulers too resorted to be swingeing taxes. But the Muslim rulers confided that even they could not be so inhuman so as to extract to the last, whatever was earmarked. The British being the colonial rulers, had no qualms to realise land tax averaging between 80 to 90% of the rental. Taxes and revenue were so high that, peasants were forced to give up their lands; tax defaulters were victimised and tortured till the last bit of their assets were forcefully extracted. India became a scene of mindless plunder, loot, extraction and rapacity.

Within 30 years, the revenue collected from Bengal alone skyrocketed from 817,553 pounds to 2,680,000 pounds. However, the entire income generated by the officials of the East India company was simply transferred to the British treasury in England, as it was considered the income of British expatriates. India was left high and dry; no amount was left for investment in land like irrigation, fertilisers, buying of seeds or pesticides. The English restricted their purchases to goods manufactured only in Britain, because of which, the manufacturers of Indian luxury goods, like the weavers of the world famous muslin cloth and of fine silk were rendered totally jobless. Paul Baran calculated that 8% of India's Gross National Product was transferred to Britain each year. Dadabhai Naoroji, the first elected Indian member of the British House of Commons, argued that India had exported an average of 13,000,000 pounds worth of goods to Britain each year, from 1835 to 1872, with no corresponding investment in India. Incidentally, in 1901, William Digby calculated, with remarkable precision, the net amount extracted from India in the 19th century itself, at 4,187,922,732 pounds.

There is no denial of the fact that the British rule in India, went by the simple logic of capitalism, the only objective being maximisation of profit. The British Empire in India was a creation of merchants, and it was still at heart a commercial enterprise, guided by the ups and downs of the market.

Dadabhai Naoroji wrote a book, 'Poverty and Un-British Rule in India'. While arguing the case for India and also to support Irish home rule, and appealing in futility to the better nature of the British, he quoted an indictment of Mr. Montgomery Martin: Mr. Montgomery Martin, after examining the condition of some provinces of Bengal and Bihar, said in 1833 in his Eastern India Despatch: 'It is impossible to avoid remarking two facts as peculiarly striking, first the richness of the country surveyed, and second, the poverty of the inhabitants....The annual drain of 3,000,000 pounds on British India, has amounted in 30 years, at compound interest, to the enormous sum of 723,900,000 pounds. So constant and accumulating a drain, even in England, would soon impoverish her. How severe then must be its effects on India when the wage of a labourer is from two pence to three pence a day.'

Incidentally, Indian indentured labour having commercial skills also made a huge contribution to consolidate the rule of the British and to strengthen the British Empire even in the far-off British colonies. Indian labour was extensively used to develop plantation agriculture in Malaya. Burma was turned into the rice bowl of Asia exclusively through Indian labour. Amidst the dense forests of Uganda in Africa, Indian labour was used to lay the railway lines through the animal infected jungles and braving inclement weather, affliction of various diseases and regular attack of pestilence. In Kenya, it was Indian labour and Indian technicians who established overhead electric lines. It was the same story in Ethiopia and in far-flung islands in the Pacific, like Fiji. But for such stupendous work, India was denied any reward or benefit from the British imperials.

Transportation to penal colonies became a preferred method of solving the problem of overcrowding in the prisons of England. Britain adopted this method of supplying manpower to the under populated British colonies. The British colony in Ross Island developed in the late nineteenth century and early twentieth century. In the 19th century, a large number of convicts and indentured labourers were transported to the dense forests of Andaman and Nicobar Islands, specially Ross Island, where they were chained to the trees, flogged and forced to clear the forests of huge trees for habitation; some labourers were even crushed to death from the falling of huge trees. The inhuman treatment of the slaves and total lack of respect for life, is too pathetic to describe in words. In the era of Company rule, the British were notorious for completely disregarding any kind of contract, treatise, solemn commitment and even payments for any work performed by the labourers. In fact, there are many instances of inhuman and brutal treatment of slaves and labourers, which can put to shame any civilised society, which the English claimed to be.

The British government was part and parcel of the privately controlled trade in the indentured labour market. From 1787, Indian convicts were transported to Malaysia and Indonesia respectively. It was by mutual agreement that Malaysia was left to the British and Indonesia, to the Dutch. It may be noted that the trade of slaves from Africa to the new colonies of America flourished till the 1833, when slave trade was abolished by the British Parliament. Paradoxically, the huge compensation was paid, not to the hapless slaves, but to the slave owners for the loss of their commodities, as the slaves were considered as nothing other than sellable commodity. Incidentally quite a large chunk of slave owners were Christian church priests.

After the reign of the governance passed to the Crown, there was some notable improvement. However, the same extortion continued to be committed under the pretence that the British under Colonial rule, would ensure peace and security to the Indian subjects. Will Durant scathingly remarked 'hypocrisy was added to brutality while the robbery went on'. Shashi Tharoor quoted the words of Cambridge Imperial historian John Seeley who in his book, 'Expansion of England', had claimed that the conquest of India was not in its proper sense, a conquest at all. The joke went about that the British had stumbled onto a vacuum and acquired their empire 'in a fit of absence of mind'. The starker reality was that large-scale economic exploitation was only possible under an umbrella of effective economic and political control. The company's expansion flowed from a series of racial decisions made in response to the then events and a desire to seize opportunities that presented to the beady eyes of the company officials, rather than some imperial master plan. They followed remorseless logic to justify the British Empire in India; as Clive said: 'to stop is dangerous; to recede ruin'. Kingdom after kingdom was annexed by the simple expedient of offering its ruler a choice between annihilation in war or a comfortable life in subjugation. When war was waged, the costs were paid from the taxes and tributes extracted from the Indians. Indians paid, in other words, for the privilege of being conquered by the British.

Even Lord Macaulay, a highly decorated official of the Company, was moved to write about the misgovernment of the English, which was 'carried to such a point as seemed incompatible with the existence of society.... The servants of the Company forced the natives to buy dear and sell cheap.... Enormous fortunes were thus rapidly accumulated at Calcutta, while 30 billion human lives were reduced to the extremity of wretchedness. They had never (had to live) under tyranny like this...' Macaulay added that whereas evil regimes could be overthrown by an oppressed people, the English were not so easily dislodged.

At the time of the Sepoy Mutiny of 1857, The East India Company boasted of an army of 2,60,000 and had annexed a quarter of a million square miles from Indian rulers. A vexed question arises in the related context: what the total extraction by the British from India was. Minhaz Merchant, the Indian surveyor and economic commentator computed the sum of reparation from India to Britain over the period of 200 years;

he calculated the amount to 3 trillion pounds in today's money, the sum being larger than the entire GDP of the year 2015.

By the end of the 19th century, India was the biggest source of revenue extraction for the British. India was not only the biggest purchaser of British exports, but ironically enough, was the only source of maintenance of highly placed British civil servants. India had also to bear the full burden of pay of the British soldiers, including their retirement or termination benefits. In a nutshell, it can be said that the entire burden of maintenance of colonial rule of the British had to be borne by India. It will be interesting to note that 'after the service of 24 years, punctuated by four years of home leave furlough', the British civil servant was entitled to retire at home on a generous pension paid by the Indian tax payers. Ramsay McDonald estimated in the late 1920s that around 7,500 Englishmen were receiving around 20 million pounds annually from India as pension.

While British revenue soared, the national debt of India multiplied exponentially. Apart from the cost of maintaining a huge British Indian army in India, ostensibly to maintain India's security, India had to bear the entire expenditure of a variety of colonial expeditions from Burma to Mesopotamia, all to further the glory of the British Empire. As Shashi Tharoor points out in his book, The Era of Darkness, the cost of deployment of the British Indian army overseas in the 19th century and in the first decade of the 20th century, was funded by India. In 1922 for instance, 64% of the total revenue of the Government of India was devoted towards paying off the British Indian troops dispatched abroad. The total payment of money to the Company's shareholders, pensions to retired officials and dividends to railway investors amounted to 30 million pounds a year, which was a total loss for India. This left India completely depleted and left it to the vagaries of poverty, suffering and famine.

William Digby stated that the salary of the Secretary of State for India in 1981 was equal to the average annual income of 90,000 Indians and it was paid for by the taxes realised from the Indians subjects. Any British soldier posted to India, had to be paid, equipped and fed and finally to be pensioned off by the government of India and not Britain. There was a shameless disparity between the ranks and pensions of the Indian and the British soldiers. Even the extra rations allotted to the British is worth noting: the British soldiers were allotted a ration which included biscuits, rice, flour, raisins, wine, pork and beef, all of which were products of India, but Indian soldiers not authorised to enjoy any of these. Indeed, as William Durant observes, 'no other army in the world consumed so large a proportion of public revenue'.

'It is an exhausting drain upon the resources of the country, the issue of which is replaced by no reflex; it is an extraction of the life blood from the veins of national industry which no subsequent introduction of nourishment is furnished to restore'.

In the opinion of Mr. F. J. Shore, 'The halcyon days of India are over; She has been drained of a large proportion of the wealth she once possessed and her energies have been cramped by a sordid system of misrule to which the interests of millions have been sacrificed for the benefit of the few....The gradual impoverishment of the people and country, under the mode of rule established by the British Government has hastened their fall'.

References

Dodwell, D. (2022). The Cambridge History of India; Volume VI. Legare Street Press.

Jagmohan (2016). Triumphs and Tragedies of Ninth Delhi. Allied Publishers Pvt Ltd

Majumdar R.C., Raychaudhuri H.C., & Datta K., (1980) An Advanced History of India- 4th edition, Macmillan, India

Marshall, P. J. (1990). British Bridgehead Eastern India 1740–1828. Orient Blackswan.

Mill, J. (1848) The history of British India. Facsimile Publisher.

Sharma, R. A., & Tewari M. (2012). Delhi- Biography of a city, Aakar Books

Singh, U. (2006). Delhi: Ancient history. Social Science Press.

Sinha, N. K. (1996). The History of Bengal, 1757–1905. B R Publications

Smith, V. A. (1954). The Oxford Student's History of India, Oxford Clarendon Press

Spear, P., Spear, T. G. P., & Gupta, N. (2002). The Delhi Omnibus. Oxford University Press

Tharoor, S. (2016). An Era of Darkness: The British Empire in India. Aleph Book Company.

www.ingramcontent.com/pod-product-compliance
Lightning Source LLC
LaVergne TN
LVHW041155150826
845673LV00001B/167

* 9 7 9 8 8 9 6 1 0 6 8 0 7 *